MW00776307

CLINICAL PSYCHOANALYSIS

ed By

Steven J. Ellman

rs: *A Contemporary Perspective*

e Origins and Originality

tal Genius of Winnicott

ion and the Language of Love

d the Vulnerable Self
eppen, Editors

**Developmental Basis for
ention**
Monk, Carol Kaye,

pproach to the

oskowitz, Editors

The Library of (

A Series of Books Edit

Freud's Technique Pape
Steven J. Ellman

In Search of the Real: *Th*
of D.W. Winnicott
Dodi Goldman

In One's Bones: *The Clini*
Dodi Goldman, Editor

The Language of Pervers
Sheldon Bach

Omnipotent Fantasies a
Carolyn S. Ellman and Joseph R

The Neurobiological and
Psychotherapeutic Interv
Michael Moskowitz, Catherine
and Steven J. Ellman, Editors

Enactment: *Toward a New A*
Therapeutic Relationship
Steven J. Ellman and Michael M

℘

ENACTMENT

Toward a New Approach to the Therapeutic Relationship

Edited by
Steven J. Ellman, Ph.D.
Michael Moskowitz, Ph.D.

JASON ARONSON INC.
Northvale, New Jersey
London

This book was set in 10 pt. Cheltenham by Alpha Graphics of Pittsfield, NH, and printed and bound by Book-mart Press of North Bergen, NJ.

Library of Congress Cataloging-in-Publication Data

Enactment : toward a new approach to the therapeutic relationship /
    Steven J. Ellman, Michael Moskowitz, editors.
        p.   cm.
    Includes bibliographical references and index.
    ISBN 1-56821-584-3 (alk. paper)
    1. Acting out (Psychology)   2. Psychotherapist and patient.
  3. Psychotherapy.   4. Transference (Psychology)
  5. Countertransference (Psychology)   I. Ellman, Steven J.
  II. Moskowitz, Michael.
  RC489.A34E52   1998
  616.89'17—DC21   97-45933

Printed in the United States of America on acid-free paper. For information and catalog write to Jason Aronson Inc., 230 Livingston Street, Northvale, NJ 07647-1731. Or visit our website: http:/ /www.aronson.com

Contents

Editors and Contributors vii

Introduction xi
 Steven J. Ellman
 Michael Moskowitz

1 **Freud's Struggle with Enactment** 1
 Steven J. Ellman

2 **General Problems of Acting Out** 19
 Phyllis Greenacre

3 **Countertranference and Role-Responsiveness** 29
 Joseph Sandler

4 **Acting Out: A Reconsideration of the Concept** 37
 Dale Boesky

5 **On Countertransference Enactments** 63
 Theodore J. Jacobs

6 **Clinical and Theoretical Aspects of Enactment** 77
 James T. McLaughlin

7 **The Evocative Power of Enactments** 93
 Judith Fingert Chused

**8 The Role of Countertransference Enactment
in a Successful Clinical Psychoanalysis**   **111**
Owen Renik

**9 Between the Scylla and Charybdis of
Psychoanalytic Interaction: A Discussion of
Owen Renik's Chapter**   **129**
Stanley Grand

10 Enactment: What Is It and Whose Is It?   **139**
Harriet I. Basseches

11 Is Enactment a Useful Concept?   **149**
Paula L. Ellman

**12 Enactments Leading to Insight for Patient,
Therapist, and Supervisor**   **157**
Fonya Lord Helm

**13 The Fixity of Action in Character Enactments:
Finding a Developmental Regression**   **169**
Nancy R. Goodman

14 Enactment, Transference, and Analytic Trust   **183**
Steven J. Ellman

Credits   205

Index   207

Editors and Contributors

Harriet I. Basseches, Ph.D., is President, Executive Board of the New York Freudian Society. Co-chair of the Executive Board of the Confederation of Independent Psychoanalytic Societies of North America (IPS), she is also Associate Clinical Professor of Psychology at the George Washington University Psy.D. Program in Clinical Psychology. She has a private practice of psychoanalysis and psychotherapy in Washington, DC.

Dale Boesky, M.D., is Training and Supervising Analyst at the Michigan Psychoanalytic Institute and Clinical Associate Professor of Psychiatry at Wayne State University School of Medicine. A frequent presenter at the American Psychoanalytic Association, he is former Editor-in-Chief of *Psychoanalytic Quarterly* and served on the editorial board of the *International Journal of Psycho-Analysis*.

Judith Fingert Chused, M.D., is Training and Supervising Psychoanalyst at the Washington Psychoanalytic Institute, as well as Clinical Professor of Psychiatry and Behavioral Sciences and Clinical Professor of Pediatrics at the George Washington University School of Medicine. She is on the editorial board of the *International Journal of Psycho-Analysis* and *Psychoanalytic Quarterly*, and is an editorial reader for the *Journal of the American Psychoanalytic Association* and *Psychiatry*.

Paula L. Ellman, Ph.D., is a clinical psychologist-psychoanalyst in private practice in Rockville, MD. She is a member of the New York Freudian Society and a graduate of its Washington, DC Program. Assistant Clinical Professor of Psychology at George Washington University Psy.D. Program in Clinical Psychology, she is on the faculty of the Washington School of Psychiatry where she supervises and teaches.

Steven J. Ellman, Ph.D., is Past Co-Chair of the Independent Psychoanalytic Societies. He is Past President and Program Chair of the Institute for Psychoanalytic Training and Research (IPTAR) in New York City, Professor in the Doctoral Program in Clinical Psychology at the City University of New York, and faculty member and supervisor in the New York University Postdoctoral Program in Psychotherapy and Psychoanalysis. His books include *Freud's Technique Papers: A Contemporary Perspective* and *The Mind in Sleep.*

Nancy R. Goodman, Ph.D., is a psychologist-psychoanalyst in private practice in Bethesda, MD. A member of the New York Freudian Society, having graduated from its Washington, DC program, she teaches and supervises in various programs including the Washington School of Psychiatry and George Washington University. Dr. Goodman researches and writes on psychoanalytic listening, Holocaust trauma, and female development.

Stanley Grand, Ph.D., practices psychoanalysis in New York City. He is a Fellow and Past President of IPTAR. He is also Training and Control Analyst at the New York Freudian Society and Supervising Analyst at the New York University Postdoctoral Program. Dr. Grand is Professor Emeritus at The Health Sciences Center, S.U.N.Y., Downstate.

Phyllis Greenacre, M.D. (1894–1989), served as President of the New York Psychoanalytic Institute where for many years she was Training and Supervising Analyst. She was Director of the outpatient clinic at the Payne Whitney Psychiatric Hospital and Clinical Professor of Psychiatry at Cornell University Medical College. She also served as President of the American Psychoanalytic Association. Her many publications include the classics *Emotional Growth: Psychoanalytic Studies of the Gifted and a Great Variety of Other Individuals* and *Trauma, Growth, and Personality.*

Fonya Lord Helm, Ph.D., is a psychoanalyst and clinical psychologist practicing in Cabin John, MD, a suburb of Washington, DC. She is Assistant Clinical Professor of Psychology at George Washington University and Instructor at the New York Freudian Society's Washington, DC training program in psychoanalysis. Currently a faculty member of the Washington School of Psychiatry, Dr. Helm for ten years was Chair of the Dynamics of Psychotherapy Training Program.

Theodore J. Jacobs, M.D., is Clinical Professor of Psychiatry, Albert Einstein College of Medicine. He is Training and Supervising Analyst at the New York Psychoanalytic Institute and the Psychoanalytic Institute at New York University, and also President of the Association for Child Psychoanalysis.

James T. McLaughlin, M.D., is Training and Supervising Analyst at the Pittsburgh Psychoanalytic Institute. He is Clinical Associate Professor Emeritus of Psychiatry at the School of Medicine, University of Pittsburgh, as well as current or former editorial board member of *Psychoanalytic Quarterly, Journal of the American Psychoanalytic Association*, and the *International Journal of Psycho-Analysis*.

Michael Moskowitz, Ph.D., is a publisher at Jason Aronson Inc., and Adjunct Associate Professor in the City University of New York Clinical Psychology Program. He is co-editor (with RoseMarie Pérez and Rafael Art. Javier) of *Reaching Across Boundaries of Culture and Class: Widening the Scope of Psychotherapy* and (with Catherine Monk, Carol Kaye, and Steven Ellman) of *The Neurobiological and Developmental Basis for Psychotherapeutic Intervention*. Dr. Moskowitz is a member of the Institute for Psychoanalytic Training and Research (IPTAR) and in private practice in New York City.

Owen Renik, M.D., is Training and Supervising Analyst at the San Francisco Psychoanalytic Institute. He is currently Editor-in-Chief of *Psychoanalytic Quarterly*, Chair of the Program Committee of the American Psychoanalytic Association, and former Secretary of the Board on Professional Standards of the American Psychoanalytic Association.

Joseph Sandler, M.D., is Training and Supervising Analyst in the British Psychoanalytical Society and former President of the International Psychoanalytical Association and the European Psychoanalytical Federation. He has published numerous papers and books on psychoanalysis and allied topics, most recently *What Do Psychoanalysts Want?: The Problem of Aims in Psychoanalytic Therapy* (with Anna Ursula Dreher) and *Freud's Model of the Mind: An Introduction* (with Alex Holder, Christopher Dare, and Dreher). In 1995 he was awarded the Sigourney Prize for outstanding contributions to psychoanalysis.

Introduction

A new word has recently entered our clinical vocabulary, *enactment*, often replacing the earlier action terms *acting out* and *acting in*. Many feel that something previously inarticulated has been captured by the concept: a recognition of a process that may involve words, but goes beyond words. For some *enactment* implies a consistent area of interaction between therapist and patient in the realm of intersubjectivity; others have questioned whether the concept adds anything but confusion. In this book we look at the relationship between action and analysis beginning with Freud's papers on transference and leading to current discussions about enactment. The topic of transference is introduced early in the volume since our guiding view is that difficulties in handling transference are a major factor in enactments. We follow the evolution of Freud's ideas of action in the transference to the contemporary concept of enactment. We present the work of significant theorists who attempted to clarify the meaning of acting out. We then offer selections from the work of contemporary writers who have elevated the concept of enactment to its present status. We have also included papers by authors who view the concept of enactment as superfluous and redundant.

The choice of papers for this volume was a particularly difficult one, for the literature now abounds with papers that employ the concept of enactment. How can one decide which papers to include and how to represent this topic that is now seemingly intertwined with many of the most compelling and thorniest questions regarding the practice of psychoanalysis? The choice for the present volume is to trace the evolution of the term within the context of psychoanalysis (primarily) in the United States. In doing this we have bypassed many interesting papers by authors from other countries and other orientations, a consideration of whose work remains for another volume. Here we attempt both to mark the evolution of the concept and to consider some of the difficulties inherent in current popular formulations.

Presenting Freud's struggle with transference is consonant with the major theme of the present volume: that difficulties in dealing with transference for both analysand and analyst have been overlooked and underplayed in the psychoanalytic literature in the United States. After looking at Freud's travail, we reprint two seminal papers on the concept of acting out. Greenacre's paper gives a good sense of how the idea of acting out was used from 1950–1970 in this country. In this paper, both a reflection of the past and a gateway to newer concepts, she importantly reflects on then often pejorative connotations of the term acting out and attempts to counteract this attitude. Boesky's paper, while also addressing the concept of acting out, is one of the precursors to the literature on enactment. He first states that there is no agreed upon definition of the concept of acting out and tries to detail why this is the case. His solution to this conceptual quandary is to begin to consider the idea of various types of interactions occurring between analysand and analyst. Boesky's idea of the actualization of the transference is a sign of the emergence of the serious consideration of the complex transmissions that occur between two parties engaged in an analysis.

In a similar vein, Sandler's concept of role responsiveness attempts to account for behaviors of the analyst that had not been carefully considered in the analytic literature. He presents to us an analyst whose behavior is in response to (or expressive of) some of the patient's unconscious fantasies. This may occur for a period of time where neither analyst nor patient is aware of why these behavioral sequences are occurring. This type of interaction today might well be considered to be an enactment.

Papers by Jacobs and McLaughlin mark the beginning of the enactment literature in the United States. Although these papers cover different situations, both authors agree that enactments are much more typical than had been previously noted. They also concur that the type of interactions that characterize enactments can be therapeutically useful or at least should not be seen solely as analytic blunders by an analyst who is unable to contain his countertransference tendencies. Several years after their contributions, Chused presents a paper that helps define the limits of the enactment literature from one theoretical perspective. She concludes that while enactments are inevitable they are not therapeutic in themselves, but rather can serve as additional sources of information that, when greeted with curiosity and not guilt, can enrich the analytic work. In this paper she also brings the concept of enactment into work with children.

Renik's chapter serves as another possible logical extension of the literature on enactment. Renik proposes that the therapeutic efficacy of analysis is embedded in enactments, thus enactments are essential to the process of psychoanalysis. Renik's paper can be seen as defining the boundaries of a position that is almost diametrically opposed to that of Chused.

The last section of the book presents varying responses to prevailing literature. Grand specifically comments on and critiques Renik's position. Basseches draws a distinction between different forms of enactments: on the one side are enactments that are solely externalizations of the inner life of the particular patient. Such enactments would occur no matter who the analyst is. On the other side are enactments that are the result of a mutual transference–countertransference interaction. Paula Ellman tries to show that the idea of enactment is in fact redundant and is contained in a conceptually clearer manner in the concepts *transference, transference neurosis,* and *countertransference.* Fonya Helm takes the position that enactments are both expectable and useful inasmuch as they allow for the uncovering and potential mastery of experiences that had previously only been felt and acted without conscious awareness of their sources and meanings. She further illustrates that when enactments go unrecognized in the therapeutic interaction they may be transformed and re-enacted in the therapist–supervisor relationship. Nancy Goodman defines a category of enactments as character enactments. These refer to action patterns that express the character structure of an individual and repeatedly create difficulties in that person's love or work life. The fixity of these enactments is hypothesized to relate to their defensive-regressive functions, particularly with reference to separation-individuation conflicts.

Steven Ellman's final chapter is not so much a summary as an attempt to offer a theoretical context for a theoretical term. Here he examines the utility of the concept and gives a brief historical explanation of why the concept is important in today's psychoanalytic community. He also constructs a more precise definition of the term and in so doing creates several new distinctions or at least several new terms.

A Word about the Term Enactment

In point of fact it is hard to decide when the term *enactment* started to be used in psychoanalytic discourse. Modell (1990), for example, credits Eagle (1984) with introducing the term. Many clinicians see Jacobs and McLaughlin as beginning to use the concept during the same time period. In fact Kohut (1977) had used a very similar concept to the one that Eagle introduced. Modell states that Eagle introduces the term enactment, which is similar to what he has called symbolic actualization (p. 137). Interestingly, Modell, Eagle, and Kohut all maintain that these nonverbal behaviors are in some way at the heart of the therapeutic process. Kohut uses the term action–thought for what he considers to be the nonverbal carrier of messages (p. 37) that when appropriately responded to, enable a patient to engage in an enactment (p. 47) demonstrating that the healing of the structural defect would take place or has already taken place. In the example that Kohut uses, he attempts to show that enactments are the beginning of a demonstration of therapeutic efficacy. McLaughlin and Jacobs use the term in a quite different manner, yet both of them suggest that enactments are frequent occurrences in the analytic process.

We have entered into this discussion in a deliberate manner, realizing that we are using the term enactment without defining the concept. But such is the state of the literature with regard to this increasingly important concept. In his summary chapter Ellman presents a clear and useful definition. It remains to be seen whether this definition will be accepted.

Steven J. Ellman
Michael Moskowitz

REFERENCES

Eagle, M. (1984). *Recent Developments in Psychoanalysis: A Critical Evaluation.* New York: McGraw Hill.
Kohut, H. (1977). *The Restoration of the Self.* New York: International Universities Press.
Modell, A. H. (1990). *Other Times, Other Realities: Toward a Theory of Psychoanalytic Treatment.* Cambridge, MA: Harvard University Press.

1

Freud's Struggle with Enactment

STEVEN J. ELLMAN

A brief review of Freud's ideas about transference gives us an example of how the creator of psychoanalysis struggled with what we would today call enactments. Freud began to recognize the clinical importance of transference in his confrontations with Dora (Freud 1900). He tries to influence her by attempting to force Dora to accept the correctness of his interpretations. Freud at that point in time does not consider his consistent encounters with Dora as efforts to influence her, nor does he see himself as being influenced by her. It was only when he wrote the postscript to the case some two to three years after he last saw her that he began to understand the power of transference in the psychoanalytic situation (Ellman 1991).

Virtually from the beginning of his career Freud is concerned with what we would today call different positions on the concept of enactment. He is fundamentally worried about actions of either analyst or analysand. The issues that Freud grappled with are basic questions that must be dealt with if an analysis is to have any chance of being a real analysis. First, Freud is anxious about physical contact between patient and analyst, particularly sexual contact. He also wanted to assure himself and the larger community (at first the medical community) that psychoanalysis is a procedure that is different from a number of other treatments that simply influence or manipulate the patient (e.g., hydrotherapy, hypnotherapy). He endeavors to show that the curative elements in psychotherapy (and psychoanalysis) are a function of the content of the treatment and *not* the relationship of the patient to the doctor. Later in his career his views will change and he will emphasize the role of transference in the treatment and therefore the relationship of analyst and analysand. But his views about transference will continue to oscillate between a commitment to his new clinical concept and a desire to see psychoanalysis as a more mechanistic procedure.

Freud as Therapist

Freud's journey in developing the psychoanalytic method starts with his leaving hypnosis and beginning his psychotherapeutic method. At this time he begins to formulate the concepts of resistance, transference, and free association. During this period (1893–1895), he is exploring the significance of hysteria and its childhood etiology. His clinical objective is to unearth and extirpate pathological memories, and at first hypnosis seems to be an ideal way of performing this psychological operation.

Making the unconscious conscious, one of the most famous later Freudian phrases, could be used to characterize Breuer and Freud's stated goal when they published "Studies on Hysteria" (1895).[1] Not only did Breuer and Freud offer a new way of understanding hysteria, but Freud's last chapter in this volume presents a remarkable view of his conversion from a hypnotherapist to a psychotherapist. In this chapter, Freud presents a new technique for bringing *pathogenic memories* to consciousness.[2] Given today's emphasis in psychoanalysis on the role of transference and enactment, it is interesting to go back to a time when Freud was involved almost exclusively in the recovery of pathogenic memories. In looking back we can note that Freud is interested in controlling the patient's activities[3] so that they are completely involved in unearthing memories that, from his view, have led to the patient's distress.

Before we begin our historical expedition, it is worth mentioning that, even when Freud was using hypnosis as a therapeutic tool, he distinguished the effects of hypnotic treatment from the effects of posthypnotic suggestion. It was his contention that when he unearthed memories, it was the process of remembering and abreacting[4] that led to symptom reduction. In his view, symptom reduction did not occur as a result of a suggestion. In fact, in any of the treat-

---

[1]At this point in time, Freud's ideas about the unconscious were not fully developed. He equivocated on the status of the secondary group of ideas. At times, this concept seems equivalent to the unconscious; at other times, he seems to be saying that the second group has ready access to consciousness. A few years later (1900), the term unconscious will begin to acquire its modern meaning.

[2]So as not to be anachronistic we might say he had a method of joining the memories in the secondary system (what later will be called the unconscious system) in a manner to make them accessible to the primary system (what later will be called the conscious-preconscious system).

[3]As we will see, these activities do not seem to include the therapeutic situation. Freud was also quite explicit about attempting to control the patient's behavior outside of the treatment situation.

[4]Abreaction occurs when memories are recovered through the cathartic method. Essentially abreation is recovering memories while having an emotional reaction. Abreacting allows one to dispel pent-up affect or energy that Freud at this time in his career thought was a factor in a variety of symptoms such as anxiety, (indirectly) phobias, and so forth.

ments that he advocated, he maintained that suggestion was never the curative element in the treatment. Freud thought that suggestion had a role, but that role was always one that helped the patient enter and continue to participate in the treatment. Although the distinction between suggestion and true therapeutic results is easy to outline, today many clinicians maintain that it is a false distinction and that boundaries between suggestion and other aspects of the therapeutic situation can never be clearly articulated.

Suggestion and Psychotherapy in "Studies on Hysteria"

Psychoanalysis started with research into hysteria, and hypnosis was the original therapeutic technique. The aim of the hypnotic technique (Breuer and Freud 1895) was to bring about the "reproduction of a memory which was of importance in bringing about the onset of the hysteria—the memory either of a single major trauma . . . or of a series of interconnected part-traumas" (p. 14). Underlying his therapeutic approach was the assumption that "hysterics suffer mainly from reminiscences" (p. 14).

These memories or reminiscences are the result of psychical trauma "or more precisely the memory of the trauma . . . [which] acts like a foreign body which long after its entry must continue to be regarded as an agent that is still at work" (p. 6). Breuer and Freud (1895) reported that, to their surprise:

> each individual hysterical symptom immediately and permanently disappeared when we had succeeded in bringing clearly to light the memory of the event by which it was provoked and in arousing its accompanying affect, and when the patient had described that event in the greatest possible detail and had put the affect into words. Recollection without affect almost invariably produces no result. [p. 6]

In this famous statement they not only proposed a partial explanation for hysteria but also stated how to treat this disorder. Freud maintained that simply providing an intellectual understanding will not be curative. Patients must be allowed to abreact or to have a full emotional reaction under hypnosis. Their cathartic method was thus dependent on the patient abreacting. While utilizing the hypnotic method, the patient's memories and verbalizations were "in accordance with the laws of association" (1895, p. 16). While the patient is hypnotized it is possible to:

> [bring] to an end the operative force of the idea which was not abreacted in the first instance (in the person's normal life), by allowing its strangulated affect to find a way out through speech; and it subjects it to associative correction by introducing it into normal consciousness (under light hypnosis). [p. 17]

In this early conceptualization about hysteria, Breuer and Freud (1895) maintained that the symptoms associated with hysteria were related to painful, anxiety-provoking memories that were not accessible to consciousness. Normally, affect associated with disturbing experiences would be worn away or discharged. When disturbing memories were not appropriately worn away or discharged, they had to be handled in some other manner.

How are we to understand the idea of affect that is worn away or discharged? The wearing occurs when a person brings an aversive situation into consciousness, re-experiences it, and is able to counteract the experience by various internal strategies. If, for instance, a situation stimulates an idea that brings up the affect of shame, a person might be able to counteract this idea by reminding himself about his positive attributes. By assuring oneself that the event that caused the affect of shame was a singular or infrequent occurrence in one's life, a person could then wear away the affect of shame. Alternatively, one might do something in reality to counteract the shameful experience. Thus, normal people are continually discharging affect or putting a memory of a disturbing or humiliating circumstance into an appropriate perspective "by considering (one's) own worth" (1895, p. 9). A normal person either can have small abreactions (discharges of affect through thought or action) or can deal with the personal insult or aversive effect more gradually "through the process of association." Forgetting, or the fading of memories, takes place when the affect is "worn away." Freud believed that memories can be recaptured when the affect is reunited with the idea or representation. This is true for memories that have pathological consequences as well as for "normal" memories.

Breuer and Freud's technique to deal with hysterics was in effect an attempt to help the person do what normal people do continuously: experience aversive situations, abreact, and then deal with the thoughts through the process of association (or rational thought). By the time "Studies on Hysteria" was published, Freud had begun to use a form of psychotherapy called the pressure technique (1895). In "Studies on Hysteria," he stated some of his reasons for abandoning the hypnotic method. He related that a number of hysterical patients refused every attempt at hypnosis. For this and other reasons, Freud decided to bypass hypnosis and utilize the pressure technique. The aim of this new technique was still the recovery of pathogenic memories, but the recovery of memories was now accomplished without the aid of hypnosis:

> When, at our first interview, I asked my patients if they remembered what had originally occasioned the symptom concerned, in some cases they said they knew nothing of it, while in others they brought forward something which they described as an obscure recollection and could not pursue further. . . . I now became insistent—if I assured them that they did know it,

that it would occur to their minds,—then, in the first cases, something did actually occur to them, and, in the others, their memory went a step further. After this I became still more insistent; I told the patients to lie down and deliberately close their eyes in order to "concentrate"—all of which had at least some resemblance to hypnosis. I then found that without any hypnosis new recollections emerged which went further back and which probably related to our topic. Experiences like this made me think that it would in fact be possible for the pathogenic groups of ideas, that were after all certainly present, to be brought to light by mere insistence; and since this insistence involved effort on my part and so suggested the idea that I had to overcome a resistance, the situation led me at once to the theory that by means of my psychical work I had to overcome a psychical force in the patients which was opposed to the pathogenic ideas becoming conscious (being remembered). A new understanding seemed to open before my eyes when it occurred to me that this must no doubt be the same psychical force that had played a part in the generating of the hysterical symptom and had at that time prevented the pathogenic idea from becoming conscious. . . . From all this there arose, as it were automatically, the thought of defense. [Breuer and Freud 1895, p. 268]

In these paragraphs Freud is telling us not only about his new technique but also about how he came upon the concept of defense.[5] In this chapter on psychotherapy, he is writing about defense and a strongly related concept, *resistance*. Freud at first used the term synonymously with defense and gradually restricted the term to denote anything that impedes the flow of the patient's associations. This distinction became more meaningful later in Freud's career when the concept of defense was being further developed. However, as early as 1894, Freud had already discovered that when defenses are operative the patient *resists* attempts to recover the pathogenic ideas or memories.

How does Freud deal with resistence? Initially, he attempts to reassure patients that if they try a little longer and harder they will think of something, but he acknowledges that this type of encouragement doesn't go very far. When the patient is resistant, Freud suggests using:

a small technical device. . . . I inform the patient that, a moment later, I shall apply pressure to his forehead, and I assure him that, all the time the pressure lasts, he will see before him a recollection in the form of a picture or will have it in his thoughts in the form of an idea occurring to him. {Breuer and Freud 1895, p. 270]

---

[5]In "The Neuro-Psychoses of Defense" (1894), Freud writes at greater length about his reasons for proposing the theory of defense.

Freud deals with resistance by trying to convince, cajole, and help focus the patient on the task at hand. The task is to associate freely. He assures the patient that he should communicate anything he thinks of, no matter how trivial. As we will see, this is similar to instructions given to his patients in psychoanalysis. Of course, in psychoanalytic sessions, Freud did not apply pressure to the patient's forehead or psyche as he does at this point in time. By using the pressure technique, Freud was trying to help patients put aside their more conscious critical facilities so that they could more easily relate their associations. What were the results of this technique?

> What emerges under the pressure of my hand is not always a "forgotten" recollection; it is only in the rarest cases that the actual pathogenic recollections lie so easily . . . on the surface. It is much more frequent for an idea to emerge which is an intermediate link in the chain of associations between the idea from which we start and the pathogenic idea which we are in search of. [Breuer and Freud 1895, p. 27]

Freud (1895) relates later in the chapter that "it is quite hopeless to penetrate directly to the nucleus of the pathogenic organization" (p. 292).

These excerpts are rich in the ideas that have shaped decades of psychotherapeutic practice and stimulated a good deal of debate. At this point, we can highlight some of the questions that have been raised.

Is Defense an Act of Will?

By this time Freud not only has confirmed the central importance of defense in psychoanalytic theory, but he has begun to show how defense is manifested in a treatment situation. From this time forward, the idea of resistance will be an essential one in psychoanalytic treatment. Freud's concept here is somewhat different from his later understanding of defense. In "Studies on Hysteria" and in a later paper "The Neuro-Psychoses of Defense," Freud (1894) talks about defense as an act of will, meaning that the person has consciously intended to banish an idea from the primary group of ideas. Conversely, this means that, if a person can concentrate hard enough then he can more easily get at (or will the return of) his pathogenic ideation. Because modern psychoanalysts are accustomed to thinking of defense as an unconscious process, this meaning of defense is not frequently used in modern psychoanalytic publications. (Werman has written a paper [1983] on suppression as a defense.) Given that Freud thought of defense as an act of will, his handling of resistance becomes more understandable. The idea of a patient's displaying resistance connotes the patient's consciously disobeying the physician. Freud saw the patient's efforts as a resistance to remembering the pathogenic ideas or memories, as well as a resistance to obeying the instructions of the physician. Because Freud felt resistance is an act of will by the patient, he attempted to counter this act of will by a greater act of will on the part of the physician. In more concrete terms, he thought it possible for the therapist to pressure the patient into complying with his instructions. Armed with this understanding of defense, Freud conceived of how he could use influence or suggestion to help the patient retrieve the memories that were causing conflict and pain.

This point, of course, is being overstated. There are also indications that Freud had at the same time a more modern understanding of defense during this same period. His thinking did not fall into neat categories. At every phase of his theorizing, one can see elements from the past, present, and indeed even the future standing side by side. During this period, however, the idea of defense as a conscious act of will was a good deal more in keeping with his treatment methods. This point of view is present in the way he conceptualized not only resistance, but transference as well. In telling of occasions of the pressure technique failing, Freud relates:

> . . . But there is yet a third possibility which bears witness equally to an obstacle, but an external obstacle, and not one inherent in the material. This happens when the patient's relation to the physician is disturbed, and it is the worst obstacle that we can come across. We can, however, reckon on meeting it in every comparatively serious analysis. . . . In my experience this obstacle arises in three principal cases:
>
> (1) If there is a personal estrangement—if, for instance, the patient feels she has been neglected, has been too little appreciated or has been insulted, or if she has heard unfavourable comments on the physician or the method of treatment. This is the least serious case. . . .
>
> (2) If the patient is seized by a dread of becoming too much accustomed to the physician personally, of losing her independence in relation to him, and even of perhaps becoming sexually dependent on him. This is a more important case, because its determinants are less individual. The cause of this obstacle lies in the solicitude inherent in the treatment. . . .
>
> (3) If the patient is frightened at finding that she is transferring on to the figure of the physician the distressing ideas which arise from the content of the analysis. This is a frequent, and indeed in some analyses a regular, occurrence. Transference on to the physician takes place through a false connection.[6] It is impossible to carry any analysis to a conclusion unless we know how to meet the resistance arising in these three ways. But we can find a way of doing so if we make up our minds that his new symptom that has been produced on the old model must be treated in the same way

---

[6]This is the first appearance of the use of transference in Freud's writings.

as the old symptoms. Our . . . task is to make the obstacle conscious to the patient . . . [pp. 301–303]

To begin with I was greatly annoyed at this increase in my psychological work, till I came to see that the whole process followed a law; and I then noticed, too, that transference of this kind brought about no great addition to what I had to do. For the patient the work remained the same: she had to overcome the distressing affect aroused by having been able to entertain such a wish even for a moment; and it seemed to make no difference to the success of the treatment whether she made this psychical repudiation the theme of her work in the historical instance or in the recent one connected with me. The patients, too, gradually learnt to realize that in these transferences on to the figure of the physician it was a question of a compulsion and an illusion which melted away with the conclusion of the analysis. [Breuer and Freud 1895, p. 304]

It is interesting that Freud sees the idea of a disturbance in the patient's relation to the physician as an *external* obstacle, even though it is met with in every serious analysis. The three types of disturbances, including what Freud calls the transference, are not the main arena of the treatment but rather are considered to be material to be mastered and gotten over as expeditiously as possible. He tells us that at first he was annoyed by the transference but now has dealt with his annoyance, since transference does not really add to his work.[7] Even in the few pages quoted, Freud vacillates in his view of transference. At times, he sees transference as an external obstacle or even as a nuisance deterring him from his main task of recovering pathogenic memories; at other times, he is surprisingly modern in his view of transference. Still, transference is restricted to distressing ideas arising from the content of the analysis, and they are ideas that are *false connections*.[8] These false connections, while important, are not the central issue for Freud's treatment to achieve success.

One of the first and most dramatic examples of transference that Freud witnessed (Breuer's treatment of Anna O.) did not help him feel secure about

---

[7]This point of view is different than that taken by Freud later and, of course, is different from the views of many modern psychoanalytic authors who would consider the transference the main vehicle of analysis.

[8]Freud at this time considered obsessive symptomatology as essentially false connections. Thus if a person defended against one idea, and obsessed about another substitute (conscious) idea, the conscious idea was a false connection. He theorized that these supervalent conscious ideas were the result of energy transfers. The process of defense was involved with making a strong idea a weak one. When this happened, there was now a new conscious strong idea, which was the false connection. Transference could be seen as just one type of false connection. Put in other terms, all false connections have a transfer of energy. For a look at Freud's views, see "The Neuro-Psychoses of Defense" (1894).

the implications of transference in a treatment situation. When Anna professed her love for Breuer, Breuer's discomfort was not lost on Freud. Freud (1914) commented that Breuer stopped his practice of hypnotherapy because of his experience with Anna O. However one may interpret Breuer's reaction to his treatment of Anna O., there can be no question that this treatment raised quite intense feelings for both Breuer and Freud. Freud was well aware of the criticisms that might be directed toward him—criticisms that he was inducing women to fall in love with him with this new technique. There was, of course, no shortage of criticism of Freud's methods. Focusing only on these external historical factors may lead us to overlook the difficulties any analyst encounters in dealing with transference. Freud was not an exception to these difficulties. In fact, we see in his treatment of Dora that the issue of transference was pivotal.

Freud's distinctions among the three types of disturbances in the patient–therapist relationship are interesting. He stresses that if a patient feels neglected or feels frightened of becoming too dependent, this is not transference but a special form of resistance that is apart from transference. Perhaps one can say that, if a patient hears something negative about this new form of treatment, it is understandable that the patient might have some reaction to these negative comments. But why would feelings of neglect or insult be considered apart from the content of the person's conflicts? Freud states that the sensitivity and suspiciousness of hysterical patients may occasionally attain surprising dimensions. This hardly seems to be a response that is situationally determined, or even necessarily the least serious conflict one might encounter in a treatment. It is clear that today these two other types of reactions would usually be considered transference reactions and, indeed, transference reactions of some importance. Freud, however, saw these two types of reactions as factors to deal with expeditiously so that one can return to the therapeutic work. He did not want to dwell on these reactions but rather felt that while they may occur, they can be dealt with quickly, allowing the real work to proceed. As Freud says earlier in this same chapter, there are some "other patients [where] . . . their personal relation to him [the therapist] will force itself, for a time at least, unduly into the foreground" (p. 266). Thus, these personal reactions force themselves into the treatment and disrupt it. By a disruption in the treatment, Freud meant that patients were no longer being able to associate and produce material related to their pathogenic memories. The recovery of the pathogenic memories was the crucial element, whereas reaction of the patient to the physician was a disturbance not intrinsic to the material. To some extent, the hypnotic technique allowed one to bypass this difficulty, but as Freud pointed out, the hypnotic technique had difficulties of its own. Moreover, based on Freud's experience and certainly Breuer's experience with Anna O., it was clearly possible for a patient to have intense reactions to the therapist even if one used hypnosis. It was Freud's destiny to deal with transference. A few years after writing the psychotherapy chapter in "Studies on Hysteria," Freud treated a young woman who helped convince him that transference is a crucial and unavoidable element in the treatment situation.

Dora

Seven years after the publication of "Studies on Hysteria," Freud wrote his first major psychoanalytic case report, "Fragment of an Analysis of a Case of Hysteria" (1905), most commonly referred to as the case of Dora. In the intervening period, Freud's ideas had both developed and changed, particularly in terms of the etiology of neuroses. He had abandoned the seduction theory as a necessary or even a usual cause of neurotic conflict. He was on his way to developing the concept of infantile sexuality. Moreover, he had just published what was perhaps his most significant work, "The Interpretation of Dreams" (Freud 1900). The case of Dora consisted mainly of the analysis of two dreams. Although Freud stated that he was publishing the case in part to help more fully understand the etiology of hysteria, it is clear that these two dreams and their relation to his newly published dream book occupied center stage for Freud. In his postscript on the case, Freud develops yet another theme that significantly changed the practice of psychoanalysis. He relates that the failure of his treatment with Dora had to do with his mishandling of the transference.

It is surprising that more investigators have not asked why Freud published a case that ended in such a frustrating manner. Most later-day commentators have either praised Freud's attempts with Dora or reanalyzed her and suggested how the treatment should have been conducted. Our focus will be to look at Freud's difficulties with Dora and with his emerging views on this troubling new concept, the transference. We will see Freud grappling with the clinical implications of this concept. It is a struggle that will continue for much of Freud's career.

Dora was a 16-year-old girl when Freud first interviewed her. The interview was conducted at her father's request. She was 18 years old when she entered treatment. She stayed in treatment from October 1900 until December of the same year. She abandoned treatment at that time and informed Freud of her decision to leave treatment during their last session (on December 31, 1900). Dora was the daughter of an upper-middle-class Austrian family whose friendship with another family (Frau and Herr K.) occupied a place of special importance in Dora's life. Dora's father was having an affair with Frau K., and Herr K. had been making advances to Dora from at least the time that she was 14 years old. Dora not only displayed a variety of symptoms, such as aphonia, chronic dyspnea, unilateral headaches, attacks of nervous coughing, periodic depression, and at times suicidal ideation, but she also obsessed with her father's relations with Frau K. Freud thought this obsession excessive, and he called these thoughts *supervalent ideation*. He used this term because he believed that "no amount of conscious and voluntary effort of thought" on Dora's part was able to dissipate or remove these thoughts. She not only was obsessed with her father's sexual liaison, but clearly felt that many of her conflicts could be resolved by changes in her father's behavior. She also desired her father's acceptance of the truth of her allegations concerning Herr K. Freud's (1905) view was that her "behavior went far beyond what would have been appropriate to filial concern. She felt and acted like a jealous wife" (p. 56). Dora's father maintained that he didn't believe her allegations about Herr K, and he considered these charges to be the fantasies of an adolescent girl. He also denied any sexual interest in Frau K. Dora's father was ostensibly turning to Freud for help in clearing up these fantasies and bringing Dora under control for her own good. Freud was suspicious of the father's motivations and realized that he wanted Dora under control at least as much for his own benefit as for hers. Dora was upsetting the delicate balance of sexual liaisons between these two families.

Even though Freud evinced skepticism about the father's motivation, he agreed to see Dora in treatment. It is interesting to look at Freud's clinical behavior with Dora. He presents interpretations early in the treatment and continues to interpret Dora's repressed sexual wishes through the last day of treatment. For example, early in the case Freud (1905) interprets that her disgust at Herr K.'s kiss was really a reversal of affect and a displacement of sensations (pp. 28–29). Dora is viewed by Freud as presenting an admixture of adolescent love, incestuous fantasies and, at rock bottom, conflicts over homosexual or lesbian relations (p. 120). This admixture is not unusual in an adolescent, but it is unusual to present this material to the adolescent without having gained some sense of her "cooperation" in the treatment. Freud's manner seems more that of a prosecuting attorney than that of an analyst. He treats Dora less as a confused and rebellious adolescent patient than as an adversary to be bested. It is, of course, a possibility that a rebellious adolescent might indeed break off a treatment even if things were handled reasonably well. But Freud did not handle the treatment well at all, and in hindsight it is easy to see that in the treatment Freud and Dora repeated conflicts that she was going through with her father and Herr K. We might ask whether we can reasonably assume that Freud enacted various conflicts during the course of this treatment. Obviously the answer to this question will depend on one's definition of enactment and whether one finds the concept useful.

First, however, let us briefly go back to Freud and Dora's last day of treatment. Freud is in the midst of analyzing the second dream of Dora. He has looked at this dream for most of two sessions. Then Freud (1905) relates the following conversation that occurred on December 31:

> She opened the third session with these words: "Do you know that I am here for the last time today?" "How can I know, as you have said nothing to me about it?" "Yes I made up my mind to put up with it till the New Year. But I shall wait no longer than that to be cured." "You know that you are free to stop the treatment at any time. But for to-day we will go on with our work. When did you come to this decision?" "A fortnight ago, I think." "That sounds just like a maidservant or a governess—a fortnight's warning." "There was a governess who gave warning with the K's, when I was on my visit to them that time at L (where she had a sexualized encounter with Herr K.), by the lake." "Really? You never told me about her. Tell me." [p. 107]

Dora then relates a story about this governess who told her that Herr K. had made love to her and then abruptly had ceased to pay attention to her. Herr K. used virtually the same seduction language with this governess as he had with Dora. Freud interprets to Dora that she was not angry at Herr K.'s proposal to her, but rather she was offended by him when she recognized the language that he used with the governess was identical to the language that he utilized in his entreaty to her. He goes on to further interpret that, like the maid, Dora wants Herr K., to leave his wife for her. In short, Freud continues the same interpretations that have already proven to be less than completely success-ful. He does not seriously consider her announcement that she is leaving treat-ment, but rather goes on with what he considers to be the analytic task, that is, unraveling Dora's *true*[9] thoughts and feelings. Whatever one's interpretation of Dora's dynamics, one thing is certain: Freud aids Dora in acting out her conflicts. He repeatedly intrudes on her without seriously considering her experience of the *analysis*. He attempts to defend his actions, but as one can see in the postscript, he develops serious misgivings about what transpired between them. If we were going to pursue the case in greater detail, one might wonder why Dora continued seeing Freud as long as she did and why she answered so many of his questions. We might also want to explain why she revisited Freud in April of 1902.

The question that we will speculate on is one that we asked before: Why did Freud write up a case where the analysis was unsuccessful? Was it simply a continuation of the dream book and exposition of his views on hysteria, or was there something else that made it a special case? Apparently Freud wrote

---

[9]True in the sense that it reflects Freud's ideas about the unconscious meaning of Dora's ver-balizations and symptoms.

up the case quite quickly (Gay 1988), and yet he didn't publish it until 1905. Gay (1988) indicates that Freud was "evidently disheartened by his friend Oscar Rie's critical reception of the manuscript and also by the decay of his most impassioned friendship" with Fliess (p. 246). This no doubt explains some delay in the publication, but it hardly seems to account for the length of the delay, particularly since Freud was submitting other manuscripts during this period.

There is much evidence that Freud's realization of what had transpired with Dora came to him gradually, and probably with a reasonable amount of psychological pain and conflict. The measure of his genius and character is that he could eventually look at his failure and learn an important lesson that began to change the way he and generations of analysts after him conceived of patients' responses in analysis. Despite the fact that Freud was able to reassess his treatment of Dora, he was still tied strongly to his pathogenic memory model. Before we look again at his tie to the pathogenic memory model, let us examine his views on transference.

Freud (1905) states in the postscript, "during psycho-analytic treatment the formation of new symptoms is invariably stopped. But the productive powers of the neurosis are by no means extinguished; they are occupied in the creation of a special class of mental structures, for the most part unconscious, to which the name of 'transferences' may be given" (p. 116).

Freud (1905) goes on to present a harbinger of his later views on the clinical significance of transference:

What are the transferences? They are new editions or facsimiles of the impulses and phantasies which are aroused and made conscious during the progress of the analysis; but they have this peculiarity, which is characteristic for their species, that they replace some earlier person by the person of the physician. To put it another way: a whole series of psychological experiences are revived, not as belonging to the past, but as applying to the person of the physician at the present moment. Some of these transferences have a content which differs from that of their model in no respect whatever except for the substitution. These then—to keep to the same metaphor—are merely new impressions or reprints. Others are more ingeniously constructed; their content has been subjected to a moderating influence—to sublimation, as I call it—and they may even become conscious, by cleverly taking advantage of some real peculiarity in the physician's person or circumstances and attaching themselves to that. These, then, will no longer be new impressions, but revised editions. [p. 116]

In this cogent statement of transference, Freud presents a small model of the different varieties of transference. To be more precise, Freud is pointing out that what is transferred may appear largely uninfluenced or may be subject to change by conscious or preconscious influence. In the next paragraph, Freud (1905) addresses for the first time the significance of transference as a crucial process in analytic therapy:

> If the theory of analytic technique is gone into, it becomes evident that transference is an inevitable necessity. Practical experience, at all events, shows conclusively that there is no means of avoiding it, and that this latest creation of the disease must be combated like all the earlier ones. This happens, however, to be by far the hardest part of the whole task. It is easy to learn how to interpret dreams, to extract from the patient's associations his unconscious thoughts and memories, and to practice similar explanatory arts: for these the patient himself will always provide the text. Transference is the one thing the presence of which has to be detected almost without assistance and with only the slightest clues to go upon, while at the same time the risk of making arbitrary inferences has to be avoided. Nevertheless, transference cannot be evaded, since use is made of it in setting up all the obstacles that make the material inaccessible to treatment, and since it is only after the transference has been resolved that a patient arrives at a sense of conviction of the validity of the connections which have been constructed during the analysis. [pp. 116–117]

This marks a turning point; Freud is again considering transference to be an inevitable necessity but now there is a new sense of urgency. Approximately seven to nine years earlier his views on transference were similar, but he did not recognize the crucial role of transference for his new clinical work. Not only is transference essential, it is the vehicle that allows the patient the "conviction of the validity of the connections" made in an analysis. In "Studies on Hysteria," Freud had already stated that "recollection without affect almost invariably produces no result." When he said this he was, of course, talking about the cathartic method, but this view remained unchanged: whatever the psychotherapeutic technique, the affect and the idea or mental representation must be experienced together in the treatment. In Freud's new developing analytic method, the idea and the affect and the conviction about the connections come via the transference. This is true even though Freud (1905) tells us it is "the hardest part of the whole (analytic) task" (p. 116).

Lessons from Dora

We know that on the basis of his clinical experience with Dora, Freud came to recognize that his failure in the case had to do with his lack of attention to

Dora's repetitions of her conflicts in the treatment. Thus, Freud ignored the transference and concentrated on her sexual conflicts as he came to understand them through his analysis of her dreams, her associations to the dreams, and her history. He has stated that he wrote the case history of Dora as a continuation of his dream book. There are indications that Freud was disappointed again to come up against transference and to find out about this new essential component of his evolving treatment method. It may be that his discovery and his reactions are a prototype for the analyst in training. It is quite frequent for an analyst to push away the transference and *regress* to the stance of a hypnotist, especially when the patient is manifesting signs of a transference reaction in which hostile wishes are expressed (negative transference). Most (perhaps all) beginning analysts have difficulty in dealing with transference manifestations and find it easier to point out to the patient the unconscious meaning of a fantasy or to trace a patient's behavior or thoughts to their historical roots. In doing this, the transference is often avoided. Freud's discovery of the analytic method is prototypic of the way most people come to know the analytic method. Freud was trying to avoid the implications of the transference by attempting to unravel Dora's pathogenic memories. Whether or not Freud's reactions can be considered prototypic, one can say that transference was the last major concept that Freud put forth in terms of his ideas on psychoanalytic technique.

Dora was the end of an era. After his experiences with her, Freud's conceptualization of the treatment situation would never be the same. In his experiences with Dora, he encounters transference in the clinical situation, and he is transformed into an analyst. This transformation was not an immediate one (nor a fully lasting one), and it took Freud several years after he had seen Dora for the last time to come to terms with his new insights.[10] His delay in the publication of the case was symptomatic of the time he needed to address yet another upheaval in his understanding of the clinical situation.

Enactment and the Freudian Legacy

Although Freud tells us that transference is the hardest part of the treatment, he does not really tell us how he came to this realization. It is left for

---

[10]Bird (1972), an author we highlight in the transference section, has previously presented a similar view. He maintains that as a result of Freud's "own self-analysis, did he come to an understanding of the significance of transference." After he had understood transference via his relationship to Fliess, then he could apply to Dora "what he had learned in himself." Whether or not Freud learned about transference in his self-analysis, it is likely that his delay in publication of the manuscript was because of his difficulties with the clinical implications of transference.

readers to infer that Freud had personal difficulty in handling a contumacious young woman. Although she was willing to tolerate Freud's interventions, she never allowed him to have the effect that he desired. He wished her to join him in his interest in the meanings of her dreams, her symptoms, and most of all in his psychotherapeutic method. She was unyielding in her reluctance to become one of Freud's subjects. She wanted other things and saw Freud in some ways as another man who was intrusive, exciting, attempting to penetrate her, and most of all as a man who wanted to use her for his own purposes.

McLaughlin (Chapter 6, this volume) defines an enactment as a time in treatment when both analyst and analysand believe that they are being influenced by the other. In this treatment, it is clear that Freud thought that he was being manipulated by Dora even when she came back to see him after a two-year hiatus. He states, "Dora came to see me again: to finish her story and to ask for help once more. One glance at her face, however, was enough to tell me that she was not in earnest over her request" (1905, pp. 120–121). He knows right away that she is not serious about treatment, and he is immediately suspicious about her intentions. Here it is clear that Freud experiences Dora as the reason for his failure.[11] She is the cause of his reaction but he does not at this point look in both directions (inward as well as outward) as he will counsel analysts to do a decade later (Freud 1912).[12] Of course, put in these terms there is clearly an anachronistic flavor to this view of the interaction between Dora and Freud. Freud had no guidelines to help with what we now term his enactments. His view of the task of the therapist (analyst) was to be an agent who uncovered pathogenic memories. Once this was done, the encounter was finished. The pathogenic memory model would not have led to the concept of enactment. Freud had to allow transference into the treatment before we could proceed to the idea of enactment.

REFERENCES

Bird, B. (1972). Notes on transference: universal phenomenon and hardest part of analysis. *Journal of the American Psychoanalytic Association* 20:267–301.
Breuer, J., and Freud, S. (1895). Studies on hysteria. *Standard Edition* 2:1–306.
Ellman, S. J. (1991). *Freud's Technique Papers: A Contemporary Perspective.* Northvale, NJ: Jason Aronson.

---

[11]Obviously Freud was not turning her away, but from his reaction it appears as if he is not willing at this time to seriously consider that Dora is in need of assistance.

[12]Here I am referring to Freud's concept of evenly hovering attention. This concept is intended to allow the analyst to focus on both internal and external events depending on their relevance to the psychoanalytic situation.

Freud, S. (1894). The neuro-psychoses of defense. *Standard Edition* 3:45–61.

—— (1900). The interpretation of dreams. *Standard Edition* 4/5.

—— (1905). Fragment of an analysis of a case of hysteria. *Standard Edition* 7:1–122.

—— (1912). Recommendations to physicians on the psycho-analytic method of treatment. In *Collected Papers*, vol. 2, pp. 342–366. New York: Basic Books, 1959.

—— (1914). On the history of the psycho-analytic movement. *Standard Edition* 14:7–66.

Gay, P. (1988). *Freud: A Life for Our Times*. New York: Norton.

Werman, D. S. (1983). Suppression as a defense. *Journal of the American Psychoanalytic Association* 31:405–415.

2

General Problems of Acting Out

PHYLLIS GREENACRE

Not very much has been written about the problems of acting out in the course of analysis, although they are most difficult to deal with, frequently interfere with analysis, and sometimes escape detection unless and until they become flagrant. Perhaps the earliest extensive discussion of acting out appeared in Freud's "Psychopathology of Everyday Life" (1901) under the headings "Erroneously Carried-out Actions" and "Symptomatic and Chance Actions." Particularly the latter chapter included some illustrations of what was later called acting out. At that time, however, such actions were generally considered from the angle of what other elements in the current situation were being displaced onto and concealed by them, and less emphasis was placed on their significance in relation to the earlier history of the patient. Perhaps the most systematic description of acting out has been presented by Fenichel (1945) who defined it tentatively as

> . . . an acting which unconsciously relieves inner tension and brings partial discharge to ward off impulses (no matter whether these impulses express directly instinctual demands or are reactions to original instinctual demands, e.g., guilt feelings); the present situation, somehow associatively connected with the repressed content, is used as an occasion for the discharge of repressed energies; the cathexis is displaced from the repressed memories to the present derivative, and the displacement makes this discharge possible. [p. 197]

Fenichel notes that this definition does not adequately differentiate acting out from other neurotic activity and emphasizes that in the former the quality of *action* is in itself especially conspicuous and important, and that it is generally a fairly organized activity, not merely a single movement, gesture, or mimicked expression. He further differentiates that by displacement and by rationalization it is generally ego-syntonic, and that it "... shares with transference an insufficient differentiation between the past and the present, an unwillingness to learn, a readiness to substitute rigid reactive patterns for adequate responses to actual stimuli." Acting out, in other words, is a special form of remembering, in which the old memory is reenacted in a more or less organized and often only slightly disguised form. It is not a clearly conscious visual or verbal recollection, nor is there any awareness that the special activity is motivated by memory. His behavior seems to the subject to be plausible and appropriate, although to the analyst and to the patient's friends it appears singularly disproportionate and inappropriate.

It would seem that in acting out there may be special problems in accepting and understanding current reality either because of (1) specific problems in the immediate real situation, (2) special persistence of memories of earlier disturbing experiences, or (3) an inadequate sense of reality. These also apply to the development of many symptoms and attitudes, but in the case of acting out there is a compulsion to reproduce repetitively a total experience or episode rather than to select some small part of it as a token representation. It may be translated into new terms or forms, but the experience in memory retains its original organization to an appreciable degree.

Fenichel notes the quality of motility or action[1] that pervades all acting out, as the very term states. He speaks of "... an allopsychic readiness—perhaps constitutional—to act..." as being one of the contributing factors, discusses the fact that being in analysis favors and utilizes acting out in the transference, and that the analytic process itself may somewhat stimulate acting out in predisposed individuals, in that it educates the patient to produce less and less distorted derivatives of repressed impulses, while it mobilizes and provokes all repressed impulses. For these reasons, acting out is relatively more frequent in persons who are undergoing analysis. It is to be particularly guarded against when it occurs outside of the transference because it interferes with the analysis by discharging tensions in an unanalyzable way, and because it may create reality problems in the patient's life of far-reaching and detrimental import. It may be useful, however, to differentiate between neurotic behavior and neurotic acting out. Doubtless these two are related, but acting out implies organized activity, which is generally based on a tendency to action, especially in those patients who show numerous instances of acting out during analysis.

----

[1]The term *acting* is used by Anna Freud in *The Ego and the Mechanisms of Defense* (Chapter 2) in the sense in which *acting out* is used here.

In dealing further with the subject of acting out, this discussion is limited to considerations of first, its genesis, and second, suggestions as to technique. It will be necessary to limit the discussion mainly to habitual neurotic acting out in contrast to psychotic acting out in which the unconscious memories and attitudes take over the current situation so completely that the stimuli of the latter may be scarcely discernible. We would also differentiate isolated, occasional, or really symptomatic acting out during the course of analysis from those conditions in which the acting out is frequent, habitual, or characteristic of tendencies evident in the entire life of the patient. It is obvious that the impulsiveness is based on an inability to tolerate frustration, a special disturbance of reality and of self-criticism, the quality of marked motility or activity often of a dramatic character—all especially characteristic of the extremely severe neuroses, which sometimes appear perilously close to psychoses and the psychopathies.

In the *genesis* of habitual acting out, Fenichel (1945) mentions oral fixation with its high narcissistic need and intolerance of frustrations, the heightened constitutional motility, and the presence of severe early traumata (producing a repetitive, abreactive acting out similar to the traumatic neuroses) as being factors producing tendencies to action and therefore contributing to acting out. While all these factors seem of undoubted importance, I would add two more: a special emphasis on visual sensitization producing a bent for dramatization (derivatives of exhibitionism and scopophilia) and a largely unconscious belief in the magic of action. The need for dramatization may be one of the factors that is most influential in turning tendencies to neurotic action into acting out, in that it predisposes to retention of the episode in memory as a scene or an organized memory rather than to the selection of parts of it for repetition. Such people often believe that to do a thing in a dramatic or imitative way—to make it look as though it were true—is really the equivalent of making it true. It is obvious that this works also to ward off with magic activity as well as to produce by imitative approximation.

It may be, however, that the common genetic situation, which combines with or sometimes partly produces these characteristics, and the accompanying general tendency to act out consist in a distortion in the relation of action to speech and verbalized thought, arising most often from severe disturbances in the second year and showing its effects in the following months as well. Repeated clinical observations of patients who habitually acted out first led me to consider these relationships of speech and action: (1) Even when the action involved in acting out includes speech, the latter is usually secondary to the action, which is the more important function. Sometimes the speech itself seems, through its own motor qualities of pitch and intensity, to participate in the motor discharge of tension rather than to participate through establishment of communication or any distillation of the situation into thought. (2) In many patients who frequently act out in the analytic situation, such periods are characterized by an extraordinary large number of distortions of language—slips, malapropisms, spoonerisms, pseudoaphasias, and even a heightened tendency to punning and klang assocations. In one patient in whom I was able to work out the origin of this disturbance rather clearly, the acting out in the analytic situation was often associated with a silly-sounding preoccupation with proper names, in various klang combinations, for all the world like the sound–mouthing explorations of a 2- to 3-year-old child. This had originally been used by the patient to ward off grief and anxiety at the age of 4 when she lost through death from lockjaw an older male cousin. She had turned to him with a displaced oedipal attachment after feeling deserted by both parents subsequent to the birth of a younger brother. Even earlier this child had frequently been taken by her nurse on daily walks to the nurse's home, and had been the passive witness of sexual scenes. She was warned not to tell and gained much praise from the nurse for keeping the secret. A precocious and attractive child, predisposed anyway to an excess of adulation, she spoke early, well, and clearly; but under the pressure of keeping the secret, she developed a special tendency to amusing prattle in which she made shrewd remarks, doubtless "half-revealing and all-concealing" her secret. It seems probable that in this situation the child, who was thus already neurotically disturbed, incorporated her infantile concept of the disease, lockjaw, into her repetitive mouthing of variations of the cousin's name with such a cute effect that her "mourning" by identification became an attractive joke, and the cornerstone of a disturbance of character development. She became a great practical joker, punster, and "gag" producer throughout her life, and she both talked and acted in order to avoid feeling.

The various types of association of word sounds, their relation to the period in which identity is established (with a separation of the self from the outer world, and an acceptance of the existence of two sexes), as well as their connection with names and natural functional sounds are beautifully apparent in a book for children: *The World is Round*, by Gertrude Stein. Examination of the psychogenesis of development proves that this is certainly a period in which speech and other motor functions, especially those of locomotion and of imitative action, may become subject to special complex involvements. It is my impression that the motility of acting out comes more from these than from inherently constitutional sources, at least in the sense of the congenital constitution. This is a period when both speech and walking are begun and are gradually being mastered. The orality of which Fenichel (1945) speaks is certainly important and has generally already been determined either by constitution or by the vicissitudes of the individual infant experience. It is certainly true

that the orally frustrated child expresses its distress through heightened dif-
fuse motility, and that oral frustration or special forms of indulgence may produce a general inability to tolerate other frustrations. It is also true that the
persistence of oral demands may be but the most conspicuous focus of a general state of emotional tension during the first months of life, and that this is a
source from which heightened disturbances at any later time occur. The special character of any early oral trauma may further play into delay, distortion,
or diversion of speech functioning.

During the second year of infancy, however, when mastery of speech and
of the special motility of walking is being accomplished, sphincter control is
also in the process of establishment. Not infrequently speech and mouth movements become combined with or influenced by the expulsive sphincter movements of bladder and bowel, and the character of the speech is clearly marked
with imprints derived from other body ejecta. General motor behavior, too, is
influenced, but not so often involved in an inhibitory way, by the struggle for
mastery of the body excretory processes. Activity seems rather to be increased
by the effort to control the excreta, and the first communications in regard to
these are generally in terms of gestures or infantile, often onomatopoeic, terms
that may persist strikingly well into adulthood.

It has seemed, then, that in those patients who tend chronically to act out
there was often (1) more or less emotional disturbance in the early months of
infancy with increased orality, diminished tolerance for frustration, and a heightened narcissism and (2) speech that was inhibited, delayed, or otherwise disturbed in development relatively more than motor discharge, which might
progress well into walking and in any event take over the burden of the increasing need for communication because of the greater tensions and pressures
of the period of toilet training. It is, however, the disturbance of the function of
speech, rather than merely of the form, which is important. In some instances
the child learns to articulate very well, but the speech becomes degraded in
its functioning, being used for exhibitionistic purposes rather than for communication. This emphasis on the cuteness of the speech with subsequent dimin-
ishing of its utility value may occur about equally in children with unclear
speech and in those with precociously clear verbalization, sometimes based
on their amusing imitations of elders. In either event, speech functioning is
exploited or even largely diverted into services other than those of communication. In other instances in which any slight uncertainty of speech was de-
rided, an inhibition of speech and an almost complete dependence on action
may occur.

Under either set of circumstances, there is an inevitable increase in rapport by looking. Dr. Anna Katan, in an unpublished communication, has verified the importance of repeated primal scene experiences in influencing act-

ing out. In her experience, the child who is repeatedly subjected to primal scenes may undergo heightened visual erotization through participation by looking. But not infrequently, by its crying, the child excites the anger of one or the other parent and so is drawn into active participation. This may, if repeated, definitely increase both the scopophilic-exhibitionistic elements of the character and the preverbal acting into the situation, which later contributes to acting out.

Anyone who works much with severe neurotics becomes aware how much their communication is in terms of body language—whether of involuntary body tensions, gestures, transitory somatic changes, or acting out. All these forms of communication, even when they appear within the analytic situation, are peculiarly difficult to analyze and may be obstacles to analysis, probably because they essentially belong to a preverbal form of thinking and represent an actual earlier difficulty in making this transition in the life of the child. The capacity to verbalize and to think in verbal terms seems to represent an enormous advance not only in the economy of communication, but also in a focusing of the emotions that are associated with the content of thought. This, I believe, is an important consideration in understanding the problems of acting out.

While it seems that this disproportion between verbalization and motor activity is characteristic of most habitual acting out, it is apparent that its importance must vary greatly with the degree and type of acting out. It is always determined in considerable measure by the pressure of the specific content of the individual piece of acting out. This will then be reproduced repeatedly as it is elicited by current stimuli, as though to ward off danger "by doing it first," or to repeat the past event as though "to see it again" and prove it to be less noxious, very much after the fashion of the stages in the development of a sense of reality. Indeed, an incompletely developed sense of reality has appeared characteristic of many of these patients. But chronic or habitual acting out is a repetition of past events and an establishment of transference relationships with too great a burden, from the second year of life. Both are lived out and presented without the sufficient emotional equipment or the methods of communication that belong to later development. This symptom complex is intensified when, in addition, a weak and narcissistic ego persists because of other causes. In most instances this very narcissistic weakness of the ego, with its accompanying overdependence on dramatic activity rather than on work-directed activity as a means of expression, is associated further with tendencies to exaggerated and somewhat detached fantasies, which in turn impair the sense of reality or at the very least jade the perception of reality.

In one of his early papers on technique, Freud (1914) discussed the subject of acting out, in accordance with the technical developments of that period and advised against encouraging it:

Allowing "repetition" during analytic treatment, which is the latest form of technique, constitutes a conjuring into existence of a piece of real life, and can therefore not always be harmless and indifferent in its effect on all cases. The whole question of "exacerbation of symptoms during treatment," so often unavoidable, is linked up with this. . . . [For the physician] recollection in the old style, reproduction in the mind, remains the goal of his endeavors. . . . He sets about a perpetual struggle with the patient to keep all the impulses which he would like to carry into action within the boundaries of his mind, and when it is possible to divert into the work of recollection any impulse which the patient wants to discharge in action, he celebrates it as a special triumph for the analysis.

Anna Freud, much later (1936), summarized the increased knowledge to the analyst of the analysand's ego reactions obtained from observations of acting out but stated that this is, peculiarly, seldom usable for therapy, as in the very process ". . . the ego continues to function freely or if it makes common cause with the id and simply carries out its behests, there is little opportunity for endopsychical displacements and the bringing to bear of influence from without." It seems probable that in these relationships lie the reasons for the therapeutic limitations of such methods as group analysis and the psychodrama, no matter how much they may relieve immediate strains and tensions. Anna Freud implies that habitual acting out cannot be analyzed.

It would seem that the three techniques known for the management of acting out are interpretation, prohibition, and strengthening the ego (Fenichel 1945). These techniques are applicable in varying degrees according to the specific nature of the acting out, the structure of the ego, and whether the acting out occurs inside or outside the analytic situation. Beyond the general prohibition against making important decisions affecting the analysand's life during the course of the treatment, prohibition of acting out is not easy. Analysis would soon become little more than guidance among many prohibitions, provided the analyst were sufficiently astute to anticipate the exact nature of the dangers the patient would encounter; furthermore, because in its very nature acting out is ego-syntonic and the patient is not aware of its destructive nature, it comes to the attention of the analyst in most instances after its occurrence (if at all), and sometimes it is not reported or is only indirectly reported.

Interpretation would certainly seem to be the method of choice, but it is inevitably limited to those patients who have reasonably well-integrated egos and those in whom the acting out occurs only sporadically and in accordance with especially laden earlier traumata that are being revived in the course of the analysis. In my experience, however, too early interpretation of some of these traumata will reactivate accessory or related ones and may set in motion a temporary tendency to act out in a patient who previously has not done so. It may then be as much a question of the timing as it is of the accuracy of the interpretation of the specific memory content, the conflictful childhood situation, which is the nucleus of the later disturbance.

Another kind of interpretation is necessary, however, to strengthen the ego and develop adequate self-criticism, which must precede or overlap analysis of id contents in patients who engage in widespread and diverse acting out apart from the analytic situation. Generally such patients reveal these tendencies in their lives before they come into analysis—whether in the frankly impulse-ridden behavior that is apparent in the history, or in generalized restraint and inhibition that wall off and disguise the latent impulsiveness. Frequently in the latter cases, habitual acting out becomes apparent only after analysis is well advanced. This is especially true in patients who have suffered an infantile psychosis that has become encapsulated. Such patients must have extensive periods of analysis during which id contents are dealt with only as much as is absolutely necessary. Many such patients bring graphic and interesting dreams and seem to have a flair for understanding symbolism. Some interpretations may have to be given which may *seem* to be accepted but are utilized only for narcissistic gratification. It is the narcissism rather that needs most to be analyzed. Patients may seduce unwary analysts into working too quickly with this deeper material at a time when it cannot be assimilated by the patient, only increases anxiety, and may even be used as a justification for acting out in deeds or talk outside of the analytic situation. Such patients may tend to distort an interpretation into an authoritative direction or take a dream as a portent.

In connection with a discussion of the forerunners of early anxiety (Greenacre 1941), I attempted to describe my own methods of dealing with a group of patients many of whom showed this tendency to frequent acting out. Adding to the material of that paper, the following points of special importance in habitual acting out, associated with poor ego structure, seem worth mentioning. It is usually important that the positive transference should be especially well established before any id content is interpreted even though it may have been presented before. In many cases, there seems little difficulty in gaining a positive transference, as affectively hungry patients will form an immediate but too demanding type of transference and will readily sense and exploit a sympathetic countertransference. Other patients will exhibit a rather showy type of positive transference, which is, however, shallow and quickly reveals itself as too susceptible to acting out both in the transference and outside. Both types of apparently quickly established positive transference need time for their solidification. Some of these patients certainly can never form a sufficiently firm transference to be analyzed.

Interpretation of the patient's *narcissism* must be begun early and pursued patiently. Among other narcissistic phenomena, the inability to distinguish fantasy from reality goals and tacit reliance on magic are outstanding. The latter reveals itself in a special picturesqueness of language and behavior (to make it look as though it were true is to make it true), also in overplaying the significance of coincidence. Relatively soon it is possible to acquaint the patient directly with his overreadiness to act and with the fact that this is one of his ways of warding off anxiety. This generally leads to the patient's awareness of his basic state of tension and his susceptibility to anxiety, which has been concealed by activity, spuriously rationalized as productive. It will become necessary at some time during the first months of the analysis for the patient to be acquainted directly with the evidences of his very early disturbances, manifest in his body language, symptomatic acts within the analytic situation and in behavior outside. The objective is not so much to understand at first the fully detailed significance of such behavior, but rather to understand that the patient is using this as a way of communication and that it is robbing him of the possibility of a fuller possession of his capacity for expression. Although it may be necessary to use an intellectualized approach about just these problems, this is done in order to cultivate the patient's self-scrutiny and self-criticism. If this is accomplished, the patient will begin to make his own prohibitions and much of the battle with acting out will have been won. This is accomplished only at the expense of considerable pain because of the narcissistic wounds and reductions involved but may be compensated by a definite feeling of growing competence, which is appreciated by the patient. Only when this is well under way can the analysis of the id be developed to the fullest extent.

There is still the question of how fully the contents of the preverbal period, which have given rise to and are sometimes contained in the acting out, can be converted into verbal (thought or spoken) expressiveness, and so relieved. That the general manner of the patient's expressiveness may be changed from acting out to verbalization has been proved in my clinical experience. Some patients may always have to guard against tensions too great to be tolerable, never getting relief by working through the traumata of these earliest months to a degree comparable to what may be attained for those whose pathogenic conflicts have occurred in the period of verbalization.

One further consideration has suggested itself from the angle of the analyst's reaction to the patient who acts out. Fenichel (1945) mentions that some analysts provoke, enjoy, or encourage dramatic acting out in their patients and overstress its possible benefit as abreaction, rather than really analyze it. This seems occasionally the problem of young and inexperienced analysts but may also occur among analysts who themselves tend to act out, either directly or in an inhibited form, and to enjoy this vicariously in their patients. This may be of greater frequency and importance than one might at first think. It occurs among analysts who display no overt acting out but who react as some severely restrained adults who enjoy and tacitly applaud the impulsive behavior of their children who dare to do what they themselves have not been permitted. This is seen strikingly in the parental attitudes that form the background of many impulse-ridden psychopaths. An attitude of overanxiety on the part of the analyst about the patient's acting out is frequently sensed and reacted to by the patient, who then unconsciously gratifies his sadism as well in the acting out and gets a spurious sense of power and independence through it. If the analyst behaves in either of these ways to any appreciable degree, acting out will continue no matter how much its specific content is interpreted.

A final question, which may only be posed, is the relation of acting out to conversion hysteria. It is obvious that, symptomatically, acting out is common in conversion hysteria. This diagnosis is made much less frequently than it used to be either because the enurosis actually does not appear so often or because we now tend to see in it a set of much deeper disturbances than we used to, and we tend to group these cases rather with the narcissistic neuroses. It is a subject worthy of further study.

REFERENCES

Fenichel, O. (1945). Neurotic acting out. *Psychoanalytic Review* 32:197.
Freud, A. (1936). *The Ego and the Mechanisms of Defense.* Chapter 2. London: Hogarth.
Freud, S. (1901). The psychopathology of everyday life. *Standard Edition* 6.
—— (1914). Remembering, repeating and working-through. *Standard Edition* 12:145–156.
Greenacre, P. (1941). The predisposition to anxiety, part 2. *Psychoanalytic Quarterly* 10:66–94.

3

Countertransference and Role-Responsiveness

JOSEPH SANDLER

As we know, the term *countertransference* has a great many meanings, just as the term *transference* has. Freud first saw countertransference as referring to the analyst's blind spots, which presented an obstacle to the analysis. From the beginning, countertransference was consistently seen by Freud "as an obstruction to the freedom of the analyst's understanding of the patient." In this context Freud regarded the analyst's mind as an "instrument . . . , its effective functioning in the analytic situation being impeded by counter-transference." Countertransference in the analyst was equated with the resistance in the patient (Sandler, Dare, and Holder 1973).

As far as *transference* is concerned, Freud saw it first as a hindrance but later regarded it as an indispensable vehicle for the analytic work. However, he did not take a similar step in regard to countertransference. This inevitable step was taken after Freud. It was a crucial development in the psychoanalytic literature when the countertransference

> began to be seen as a phenomenon of importance in helping the analyst to understand the hidden meaning of material brought by the patient. The essential idea . . . is that the analyst has elements of understanding and appreciation of the processes occurring in his patient, that these elements are not immediately conscious and that they can be discovered by the analyst if he monitors his own mental associations while listening to the patient. [Sandler, Dare, and Holder 1973]

The first explicit statement of the *positive* value of countertransference was made by Paula Heimann (1950). Others have written on and developed the topic.

However, the two papers by Heimann (1950, 1960) have to be singled out as landmarks in the change of view of countertransference. She started by considering countertransference as referring to all the feelings that the analyst may experience toward his patient. Heimann remarks that the analyst has to be able to *"sustain* the feelings which are stirred up in him, as opposed to discharging them (as does the patient), in order to *subordinate* them to the analytic task in which he functions as the patient's mirror reflection." She assumes "that the analyst's unconscious understands that of his patient. This rapport on the deep level comes to the surface in the form of feelings which the analyst notices in response to his patient, in his 'countertransference'" (Heimann 1950).

I shall not mention the other important writings in this field, except to say that, of course, countertransference had been written about before Heimann's work and it had been pointed out that countertransference is a normal phenomenon. But what seems to have been stressed has been the differences between what one might call the "appropriate" and "useful" countertransference on the one hand and the "dangerous" or "undesirable" countertransference response on the other. Heimann's contribution was to show clearly that the reaction of the analyst may usefully be the first clue to what is going on in the patient.

In *The Patient and the Analyst* the literature on transference was discussed in some detail, and we concluded by commenting that, in our view:

> . . . transference need not be restricted to the illusory apperception of another person . . . , but can be taken to include the unconscious (and often subtle) attempts to manipulate or to provoke situations with others which are a concealed repetition of earlier experiences and relationships. It has been pointed out previously that when such transference manipulations or provocations occur in ordinary life, the person toward whom they are directed may either show that he does not accept the role, or may, if he is unconsciously disposed in that direction, in fact accept it, and act accordingly. It is likely that such acceptance or rejection of a transference role is not based on a conscious awareness of what is happening, but rather on unconscious cues. Transference elements enter to a varying degree into all relationships, and these (e.g. choice of spouse or employer) are often determined by some characteristic of the other person who (consciously or unconsciously) represents some attribute of an important figure of the past. [Sandler, Dare, and Holder 1973]

In our conclusions about transference we took the step of extending the notion of the patient's *projection* or *externalization* of some aspect of the past or of a figure of the past, on to the person of the analyst, to *all* his attempts to manipulate or to provoke situations with the analyst. I believe such manipulations to be an important part of object relationships in general, and to enter in trial form into the "scanning" of objects in the process of object choice. In the transference, in many subtle ways, the patient attempts to prod the analyst into behaving in a particular way and unconsciously scans and adapts to his perception of the analyst's reaction. The analyst may be able to "hold" his response to this prodding in his consciousness as a reaction *of his own*, which he perceives. I would make the link between certain countertransference responses and transference via the behavioral (verbal and nonverbal) *interaction* between the patient and the analyst. Heimann went as far as to point out that the analyst's response to the patient can be used as a basis for understanding the patient's material, often by something which he catches and holds in himself. I should like to try to elaborate.

No one can doubt the value of the analyst's continuing analysis of his or her countertransference. We can, I believe, start by assuming that the understanding of countertransference *is* important. My own interest in the subject has run parallel with an interest in the psychoanalytic psychology of object relationships, and what I present in the following is based on the assumption that a relationship or, to say the least, an interaction, develops between the two parties to the analytic process. We are all aware of the special features of the analytic situation, with its capacity to induce the regressive revival of the past in the present, in a way that is usually entirely unconscious in or rationalized by the patient. On the other hand, we have the use made by the analyst of his special skills, including the employment of such capacities as that for free-floating attention, for self-analysis, and for the maintenance of what Winnicott (1960) has called the "professional attitude." By free-floating attention I do not mean the clearing of the mind of thoughts or memories, but the capacity to allow all sorts of thoughts, daydreams, and associations to enter the analyst's consciousness while he is at the same time listening to and observing the patient.

I have mentioned the interaction between the patient and the analyst, and this is in large part (though, of course, not wholly) determined by what I shall refer to as the intrapsychic role-relationship that each party tries to impose on the other. One aspect of such a role-relationship can be appropriate to the task in hand, that is, to the work of analysis. Certainly from the side of the *patient* we may see a whole variety of very specific role-relationships emerge. What I want to emphasize is that the role-relationship of the patient in analysis at any particular time consists of a role in which he casts himself, and a *complementary* role in which he casts the analyst at that particular time. The patient's transference would thus represent an attempt by him to impose an interaction, an interrelationship (in the broadest sense of the word), between himself and the analyst. Nowadays many analysts must have the conviction (or at least the uneasy feeling) that the conceptualization of transference as the patient's libidinal or aggressive energic cathexis of a past object being transferred to the image of the analyst in the present is woefully inadequate. The patient's unconscious wishes and mechanisms with which we are concerned in our work are expressed intrapsychically in (descriptively) unconscious images or fantasies, in which both self and object in interaction have come to be represented in particular roles. In a sense the patient, in the transference, attempts to *actualize*[1] *these in a disguised way*, within the framework and limits of the analytic situation. In doing so, he resists becoming aware of any infantile relationship that he might be attempting to impose. I want to emphasize the difference between the manifest content of what the patient brings and the latent unconscious content (in particular the infantile role-relationships that he seeks to express or *enact*, as well as the defensive role-relationships that he may have constructed). If the patient keeps to the rules he will report rather than enact, and our clues, as analysts, to the unconscious inner role-relationship, which the patient is trying to impose, come to us via our perceptions and the application of our analytic tools.

One could regard even the simplest instinctual wish as, from early in life, a wish to impose and to experience a *role-relationship* as a vehicle of instinctual gratification. However, what I have to say here applies not only to unconscious instinctual wishes but *to the whole gamut of unconscious (including preconscious) wishes related to all sorts of needs, gratifications, and defenses.*

Parallel to the free-floating attention of the analyst is what I call *free-floating responsiveness*. The analyst is, of course, not a machine in absolute self-control, only experiencing on the one hand, and delivering interpretations on the other, although much of the literature might seem to paint such a picture. Among many other things, he talks, he greets the patient, he makes arrangements about practical matters, he may joke and, to some degree, he may allow his responses to depart from the classical psychoanalytic norm. My contention is that the analyst's overt reactions to the patient as well as in his thoughts and feelings what can be called his *role-responsiveness* shows itself, not only in his feelings but also in his attitudes and behavior, as a crucial element in his "useful" countertransference.

The following two examples illustrate what I mean.

Case Study 1

A patient, aged 35, had not had any previous analysis and had little knowledge of the analytic process. He was referred to me because of extreme anxiety about making public presentations of his work, although he felt absolutely

---

[1] I want to use the term *actualization* in the dictionary sense of the word, not in the specific technical senses in which it has been used by certain writers. *The Oxford English Dictionary* defines *actualization* as "a making actual; a realization in action or fact" and *actualize* as "to make actual, to convert into an actual fact, to realize in action."

competent and at ease in private and informal discussions. He had had a very narrow education, was the son of Eastern European immigrants, but because of his great financial and organizational skills had risen to a high position in a large financial organization. In the initial interview I found that he responded extremely well to trial interpretations, and I felt that work with him was going to be rewarding and a pleasure. During the first week or two of his analysis I found that I was talking very much more than I usually do. I should say that I am not an unduly silent analyst. After a little while I felt that something was making me anxious in regard to this patient. Some self-analytic reflection on my part showed me that I was afraid that he would leave, that I was anxious to keep him, to lower his anxiety level so that he would stay in analysis, and that I was talking more than usual in order to avoid the aggressive side of his ambivalent feelings. When I saw this, I felt relieved and reverted to my more usual analytic behavior. However, I noticed at once the urge to talk during the session and became aware that the patient, by a slight inflection of his voice, succeeded in ending every sentence with an interrogation, although he did not usually formulate a direct question. This gave me the opportunity to point out to him what he was doing (he was unaware of it, just as I had been unaware of it in him) and to show him how much he needed to have me reassure him by talking. He then recalled how he would feel extremely anxious as a child when his father returned home from work, and he would compulsively engage his father in conversation, asking him many questions in order to be reassured that his father was not angry with him. His father had been a professional fighter and was very violent. The patient was terrified of him but needed his father's admiration and love, to be the preferred child. (Later in the analysis we were, as one might expect, to see his fear of his own hostility to his father.) He told me that his father had the habit of not listening and not responding, and how frightening this was. The patient then realized that from early childhood onward he had developed the trick of asking questions without directly asking them, and this had become part of his character, being intensified in situations where he feared disapproval and needed supplies of reassurance from authority figures.

The point here is that, apart from the "ordinary" elements in his analytic work, the analyst will often respond overtly to the patient in a way that he feels indicates *only* his own (the analyst's) problems, his own blind spots, and he may successfully resort to self-analysis in order to discover the pathology behind his particular response or attitude to the patient. However, I want to suggest that very often the irrational response of the analyst, which his professional conscience leads him to see entirely as a blind spot of his own, may sometimes be usefully regarded as a compromise-formation between his own tendencies and *his reflexive acceptance of the role that the patient is forcing on him.*

Naturally, some analysts are more susceptible to certain roles than others, and also the proportion of the contribution from the side of the patient and from the side of the analyst will vary greatly from one instance to another. Of course, not all the irrational actions and reactions of the analyst are reflections of the role into which he is maneuvered by the patient. What I wanted to show in this example was simply how the patient, by a rather subtle element in his behavior, evoked an overt response from the analyst, which at first seemed to be *only* irrational countertransference. I am absolutely opposed to the idea that all countertransference responses of the analyst are due to what the patient has imposed on him.

Case Study 2

A patient in her late twenties, a schoolteacher, came to treatment because of social and sexual difficulties. After some time it became clear that she was terrified of her penis envy and of her hostility toward her mother. She had multiple phobic anxieties and needed, mainly through intellectualization and organizational control of others, including her teaching, to structure her world so that she always knew exactly "where she was." Her need to do this emerged in the transference, and after some three years of analytic work her psychopathology had become much clearer and she was much improved and happier. However, one strand of material had remained rather obscure. From the beginning she had cried during each session, and I had routinely passed her the box of tissues whenever she began to cry. Now I did not know why I did this but, having begun the practice, I did not feel inclined to change it without some good reason. Without knowing why, I had not felt it appropriate to take up her failure to bring her own tissues or a handkerchief, although with other patients I would have done this. There were many determinants of her crying, including her mourning for the mother she wanted to kill off, for the father she felt she had to give up, and so on. It transpired that when she was about 2 years old and a second child, a brother, had been born, she felt that she had lost her mother's attention. She remembered that at about 2½ years of age she was relegated to playing on her own in the backyard while her brother was being washed and changed. At this time she had also been sent to a nursery school where she had the memory of being very withdrawn, climbing into the rabbit hutch, and cuddling a white rabbit. She had later learned that after a short while at this school she was diagnosed as "autistic" by the school psychologist, was apparently very regressed, and had uncontrollable rages and tantrums. By this point in her analysis we were able to get at the repetition in the present of her fear of soiling and disgracing herself, and her need to control her objects as she had to control her sphincters. However, there was clearly something that was an important unconscious fantasy for her that had not been elicited. I had the feeling that we were somewhat stuck in the analytic work. One day something rather unusual happened in the analysis. She had begun to cry silently but this time I failed to respond, and she suddenly began to upbraid me and criticize me for not passing her the tissues. She became quite panicky and began to accuse me of being callous and uncaring. I responded by saying that I did not know why I had not passed her the tissues at that particular point, but if she could go on talking perhaps we could both understand more about it. What emerged then was material that lent a great deal of specificity to something we had not been able to crystallize previously. It became clear that her great need for control and for structures in her life was based not on a fear of soiling herself but rather on a fear that she would coil or wet herself *and that there would not be an adult around to clean her up.* This turned out to be the fear that dominated her life. It was a specific fantasy that seemed to have been elaborated during the late anal phase, under the impact of the mother's withdrawal from her because of the birth of the second child. The discovery and working through of this specific fantasy marked a crucial point in her analysis. I do not want to go into any more detail about her material, except to say that I think that I must have picked up unconscious cues from the patient that prompted me to behave in a certain way in her analysis, both to keep passing her the tissues and then to omit doing so. (It would be pure speculation to link the two and a half years of analysis with the age when her anxiety started.) I believe that this patient had forced me into a role, quite unconsciously on her part and on mine, corresponding to that of a parental introject, in which I enacted that part, first of the attentive mother and then suddenly that of the parent who did not clean her up. In the session I was not available to make sure that she was clean, just as she felt that, with the birth of her brother, her mother had not been there to clean her, being busy paying attention to the new baby.

Because the length of this presentation is limited, I cannot go into this rich topic any further, and in conclusion I shall restrict myself to one or two points. I have suggested that the analyst has, within certain limits, a free-floating behavioral responsiveness in addition to his free-floating conscious attention.

Within the limits set by the analytical situation he will, unless he becomes aware of it, tend to comply with the role demanded of him, to integrate it into his mode of responding and relating to the patient. Normally, of course, he can catch this counter-response in himself, particularly if it appears to be in the direction of being inappropriate. However, he may only become aware of it through observing his own behavior, responses, and attitudes, *after these have been carried over into action.* What I have been concerned with in this chapter is the special case of the analyst regarding some aspect of his own behavior as deriving entirely from within himself when it could more usefully be seen as a *compromise* between his own tendencies or propensities and the role-relationship that the patient is unconsciously seeking to establish. I should add that I do not find the terms *projection, externalization, projective identification,* and *putting parts of oneself into the analyst* sufficient to explain and to understand the processes of dynamic interaction that occur in the transference and countertransference. It seems that a complicated system of unconscious cues, both given and received, is involved. This is the same sort of process that occurs not only in the aspects of transference and countertransference discussed here but in normal object relationships and in the process of temporary or permanent object choice as well.

REFERENCES

Heimann, P. (1950). On counter-transference. *International Journal of Psycho-Analysis* 31:81–84.
—— (1960). Counter-transference. *British Journal of Medical Psychology* 33:9–15.
Sandler, J., Dare, C., and Holder, A. (1973). *The Patient and the Analyst: The Basis of the Psychoanalytic Process.* London: Allen & Unwin.
Winnicott, D. W. (1960). Counter-transference. *British Journal of Medical Psychology* 33:17–21.

4

Acting Out: A Reconsideration of the Concept

DALE BOESKY

Repetition is the only form of permanence which nature can achieve.
George Santayana

The term *acting out* has been used to describe *inter alia* criminal behavior, delinquency, drug addictions, severe character neuroses, sexual perversions, the general tendency of human beings to behave sometimes in an irrational way, and also to describe a wide range of behavior of patients during the course of psychoanalytic treatment. It has therefore been easy to agree that the term acting out has been too loosely applied. Blos (1978) stated that "the concept of acting out is over-burdened with references and meanings . . . and needs further clarification." (For clinically focused discussions of the definition of acting out see Blum 1976 and Infante et al. 1976.)

At the conclusion of the 1968 Copenhagen symposium, "Acting Out and Its Role in the Psychoanalytic Process," Calef (1968) reported: ". . . We could not agree on the clinical description of the entity under discussion and therefore it remained unclear just what the metapsychological formulations were intended to encompass and explain." Many analysts then and later have commented on the conceptual confusion caused by the failure to specify the boundaries of the concept of acting out (Blum 1976, A. Freud 1968, Loewald 1971, Rangell 1968, Sandler 1970, Sandler et al. 1973). In general there has been a tendency to accept the view that a return to the precision of the narrower definition of acting out as integrally linked to a therapeutic relationship would go far toward eliminating some of our present confusion. For example, Loewald (1971) stated: "It is important to keep in mind that acting out is a concept which is strictly related to the concept of reproduction in the psychic field . . . to designate an action as acting out makes sense only insofar as action is seen under the perspective of an alternative to reproduction in the physical field."

Beres (1965), on the other hand, has questioned whether even then it would be possible to state a clinical definition of acting out that would truly differ from other clinical phenomena such as perversion. His closely reasoned questions can be paraphrased in approximately this way: If the essence of the narrow definition of acting out is to be the repetition (in or out of a therapeutic relationship) of repressed memories, how would that differ from certain perversions or from a variety of other forms of enactment of unconscious fantasy or neurotic behavior? After an effort of two years' duration, the Kris Study Group on Acting Out chaired by Beres could not reach unified agreement on a suitable clinical definition of acting out.

The concept of acting out has been the subject of two books (Abt and Weissman 1976, Rexford 1978); a symposium at the Copenhagen congress (A. Freud 1968, Greenacre 1968, Moore et al. 1968, Rangell 1968); two panels of the American Psychoanalytic Association (Kanzer 1957, Panel 1970); and numerous papers.

Nevertheless, there continues to be considerable confusion about the nature of acting out, and it is apparently necessary for us to rediscover the significance of an important, well known, but neglected clinical fact (see Brenner 1968, 1976). In *every* analysis at certain times there are behavioral or action communications. The oscillation between the intrapsychic-introspective-reporting mode and the sphere of action remains unclear and awaits systematic understanding. Because there is available a comprehensive review of the large literature on acting out by Rexford (1978), I will here comment only on a small number of prior contributions that touch most directly on the scope of this paper.

Acting Out Reconsidered

In 1914 Freud wrote the paper "Remembering, Repeating, and Working-Through." It is an extraordinary paper that contains a famous passage that is familiar to all analysts: "The patient does not *remember* anything of what he has forgotten and repressed, but *acts* it out. He reproduces it not as a memory but as an action: he *repeats* it, without, of course, knowing that he is repeating it" (p. 150). In his editor's note, Strachey comments that this paper is noteworthy for containing the first appearance of the concepts of the repetition compulsion (p. 150) and of working-through (p. 155). Although Freud (1905) used the term "acting out" earlier to explain why Dora quit her analysis, it was not until this 1914 paper that he gave a systematic definition and discussion of acting out:

For instance, the patient does not say that he remembers that he used to be
defiant and critical towards his parents' authority; instead, he behaves in
that way to the doctor. He does not remember how he came to a helpless
and hopeless deadlock in his infantile sexual researches: but he produces
a mass of confused dreams and associations, complains that he cannot
succeed in anything and asserts that he is fated never to carry through what
he undertakes. He does not remember having been intensely ashamed of
certain sexual activities and afraid of their being found out; but he makes it
clear that he is ashamed of the treatment on which he is now embarked
and tries to keep it secret from everybody. And so on . . . [or] . . . He is silent
and declares that nothing occurs to him . . . as long as the patient is in the
treatment he cannot escape from this compulsion to repeat: and in the end
we understand that this is his way of remembering. [p. 150]

Notice how different Freud's examples of acting out were from the variety of behaviors we currently associate with the term. Freud's patients acted
out when they produced masses of confusing dreams: when they disparaged
themselves, when they were silent, when they experienced the analysis as a
shameful secret. To be sure, Freud spoke later in this paper of the necessary
cautions to be observed if dangerous actions spilled outside of the analysis
and threatened the analysis or the patient's safety: but the central thrust of his
discussion related to a range of behavior that is no longer commonly thought
of as acting out.

Essentially Freud was saying in 1914 that the entire transference was an
acting out:

As long as the patient is in the treatment he cannot escape from this compulsion to repeat: and in the end we understand that this is his way of remembering. What interests us most of all is naturally the relation of this
compulsion to repeat to the transference and to resistance. We soon perceive that the transference is itself only a piece of repetition. . . . The greater
the resistance, the more extensively will acting out (repetition) replace
remembering. [pp. 150–151]

Confusion has surrounded this concept whenever the effort is made to
define the term *acting out* descriptively. Fenichel (1954) offered the following
as an approximate description: "Acting out is an acting which relieves inner
tension and brings a partial discharge to warded-off impulses. . . ." Fenichel then
said that this was an insufficient explanation, but in my opinion he failed to
deal with the relevant reasons. He continued as follows:

This definition is certainly correct; but it is insufficient . . . if a person, after
having repressed an infantile sexual temptation, produces a neurotic symp-

tom . . . or if a person develops feelings toward his analyst which he once had toward his father, all these phenomena are in accord with the . . . definition but they are not "acting out" . . . [Note that this last example exactly reversed Freud's definition of acting out.] "Acting out," as distinguished from the other phenomena, is an acting, not a mere feeling, not a mere thing, not a mere mimic expression, not a mere single movement. [p. 296]

Fenichel then proceeded to exclude compulsive acts from the definition of acting out "because they are limited in their extent and . . . not as ego-syntonic." If certain rituals become ego-syntonic they can then be called acting out. I conclude my quotation of Fenichel with the following: "We rather call it 'transference' if the attitude concerns definite persons and 'acting out' if something has to be done regardless toward whom" (pp. 296–297).

We are now in a position to examine four problems posed by using this 1914 definition of acting out to account for clinical observations in psychoanalytic treatment. The most obvious question has to do with the essential emphasis on remembering as the antithesis to acting out. "Remembering" in the 1914 definition required primary emphasis because Freud's theoretical explanation for the nature of what was curative in psychoanalytic treatment at that time was rooted in the topographical model of the psychic apparatus. It was not the crude topography of the hypno-cathartic phase wherein the analyst tried to make memories conscious. In 1914 Freud was in a transitional phase with regard to his *theory* of technique. The era of this series of technique papers roughly bridges the earlier goal: to make the unconscious conscious, and the later *dictum*: where id was there shall ego be. Although his *technique* in 1914 may have represented his most advanced development as a clinician (see Lipton 1977), his theoretical explanations were still phrased in topographic terms. And so Freud's 1914 definition of acting out was anchored to his earlier topographic definition of the therapeutic task as the removal of repressions.

As we know, there are obvious and important clinical observations that do not fit with Freud's 1914 definition of acting out. Patients in analysis are actually not confined to a choice between remembering or acting (Loewald 1971). They have a range of alternatives that remains to be integrated with a modern description of acting out. Weiss (1942) observed that patients often act out emotional situations that they have *already remembered*. Moreover, certain repressed contents never were conscious and could never be remembered. Sandler et al. (1973, pp. 102–103) also noted that a problem arises if we adhere too concretely to the view that acting out is a substitute for remembering. He gave the example of certain forms of therapy that have explicitly renounced the patient's task to remember. In some of these forms of psychotherapy where remembering is in fact discouraged explicitly, there is still an

intense relationship with the therapist leading to emotional revivals and enactments[1] of earlier states that could legitimately be called acting out.

The integral linkage of Freud's 1914 definition of acting out with memory
functions is the first and most obvious theoretical problem attributable to the
topographic hypothesis. The second problem is the theoretic notion of action
viewed in topographic terms as a manifestation of shifts in the distribution of
psychic energy between the system's unconscious, preconscious, and conscious. In a somewhat oversimplified way one might say that irrationally motivated behavior was then viewed as the consequence of mobile discharge of
psychic energy governed by the primary process when certain mental contents were dissociated by repression from the system's preconscious and conscious. For example, "from the moment at which the repressed thoughts are
strongly cathected by the unconscious wishful impulse and . . . abandoned by
the pre-conscious cathexis, they become subject to the primary psychical process, and their one aim is motor discharge . . ." (Freud 1900, p. 605). Nor have
we yet solved the problem of giving a systematic theoretical accounting of action
in modern psychoanalytic theory. *It is recognized* (Rangell 1968) *that not all
action is acting out. It is not yet sufficiently understood that not all acting out involves action.* Hartmann (1964) pointed out that to this day we still have no
systematic presentation of a psychoanalytic theory of action—and that "a theory
of action based on the knowledge of structural aspects of the personality and
of its motivations is the most important contribution psychoanalysis will one
day be able to make in this field."[2]

The third problem with Freud's 1914 definition of acting out resides in his
use in that era of an instinctual definition of transference. Adherence to that
view is one of the conceptual problems with Rosenfeld's (1966) dichotomous

---

[1]Sandler (1970, 1973) has suggested substitution of the term *enactment* for acting out on the
grounds that some of the confusion about acting out arises from a mistranslation of the German
agieren. Agieren is a term of Latin origin and not a term of common idiomatic German usage.
Freud used it transitively as he did *abreagieren*, which has the same root (Laplanche and Pontalis
1973). Sandler cited Greenacre and other authors who equated the German *handeln*, which
connotes acting, with the word *agieren*, which Sterba (1946) and others have translated into the
English *acting out*. Rexford (1978, pp. 250–251) and others state that the earliest use of the term
acting out was in 1901 in Freud's "The Psychopathology of Everyday Life" wherein Freud used
the word *handeln* to describe certain faulty actions and symptomatic acts. In 1905 Freud first
used the term *agieren* to describe Dora's acting out her fantasy of revenge against Herr K. by
quitting her analysis. Sterba (1979) disagreed with Sandler and cited Freud's (1936) published
approval of Sterba's rendering of *agieren* as acting out.

[2]These prophetic words of Hartmann emphasize the complexity of establishing a psychoanalytic theory of action. This is well illustrated by the problems Schafer (1976) encountered in his
problematic attempt to do the opposite: to establish an account of psychoanalysis based on action
theory, which has so engaged philosophic attention in recent years.

definition of partial and total acting out. Anna Freud (1936) and Loewenstein (1969) have discussed a classification of transference that took account of structural considerations instead of considering only libidinal or aggressive drive derivatives. In the structural model, acting out cannot be relegated to any one of the three substructures because it entails the contributions of id, ego, and superego. Obviously also the problem of repetition in the transference, which is the key to Freud's 1914 definition of acting out, cannot be completely understood without consideration of the role of the ego and superego (Loewenstein 1969).

Actualization

Up to this point I have discussed three theoretical problems about acting out that derive from the evolving refinement of Freud's theories since 1914. The next issue is of a different kind altogether. There is an ambiguity inherent in Freud's 1914 definition of acting out. To my knowledge the first report in the vast literature on acting out that deals with this problem is that of Laplanche and Pontalis (1973): "the term acting out enshrines an ambiguity that is actually intrinsic to Freud's thinking here: he fails to distinguish the element of *actualization* in the transference from the resort to motor action—which the transference does not necessarily entail."[3]

The word *actualization* as used here by Laplanche and Pontalis connotes the ordinary dictionary sense of the word; in this sense it means making actual, converting into an actual or real fact. The term *actualize* has been used in a variety of other ways with a variety of theoretical or technical connotations—none of which is intended here. The term *actualization* has been used as I mean it by Sandler (1976a,b, and Chapter 3, this volume) in his helpful discussion of issues closely related to the topic of this paper. Although he did not *there* include acting out in any detail, I believe that his discussions of transference and countertransference as aspects of an object relationship are relevant to acting out. He said (1976b) that all wish fulfillment is brought about through some form of actualization and that our patients attempt to actualize their transference wishes in disguised ways by assuming a certain role-relationship with the analyst at any given time. "The patient's transference would thus represent an attempt by him to impose an interaction . . . between himself and the analyst" (Chapter 3, p. 31). Sandler next stated: "If the patient keeps to the *rules* he will report rather than *enact*, and our clues as analysts, to the unconscious inner role-relationship which the patient is trying to impose, come to us via our

---

[3]Gill (1979) also deals with this as a conceptual problem.

perceptions and the application of our analytic tools" (Chapter 3, p. 32, my italics). At precisely this point I believe there are advantages to going beyond Sandler's distinction of reporting *rather* than enacting. The contrast Sandler makes here, which is shared by many if not most analysts, is between reporting versus acting out, which in my opinion confuses the issues of action with actualizing. Sandler's clinical examples included a vignette about a transference interaction in which a patient subtly and for some time successfully managed to manipulate the analyst into talking more than the analyst felt he should. This patient was reporting *and* enacting, but the only observable action by the patient was verbal[4] and consisted of his attempt to shift from reporting to conversing. Sandler then presented very convincing evidence linking this transference behavior to a variety of issues concerning the patient's prior relationship with his father.

Most analysts do not include such mundane, day in and day out transference behavior under the rubric of acting out, but Freud did and we should carefully consider why he did. I propose that it is useful to divide the concept of acting out into two components: an unconscious transference fantasy and some related action or behavior. Such a separation has heuristic advantages but cannot imply a literal, functional separation. I must emphasize that throughout this discussion my proposal to consider action in its motor-behavioral aspect as separate from fantasy, image, thought, and affect is utterly artificial. My justification for isolating action to its restrictive-motor sense is to add emphasis and expositional clarity. This is analogous to Freud's (1908) suggestion to give separate consideration to the masturbatory act and the masturbatory fantasy. The relationship between the transference fantasy and the action may be complex or simple. It may be that the unconscious fantasy and the related action are isomorphic and parallel or that the related action is sharply opposed to the actualization of the fantasy. Clinical reality encompasses a large range of intermediate positions on this continuum. Although the given instance of action may ostensibly serve to deny the fantasy that propels it, the action is always contextually linked to the fantasy. Here the defensive function of the action is to block awareness of painful affects that would ensue were there not an impedance to the further actualization of the fantasy. In such instances the action may bear a relationship to the fantasy analogous in its function and complexity to the familiar relation between the manifest and latent dream (Grinberg 1968, Mitscherlich-Nielsen 1968).

Clinical experience shows that vivid episodes of re-enactment during psychoanalytic therapy, which fully deserve to be called acting out, may involve no motor action of any kind. Certain episodes of silence during analysis would

---

[4]For a discussion of verbalization as acting out see Loewald (1970) and Blum (1976).

be one example.[5] Even more representative would be the ubiquitous situation so well illustrated when the patient attempts to impose certain roles on the analyst by using no other form of behavior than conversation. In this sense verbalization is the major mode of acting out in any analysis. Indeed, sometimes the crucial acting out by the patient consists of a refusal to act (Diatkine 1968). It would then seem that there is no compelling reason to distinguish between various forms of actualization of transference fantasies solely on the basis of whether they are accompanied by motor actions.

So far I have discussed the advantages of distinguishing between actualization and action. However, the introduction of the term actualization does not solve the conceptual problems entirely and indeed introduces new ambiguities. In their discussion of anthropomorphism in psychoanalytic theory, Grossman and Simon (1969) described bridge terms that attempt to link subjective experience with objective-abstract theories that seem to explain the subjective experience. The words *tension* or *drive* are examples. Actualization is also a word with subjective as well as theoretical-objective connotations. Actualization can mean the subjective experience of feeling that an unconscious fantasy is being partially fulfilled, realized, or "coming true." Actualization can also mean the postulated processes by which a group of coherently organized activities of the ego revise compromise formations engendered by intrapsychic conflict related to emerging transference fantasies. The major advantage of the introduction of the process term *actualizing* is the connotation of intrapsychic subjective experience as contrasted with the extra-psychic, action-behavioral connotation of acting out. Yet there is the necessity to recognize that a mere change of terminology in no way eliminates the basic conceptual issues here discussed and indeed raises some new ones: for example, Can we give an adequate clinical definition of what we mean in all cases by alluding to the subjective experience of an unconscious fantasy seeming to approach actual fulfillment? Most often, it would not be a case of even nearly direct gratification. New compromise formations are the typical route to a partial fulfillment of unconscious fantasies. We would not insist on any conscious awareness that an unconscious fantasy was about to be "gratified" or "actualized." We would include in our understanding of actualization the entire spectrum of affects in the pleasure–unpleasure series.

Acting Out and Transference

We have known for some time that it is a fallacy to focus only on the pejorative aspect of acting out. It is true that Freud wished, in his 1914 paper, to

---

[5]For a discussion of silence in the special context of nonverbal communication, see particularly the 1969 (Panel) discussion.

call attention to the dangers of acting out viewed as a resistance. But more important, and curiously much more neglected subsequently, Freud was drawing attention to the invaluable and indeed unavoidable communicative aspects of acting out. One can see in that paper that Freud equated acting out with transference in just this way.[6] Both transference and acting out could constitute a resistance at one time or an indispensable vehicle to propel the psychoanalytic process forward. After all, only the newly invoked compulsion to repeat could give the patient the all-essential affective conviction that was required for working through, and it was working through that now replaced the prior concept of abreaction. Both transference and optimum workable levels of acting out (in the communicative sense) were therefore essential because: "when all is said and done, it is impossible to destroy anyone *in absentia* or *in effigie*" (Freud 1912). Freud clearly intended here to anchor his definition of working through to acting out. Acting out might occur without working through if the transference was not judiciously interpreted, but *working through could never occur without acting out* because in this sense the entire transference was an acting out. (See also Limentani [1966] for a discussion of acting out in relation to working through.)

Rangell (1968) reported a case to illustrate how misleading the pejorative attitude to acting out can be. His patient was a married homosexual man whose perverse behavior prior to and during the early phase of his analysis had been quite dangerous. These acts continued for some time during the analysis and constituted a large proportion of the analytic work. It was only when these acts became imbricated with the transference that Rangell felt he could say that they now constituted acting out with a corresponding improvement in prognosis. (See Rangell [1981] for a distinction between acting out, neurotic action, and normal action.)

It is therefore more clear why Freud simultaneously introduced these three major concepts in his pivotal 1914 paper: acting out, the repetition compulsion, and working through were integrally and intimately interrelated and were designated to describe related aspects of closely related phenomena. He could not at that time define any one of the three without the other two. Subsequent evolution of the use of these three terms shows that their simultaneous birth is too often neglected. The highly complex subsequent fate of the three concepts is beyond the scope of this chapter, but it is here proposed that refinement of our understanding of acting out in modern structural terms must include a systematic refinement of our notions of working through and the repetition compulsion.

---

[6]Kanzer (1966) discussed acting out in the context of Freud's evolving theories, but in a different context. See Kanzer (1968) where he defines acting out as a transference dominated *motility*.

Some of the confusion about the use of the term acting out relates to an issue exactly parallel to the limitation of the term transference. Shall we confine its use to psychoanalytic therapy or not? In this discussion I am using the word transference in the sense of transference neurosis. Transference as the broader aspect of the universal human tendency to seek the gratification of childhood wishes can obviously occur in any relationship and certainly does occur outside of the psychoanalytic relationship. Obviously that is not the case for the transference neurosis. Almost every usage of acting out that refers to phenomena outside a treatment relationship refers to the ubiquitous presence of unconscious motivation in any human behavior and is of course part of the basis for the present confusion about the term.

Freud did not distinguish acting out very clearly from transference nor did he seem to view them as terms that required precise separation. In 1914, after all, he was refining his theory of the psychoanalytic process and describing the more global aspects of how to conduct an analysis so that analysts would neither ignore acting out, if it threatened the safety of the patient or the viability of the treatment, nor stop it prematurely if the patient needed minor acting out for communicative reasons that would help the progress of the analysis. All transference is repetition and in Freud's 1914 definition all acting out is transference. But repetition is part of a different and larger conceptual category than transference and is not synonymous nor coextensive with transference or acting out. Some repetitions during analysis are not manifestations of transference.

Up to this point I have discussed some of the problems that arise if we try to return to Freud's 1914 definition of acting out. Before pursuing other aspects of those problems, I turn now to Freud's written views on acting out subsequent to 1914. It is generally agreed (e.g., Sandler et al. 1973) that Freud's views on acting out remained essentially unaltered in his subsequent discussions on the subject.

In "Beyond the Pleasure Principle" Freud (1920) returned to a systematic consideration of the repetition compulsion that he introduced in the 1914 paper. He took up exactly the same clinical phenomena now and re-examined these issues from a protostructural point of view.

He began again with a description (1920) of the futility of attempting to persuade the patient of the correctness of the analyst's constructions concerning the patient's past:

> He is obliged to *repeat* the repressed material as a contemporary experience instead of, as the physician would prefer to see, *remembering* it as something belonging to the past. These reproductions, which emerge with such unwished-for exactitude, always have as their subject some portion of infantile sexual life . . . and they are invariably *acted out* in the sphere of the transference . . . [italics mine] . . . When things have reached this stage, it may be said that the

earlier neurosis has been replaced by a fresh "transference neurosis." It has been the physician's endeavour to keep this transference neurosis within the narrowest limits: to force as much as possible into the channel of memory and to allow as little as possible to emerge as repetition. [pp. 18–19]

At this point Freud departed from his 1914 explanation:

> In order to make it easier to understand this "compulsion to repeat," which emerges during the psycho-analytic treatment of neurotics, we must above all get rid of the mistaken notion that what we are dealing with in our struggle against resistances is resistance on the part of the *unconscious*. The unconscious—that is to say, the "repressed"—offers no resistance whatever to the efforts of the treatment. . . . We shall avoid a lack of clarity if we make our contrast not between the conscious and the unconscious but between the coherent ego and the *repressed*. It is certain that much of the ego is itself unconscious. . . . Having replaced a purely *descriptive* [italics mine] terminology by one which is systematic or dynamic we can say that the patient's resistance arises from his ego, and we then at once perceive that the compulsion to repeat must be ascribed to the unconscious repressed. [pp. 19–20]

As I read this discussion, Freud seems to be adapting the term acting out to this new structural view. On the other hand, Freud wasn't always too careful about using the term consistently.

Contrary to the assumption that he adhered to his strictly clinical definition of 1914, Freud used the term inconsistently as many other analysts have used it, in an application ranging far indeed from his original definition. In "Moses and Monotheism" Freud (1937) wondered why the monotheistic idea made such a deep impression on the Jews. He asserted that the Jewish people repeated the primeval parricide on the person of Moses. "It was a case of 'acting out' instead of remembering, as happens so often with neurotics during the work of analysis." His final reference to acting out occurs in "An Outline of Psychoanalysis." Freud (1940) states: "We think it most undesirable if the patient *acts* outside the transference instead of remembering. The ideal conduct for our purposes would be that he should behave as normally as possible outside the treatment and express his abnormal reactions only in the transference" (p. 177). This statement repeats his 1914 views incompletely and is sometimes cited as the basis for the pejorative view of acting out (even though Freud's discussion up to this point makes it clear that the patient is driven to act instead of reporting [1940, p. 176]).

Problems of Definition

Among the paradoxes and contradictions in our extension and alteration of the term acting out, none is more striking than the fact that most analysts now use the term only in the sense *opposite* to Freud's original definition. Laplanche and Pontalis (1973) concluded that the most commonly held psychoanalytic view currently is that transference and acting out are not only distinctly separate but actually opposed to one another. It is as though acting out represents a basic refusal to acknowledge the transference—it is common to hear that the patient who regularly arrives late is "acting out to avoid the transference." It is possible to speak here of a distinction between acting out as an integral manifestation of the transference versus acting out as an effort to avoid awareness of the transference (Curtis 1979, Gill 1979). My experience suggests that such a distinction omits fuller consideration of the clinical data that often show that the avoidance of awareness of transference itself may be an expression of the transference. It is useful to observe here that this issue of acting out as an opposition to transference overlooks another clinical observation. The danger to the patient is not transference per se but unpleasant affects that threaten to cause the patient pain immediately. Although ultimately the patient is attempting to avoid remembering, it is important to restate the obvious: the patient who acts out is avoiding the experience of affects linked to transference fantasies in the immediate present. It is my view that we have arrived here at a spurious paradox. Acting out may be either an integral aspect of transference or a resistance to the same extent that transference itself is indispensable to psychoanalysis or inevitably also at times a resistance.

Laplanche and Pontalis (1973) state:

> One of the outstanding tasks of psycho-analysis is to ground the distinction between transference and acting out on criteria other than purely technical ones—or even considerations of locale (does something happen within the consulting room or not?). This task presupposes a reformulation of the concepts of *action* and *actualization* and a fresh definition of the different modalities of *communication*.

My purpose is to attempt an initial step in the direction proposed by Laplanche and Pontalis by suggesting that acting out can be defined only in terms of metapsychology and that clinical descriptive definitions of acting out will of necessity be inadequate. I use the term metapsychology here in Freud's original sense to describe the psychology of unconscious mental processes (see Brenner 1980). I propose that we view acting out as inseparable from the transference neurosis. In accordance with the principle of multiple function, what becomes relevant in the context of metapsychology is the fate of the unconscious transference fantasy and its tendency toward actualization rather than the coincidental motor action or behavior that might or might not appear as an aspect of the compromise formation engendered by the fantasy. Acting out thus expresses the psychic reality of the transference neurosis (McLaughlin 1981).

In Versus Out: A Spurious Distinction

We have seen such a radical extension of the term acting out based on descriptive considerations that it has become a part of the lexicon of our daily language and is used by many psychoanalysts as well as educated lay people simply to indicate the close relationship between any human activity and unconscious fantasy. Partially to retrench and correct for this confusion we have been offered distinctions that are linked to simplistic considerations of the meaning of the words *in* and *out* when applied to acting out.

Fenichel (1954) and Greenacre (Chapter 2, this volume) distinguished between acting out inside of analysis and acting out outside of analysis. Zeligs (1957) and Rosen (1976) discussed *acting in*, as distinct from *acting out inside the analysis*. These terminological distinctions illustrate the conceptual confusion and redundancy resulting from efforts to adhere to a clinical-descriptive definition of acting out. Acting out as a term is a bit like hay fever, which is not accompanied by a temperature elevation and is not caused by hay. These terms acting in or acting out inside the analytic situation merely locate the patient's behavior.

There are numerous examples in the literature of this concretization of the antithesis *out* versus *in*. Gray (1973) reported the advantages of stressing the focus of the patient's view during the analysis to data limited essentially to *inside* the psychoanalytic situation rather than to behavior *outside* the analytic situation. The distinction of inside versus outside is trivial if viewed as a geographical question. The antithesis of inside versus outside blurs the more relevant meta-psychological distinction of intrapsychic versus overt action, be the action on the couch, in the office of the analyst, or elsewhere in the world. Many discussions of inside versus outside confuse geography and metapsychology. The *Glossary of Psychoanalytic Terms and Concepts* (Moore and Fine 1968) voices this view as well, by noting that the term has come to be applied also to persons who externalize their conflicts and who are not in treatment and that the term acting out is often applied in a pejorative and indiscriminate sense to any antisocial activity. "It therefore lacks precision except in the context of the analytic situation." Although most considerations still indicate that the term should be narrowed in its application, two authors have given arguments against excluding certain carefully defined forms of psychopathology from the accepted boundaries of a rigorous definition of acting out.

Stein (1973) discussed the tendency to act out in certain patients as a character trait prior to starting analysis and presented a thoughtful argument for extending the term acting out to include complex repetitive behavior of certain patients over extended periods who manifested a specific disturbance in reality testing. The behavior was always ego-syntonic and represented a large group of meanings that ideally illustrated the principle of multiple function. Greenacre (1968) also advised against this tendency to resolve the conceptual problems of acting out by simple definitional exclusions. Greenacre (1950) has essentially agreed with Fenichel's definition of acting out. She stressed the acting out of certain patients who experienced serious trauma in their preverbal development. In her discussion of these patients, she referred to acting out in the expanded sense as a general propensity of such patients whether or not they were in psychoanalytic treatment. She has described a quasi-syndrome of severe early trauma, a special emphasis on visual sensitization producing a bent for dramatization . . . and a largely unconscious belief in the magic of action.[7] Separation of actualization from the action aspect would clarify further discussion of the pros and cons of a narrow versus expanded definition of acting out. I agree with Greenacre's suggestion (1968) that rather than abandon the term acting out we should try more "to understand the dynamics and effect of the substitution of action for verbal communication in the impact on the psychoanalytic treatment process."

Action, Defense, and Reality

It is this question—Why does the patient substitute action for verbal communication?—that we least understand. Some would say that it is now clear that all prior questions in this chapter merely rephrase the problem of the relation of thought to action and that we are merely manipulating terms. I could not disprove such an assertion, but I will argue here for heuristic advantages in making these distinctions. Why do patients shift to action at all? At present we know too little about the reasons why an obsessional patient sometimes contents himself with intrapsychic boundaries for his conflicts but will at other times requires a shift to the sphere of action for performance of his ceremonials in compulsive acts such as repetitive symmetrical touching. The formula "neurosis is the negative of perversion" encompasses the same complex problem and illustrates the extraordinary complexity of establishing a psychological theory of action. These issues touch on questions rasied by Calef (1968) in his summary of the discussion at the Copenhagen congress on acting out: "The most important question could not be answered. Why does a given patient choose acting out as a way of resolving or expressing conflict? Who is it that would rather enact than think? Why the choice of acting and not thinking? Why

---

[7]See also Segel (1969) for a discussion of the linkage between acting out with object loss or primal scene traumatization during childhood. Ritvo (1968) discussed the issue whether or not we can specify a relation between one form of ego alteration, acting out, and specific patterns of infantile experience. We see here another example of the problem with an overly inclusive definition of acting out.

discharge instead of delay?" I will attempt in the ensuing discussion to illustrate that the antithetic placement of action versus thinking simplifies these issues and will advocate the contrast of action to intrapsychic experience.

Freud alluded to this question but did not deal with this systematically in his 1914 paper. He observed that the patient is most likely to act out when the resistances are at a maximum. He also said that two aspects of the transference could directly increase the tendency to act out: "If as the analysis proceeds, the transference becomes hostile or unduly intense and therefore in need of repression, *remembering* at once gives way to acting out" [my italics]. Freud left this as an empirical observation,[8] and it has been repeatedly observed (e.g., Brenner 1969, 1976) that delay in interpreting the transference will cause acting out. The reasons for this are by no means clear. It is precisely this question that awaits the development of a psychoanalytic theory of action. If we altered Freud's 1914 formulation slightly, it would still be valid. Instead of saying "when the transference becomes . . . unduly intense . . . *remembering* . . . gives way to acting out," we would say today that verbalization and introspection give way to acting out. But we can barely begin to say why this is so. Viewed from the angle of defense, clinical experience easily confirms that the shift to action serves to avoid unpleasant affects evoked by emerging transference fantasies in the here and now.[9]

The vicissitudes of unconscious transference fantasies are central to the concept of acting out. It is the tendency toward actualization that promises to make transference wishes come true. The pain and poignance of transference is the tension between the actuality of the experience of the *affects* in the transference and the futility, danger, or both of ever *fully* realizing or actualizing the transference wishes. Any tendency toward actualization is a signal to the ego that a transference fantasy is about to be gratified in reality. Action at this point facilitates a compromise formation, which is required because of this defense imbalance (Cowitz 1979). Actualization means immediate danger of a defense imbalance requiring compromise formations, but this need not of necessity require action off the couch. In fact most of the acting out in the narrow definition I am using in the average analysis is confined to a verbal-conversational interaction with the analyst that involves no action other than speech. Loewald (1970) described this as follows: "Giving words to feelings is not simply a delay of gratification . . . but is a kind of gratification by verbal action, by establishing communicative links between psychic elements and levels, both within the

---

[8]Sterba (1979) said that Freud once remarked, in a clinical discussion that Sterba attended, that ultimately the issue of whether the patient will act out depended on quantitative factors.

[9]Connotations of the phrase *here and now* as discussed by Gill (1979) are outside the scope of the present discussion.

patient himself (intrapsychic communication) and between the patient and the analyst." Here Loewald proceeds to distinguish between abreaction as it is often used pejoratively versus abreaction through verbalization (see also Blum 1976).

The very fact that motor behavior outside the analysis is observable by others and even that it constitutes an event in the sphere of action heightens the reality force or reality quality of the event. Thus the shift to motor action creates an illusory reality that serves the purpose of defense. I will cite an example only to illustrate this. A man in analysis for some time became frightened of emerging homosexual transference fantasies during his analytic sessions and began a flamboyant heterosexual episode in his external life. He shifted to the sphere of action outside the analysis because he had a defensive need to prove that a false reality was true. The very fact that he and she were doing something was real. The reality of his about-to-be actualized homosexual transference feelings about the analyst were thus easier to deny. He required action to help him to create verisimilitude, just as a writer lulls his readers toward a suspension of disbelief. The writer creates ultra-detailed aspects of reality at the periphery to distract our attention from the implausible proceedings at the center. This is also similar to the magician's guile in that his prestidigitation and sleight of hand are calculated to create the illusion of reality in part by distracting our most critical perceptual functions. In this respect our patients become magicians when they act out in an effort to recruit the analyst as a witness to a reality that is spurious.

Let us keep in mind Freud's observation that acting out will increase under conditions of a hostile transference or a transference that has become too intense. In the everyday analytic work with neurotic patients, the ego of the patient is often well able to tolerate the imbalance between superego components, drive derivatives, ego ideals, and defenses, which is evoked by the threat of actualization of transference wishes. It is defensively necessary for most patients at one time or another to supplement their defenses by shifting to the realm of action and behavior when an excessive imbalance occurs. Action may in part defend *against* actualization. Just as fantasy and manual manipulation may undergo separate vicissitudes in masturbation (Arlow 1953, Freud 1908, Miller 1969), action and transference fantasy may undergo separate fates in acting out.

Acting out is often analogous in structure to dreams. This analogy has been advocated by Greenson (1966), Grinberg (1968), Mitscherlich-Nielsen (1968), and others who have compared acting out to dreams, and Moore (1968) has given some reasons for care in carrying the analogy too far. What I especially wish to compare at this point is the false reality of actions evoked by the defense imbalance engendered by emerging transference fantasies and the hallucinatory reality of dreams. Clinical experience confirms a wide range of primary process elaborations of the action component in relation to the latent transference fantasy so that some episodes of acting out are conspicuously similar in structure to dreams and others are not.[10] Furthermore the analogy to dreams is useful to extend in another direction: the day residues of dreams are quite similar to transference developments that become elaborated as *transference residues* in a piece of acting out just as day residues by primary process elaboration become integrated in the manifest and latent dream.

Among others, Bird (1957) has observed that the behavior of the analyst can be an important factor in evoking acting out. The added aspect of a possible unwitting congruence between the behavior of the analyst and pathogenic childhood object relations can be a powerful inducement to acting out. When that which *has* been actual in the past converges with that which inappropriately becomes actual by virtue of the analyst's inadvertent complicity in the present, the potential for acting out is much increased. Tarachow (1963) expressed this as an aphorism: the analysis is always vulnerable to the danger of degenerating into reality. Yet the shift to action is not inevitable and there are clinical situations where the inadvertent compliance of the analyst may give rise to a dream instead of, or in addition to, acting out. Thus the inter-relatedness of the transference fantasy and the action component may be extremely complex with full equivalence to the complexity of the inter-relationship between manifest and latent dreams. To illustrate this only schematically, the man in my prior vignette was unconsciously identified with the woman he chose for his episode of acting out. He masochistically provoked her to behave sadistically toward him just as he wished to experience himself as a hostile woman in his transference fantasy of provoking me to attack him.

It is common to describe acting out as *ego-syntonic* because patients often defend strenuously against analyzing their acting out. I suggest here a further analogy to dreams by comparing the rationalizing of acting out to the secondary revision of the dream work.

The use of ego-syntonicity to define acting out introduces another source of confusion about the definition of acting out on descriptive grounds. Beres (1965) has commented that the term ego-syntonic dates to the days when analysts used the word *ego* as a synonym for *self*. Because the ego is a group of functions, neurotic behavior can only be syntonic with certain functions of the ego as opposed to others. Thus the common distinction between symptomatic acts as opposed to acting out on the grounds of ego-syntonicity is invalid. The simple dichotomy implied by whether an episode of acting out is or is not ego-syntonic is not congruent with the complexity of clinical phenom-

---

[10]For a clinical example of acting out in relation to a dream, see Sterba (1946). Van Dam (1978) and others have compared acting out to children's play.

ena wherein we see a broad range of attitudes toward such behavior. Patients may rather willingly discuss their acting out, they may vigorously rationalize it, they may defensively argue about it, but they may also consciously withhold reporting that it has even occurred (Diatkine 1968).

These considerations about the defensive significance of the analogy between the hallucinatory reality of dreams and the verisimilitude or false reality created by acting out give rise to a conjecture. There are possible defensive implications about the relation between action, reality, reality testing, and rationalization.

Action in the painful, slow course of human development gradually becomes more and more often preceded by delay and thought as trial action (Freud 1911). Ontogenetically, action tends to precede thought. As a result of successful development, that which we have actually done in motor action was hopefully safer and more adaptive than those rejected merely-mental trial alternatives that we repudiated as unreasonable. Action may thus feel more real partly because thinking is reversible and action is often irrevocable and final. The acting out of a patient (in its action component) corresponds then in this context to the hallucinatory quality of reality in a dream. Thus sometimes a patient who acts out may assure himself that his behavior does not require analysis because it was real or actual. This is analogous to a patient who protests about his "simple" dream. "But this dream merely reproduces an actual conversation, or an actual event, so what is there to analyze?" He would not *do* something if it were irrational and since he has actually *done* it, there are 'rational' explanations for it.

Repetition, Regression, and Working Through

Loewald (1971) has described two contrasting forms of repetition that I use here to illustrate the adaptive and reorganizing aspects of certain forms of acting out:

> Psychoanalysis has always maintained that the life of the individual is determined by his infantile history, his early experiences and conflicts; but everything depends on *how* these early experiences are repeated in the course of life: to what extent they are repeated passively—suffered again even if "actively" arranged—and to what extent they can be taken over in the ego's organizing activity and made over into something new—a re-creation of something old as against a duplication of it. In such re-creation the old is mastered, where mastery does not mean elimination of it, but dissolution, and reconstruction out of the elements of destruction. We may thus distinguish between repetition as re-creation, the passive and the active form.

Acting out may therefore be a passive or an active repetition viewed from the angle of the ego's shifting dominance of functions, but Loewald proposed to exclude re-creative repetitions with progressive tendencies and to designate as acting out only those repetitions that take place to block repetition in the psychic field. In either case, the use of *regression* as an explanatory concept must be utilized with full respect for the complexity of related issues concerning ego and superego development. Not every behavioral communication is regressive. Loewald's views about repetition place the issue of the resistance versus communicative aspects of acting out in better perspective (see Van Gaard 1968). The issue of attempting to oppose the resistance versus the communicative aspect of acting out is spurious. Brenner (1969, 1976) has shown that whether something can be usefully understood during analysis does not depend on whether it was acted out, but instead it depends on the intensity of the resistance. Some intractable resistances involve no action, and some actions of the patient enhance our understanding.

The distinction made here by Loewald concerning passive, regressive, *automatic* repetitions versus active, re-creative forms of repetition may ultimately prove too schematic, yet the dialectic tension here implied seems relevant to clinical complexities of acting out. It will be recalled that Freud introduced the concept of the repetition compulsion simultaneously with his introduction of the concepts of working through and acting out. We can avoid facile assumptions that equate all acting out with regressive repetition phenomena by keeping clearly in mind the following point made by Loewald (1971).

> When we speak of repetition compulsion in psychoanalysis as a psychological phenomenon, and not as an ultimate principle inherent in cosmic processes in general, it is primarily the passive, reproductive repetition that we have in mind . . . The distinction of reproductive versus re-creative repetition can help to elucidate the relations between id, ego, and superego.[11]

Loewald concurred with the classic view by stressing the interconnections of remembering, working through, and mourning.[12] Freud, in 1914, was attempting a substantial theoretical revision of the nature of the psychoanalytic therapeutic process. He saw the inadequacy of the topographic model and replaced abreaction of affects attached to repressed memories with the concept of work-

---

[11]For a related discussion of the repetition compulsion, see Bibring (1943).

[12]For an example of a misleading separation of the concepts acting out from working through, see Robertiello (1976). An excellent discussion of action by Poland (1977) is consistent with my own views here on the relation between the action component of acting out and working through.

ing through resistances. He had not yet formulated the concept of the ego that was compelled by unintegrated aspects of its own organization to passive repetitions. He used the term acting out merely descriptively and not systematically and only to define a special category of psychological repetition. His ingenious idea served as a scaffolding, but his definition of acting out was ambiguous from the start. The entire transference was a repetition and acting out was always transference, but we were not told what part of transference was not acting out.[13]

We now can see that the suggestion in the 1968 Symposium on Acting Out to return to the original definition of acting out given by Freud in 1914, but updated to include the refinement of modern psychoanalytic theory, is complicated by virtue of the problems inherent in that original definition. We can also suggest that the valid aspects of Greenacre's and Stein's proposals to extend the use of the term acting out beyond the confines of a psychoanalytic therapeutic relationship can be preserved by viewing their valuable clinical reports in the context of the psychology of action rather than actualization. The shift *in* a psychoanalytic treatment from the introspective-verbalizing form of actualization to motor-behavioral forms remains unexplained. It may be that this shift is induced partly by a defense imbalance evoked by the overload of affects linked to emerging transference fantasies. However, it is not at all necessary that every unconsciously motivated motor action by a patient be induced by transference phenomena.

I further suggest that we redirect our attention to a neglected boundary in every analysis. I refer to the ubiquitous shifts during analysis from intrapsychic, introspective experiencing to action, behavior, and reality. Obvious and profound differences separate those patients who cross this boundary rarely from those whose bustling traffic at this frontier is a source of bewilderment and even danger. We want to know why certain patients cannot tolerate average levels of frustration, and we assume that the patient's intolerance of painful affects is crucial in determining the shift to behavior. This means we must account for the development of certain functional ego capacities or incapacities and therefore developmental considerations are more important than dynamic issues (Beres 1965). Here we touch on the complex developmental issues involved in the question as to what degree of intrapsychic structure must be achieved before we would speak of acting out in a very young child. The failure to sort out these diverse aspects of acting out is what has relegated so many discussions of acting out to the technical aspects of containment within the confines of the psychoanalytic therapeutic relationship.

---

[13]I am indebted to members of the C.A.P.S. Discussion Group 7 for this and other valuable suggestions about this topic.

There are important and obvious differences between patients who demonstrate major acting out and those who limit themselves to subtle and minor behavioral communications. Yet in our effort to understand who it is that prefers action to intrapsychic experience, and why and when this person prefers action, it may be wise not to segregate prematurely the major and minor categories. Potential, concealed similarities may yet some day provide enhanced reciprocal understanding of these issues.

The shift from introspection to action of a mild to medium variety is not only ubiquitous. The total absence of even minor acting out should alert the analyst, as would the absence of dreams, to be aware of important concealed resistances.

It is not possible in my opinion to give an adequate clinical-descriptive definition of acting out. Nor do available dynamic definitions adequately encompass all available clinical data. A given piece of behavior may be viewed simultaneously as the expression of multiple function on a large number of co-ordinates (Blos 1978); not all of these co-ordinates can yet be specified. It is not enough to say that acting out is likely to occur when resistances are markedly increased. We have long since verified this empirical observation. Our task is to specify why this is true.

Summary

I have discussed acting out to illustrate why it cannot be defined on empirical clinical grounds. Even when full recognition of whether unconscious fantasy as a factor is included in the definition, other clinical phenomena such as perversions or neurotic behavior of other types must be included as well. I believe the problem with attempting a definition has been obscured by two main factors. The first is a conceptual confusion about the unconscious fantasy versus the action components of acting out. The second is a tendency to ignore that the concept of acting out was devised in terms of the topographic rather than structural hypothesis. I have suggested the value of directing our attention to the nature of those processes involved in the ubiquitous travels by our patients to and fro across the frontier between introspection and action. There are advantages to distinguishing between the intrapsychic actualization of unconscious transference fantasy and motor action. The distinction frees us from the insoluble contradictions of a descriptive definition of acting out and makes it possible to approach acting out in the framework of metapsychology. The concept of acting out is confused if we isolate it from the integrally related concepts of working through and repetition in the psychoanalytic process. We can keep the important clinical problem of patients whose acting out is conspicuous and central to their psychopathology as an unsolved aspect of the psychology of action. The artificial but heuristically advantageous distinction between actualization of unconscious transference fantasy and action allows us to understand better the vicissitudes of transference fantasies that may include tendencies to either or both actualization and action. Here we gain the clear advantage of viewing the phenomena of acting out as integrally linked to unconscious fantasies evoked by the emerging and evolving transference in the psychoanalytic process. The unconscious fantasy is here considered to be the central organizing structure of the transference in the sense of fantasy as a compromise formation in accordance with the principle of multiple function. The patient does not act out only to avoid remembering. Psychoanalysis cannot take place without acting out any more than psychoanalysis could take place without transference. Acting out is the potential of the transference neurosis for actualization and therefore expresses the psychic reality of the transference.

REFERENCES

Abt, L., and Weissman, S., eds. (1976). *Acting Out*. 2nd ed. New York: Jason Aronson.

Arlow, J. (1953). Masturbation and symptom formation. *Journal of the American Psychoanalytic Association* 1:45–58.

—— (1971). Character perversions. In *Currents in Psychoanalysis*, ed. I. Marcus, pp. 317–336. New York: International Universities Press.

Beres, D. (1965). Kris Study Group on acting out. Unpublished.

Bibring, E. (1943). The conception of the repetition compulsion. *Psychoanalytic Quarterly* 12:486–519.

Bird, B. (1957). A specific peculiarity of acting out. *Journal of the American Psychoanalytic Association* 5:630–647.

Blos, P. (1978). The concept of acting out in relation to the adolescent process. In *A Developmental Approach to Problems of Acting Out*, rev. edition, ed. E. Rexford, pp. 153–182 (also 247–248). New York: International Universities Press.

Blum, H. (1976). Acting out, the psychoanalytic process, and interpretation. *Annual of Psychoanalytics* 4:163–184.

Brenner, C. (1969). Some comments on technical precepts in psychoanalysis. *Journal of the American Psychoanalytic Association* 17:333–352.

—— (1976). *Psychoanalytic Technique and Psychic Conflict*, pp. 122–125. New York: International Universities Press.

—— (1980). Metapsychology and psychoanalytic theory. *Psychoanalytic Quarterly* 49:189–214.

Calef, V. (1968). Symposium: Acting out and its relation to the psychoanalytic process. *International Journal of Psycho-Analysis* 49:225–227.

Cowitz, B. (1979). Personal communication.

Curtis, H. (1979). Personal communication.

Diatkine, D. (1968). Quoted by J. Laplanche. Symposium: Acting out and its relation to the psychoanalytic process. *International Journal of Psycho-Analysis* 49:230.

Fenichel, O. (1954). Neurotic acting out. In *The Collected Papers of Otto Fenichel*, second series, pp. 296–304. New York: Norton.

Freud, A. (1936). *The Ego and the Mechanisms of Defense*. New York: International Universities Press.

—— (1968). Symposium: Acting out and its relation to the psychoanalytic process. *International Journal of Psycho-Analysis* 49:165–170.

Freud, S. (1900). The interpretation of dreams. *Standard Edition* 5.

—— (1901). The psychopathology of everyday life. *Standard Edition* 6.

—— (1905). Fragment of an analysis of a case of hysteria. *Standard Edition* 7.

—— (1908). Hysterical fantasies and their relation to bisexuality. *Standard Edition* 9.

—— (1911). Formulations on the two principles of mental functioning. *Standard Edition* 12.

—— (1912). The dynamics of transference. *Standard Edition* 12.

—— (1914). Remembering, repeating, and working-through. *Standard Edition* 12.

—— (1920). Beyond the pleasure principle *Standard Edition* 18.

—— (1936). Preface to Richard Sterba's *Dictionary of Psycho-Analysis*. *Standard Edition* 22.

—— (1937). Moses and monotheism. *Standard Edition* 23.

—— (1940). An outline of psychoanalysis. *Standard Edition* 23.

Gill, M. (1979). The analysis of the transference. *Journal of the American Psychoanalytic Association* 27 (Supp.):263–288.

Gray, P. (1973). Psychoanalytic technique and the ego's capacity for viewing intrapsychic activity. *Journal of the American Psychoanalytic Association* 21:474–494.

Greenacre, P. (1968). Symposium: Acting out and its role in the psychoanalytic process. *International Journal of Psycho-Analysis* 49:211–218.

—— (1978). Problems of acting out in the transference relationship. In *A Developmental Approach to Problems of Acting Out*, rev. edition, ed. E. Rexford, pp. 215–233. New York: International Universities Press.

Greenson, R. (1966). Comment on paper by A. Limentani: A re-evaluation of acting out in relation to working through. *International Journal of Psycho-Analysis* 47:282–285.

Grinberg, L. (1968). Symposium: Acting out and its role in the psychoanalytic process. *International Journal of Psycho-Analysis* 49:171–178.

Grossman, W., and Simon, B. (1969). Anthropomorphism: motive, meaning, and causality in psychoanalytic theory. In *Psychoanalytic Study of the Child* 24:78–111. New York: International Universities Press.

Harmann, H. (1964). On rational and irrational action. *Essays on Ego Psychology*, pp. 37–68. New York: International Universities Press.

Infante, J., Stone, C., and Horwitz, L. (1976). Acting out: a clinical reappraisal. *Bulletin of the Menninger Clinic* 40:315–334.

Kanzer, M. (1957). Acting out, sublimation, and reality testing. *Journal of the American Psychoanalytic Association* 5:663–684.

—— (1966). The motor sphere of the transference. *Psychoanalytic Quarterly* 35:522–539.

—— (1968). Ego alteration and acting out. *International Journal of Psycho-Analysis* 49:431–435.

LaPlanche, J., and Pontalis, J. B. (1973). *The Language of Psychoanalysis*. New York: Norton.

Limentani, A. (1966). A re-evaluation of acting out in relation to working through. *International Journal of Psycho-Analysis* 47:274–282.

Lipton, S. (1977). The advantages of Freud's technique as shown in his analysis of the rat man. *International Journal of Psycho-Analysis* 58:255–273.

Loewald, H. (1970). Psychoanalytic theory and the psychoanalytic process. *Psychoanalytic Study of the Child* 25:45–68. New York: International Universities Press.

—— (1971). Some considerations on repetition and repetition compulsion. *International Journal of Psycho-Analysis* 52:59–66.

Loewenstein, R. (1969). Transference in the last fifty years. *International Journal of Psycho-Analysis* 50:583–588.

McLaughlin, J. (1981). Transference, psychic reality, and countertransference. *Psychoanalytic Quarterly* 50:639–664.

Miller, I. (1969). Unconscious fantasy and masturbatory technique. *Journal of the American Psychoanalytic Association* 17:826–847.

Mitscherlich-Nielsen, M. (1968). Symposium: Acting out and its role in the psychoanalytic process. *International Journal of Psycho-Analysis* 49:188–192.

Moore, B. (1968). Symposium: Acting out and its role in the psychoanalytical process. *International Journal of Psycho-Analysis* 49:182–184.

Moore, B., and Fine, B. (1968). *A Glossary of Psycho-Analytic Terms and Concepts.* New York: American Psychoanalytic Association.

Panel (1957). Acting out and its relation to impulse disorders. M. Kanzer, reporter. *Journal of the American Psychoanalytic Association* 5:136–145.

—— (1969). Motor behavior as non-verbal communication in psychoanalysis of adults. A. Suslick, reporter. *Journal of the American Psychoanalytic Association* 17:955–967.

—— (1970). Action, acting out, and the symptomatic act. N. Atkins, reporter. *Journal of the American Psychoanalytic Association* 18:631–643.

Poland, W. (1977). Pilgrimage: action and tradition in self-analysis. *Journal of the American Psychoanalytic Association* 25:399–416.

Rangell, L. (1968). Symposium: Acting out and its role in the psychoanalytic process. *International Journal of Psycho-Analysis* 49:195–201.

—— (1981). From insight to change. *Journal of the American Psychoanalytic Association* 29:119–141.

Rexford, E., ed. (1978). *A Developmental Approach to Problems of Acting Out,* revised edition. New York: International Universities Press.

Ritvo, S. (1968). Comment on M. Kanzer's paper: Ego alteration and acting out. *International Journal of Psycho-Analysis* 49:435–437.

Robertiello, R. (1976). "Acting out" or "working through." In *Acting Out,* ed. L. Abt and S. Weissman, 2nd ed., pp. 40–45. New York: Jason Aronson.

Rosen, J. (1976). The concept of acting in. In *Acting Out,* ed L. Abt and S. Weissman, 2nd ed., pp. 20–29. New York: Jason Aronson.

Rosenfeld, H. (1966). The need of patients to act out during analysis. *Psychoanalysis Forum* 1:20–29.

Sandler, J. (1970). Acting out. Basic psychoanalytic concepts. VI. *British Journal of Psychiatry* 117:329–334.

—— (1976a). Actualization and object relationships. *Journal of the Philadelphia Association of Psychoanalysis* 3 (Special Issue): 59–70.

—— (1976b). Dreams, unconscious fantasies, and identity of perception. *International Review of Psycho-Analysis* 3:33–42.

Sandler, J., Dare, C., and Holder, A. (1973). *The Patient and the Analyst,* pp. 102–103. New York: International Universities Press.

Schafer, R. (1976). *A New Language for Psychoanalysis.* New Haven, CT: Yale University Press.

Segel, N. (1969). Repetition compulsion, acting out, and identification with the doer. *Journal of the American Psychoanalytic Association* 17:474–488.

Stein, M. (1973). Acting out as a character trait. In *Psychoanalytic Study of the Child* 28:347–364. New Haven, CT: Yale University Press.

Sterba, R. (1946). Dreams and acting out. *Psychoanalytic Quarterly* 15:175–179.

—— (1979). Personal communication.

Tarachow, S. (1963). *An Introduction to Psychotherapy*. New York: International Universities Press.

Van Dam, H. (1978). Acting out in the transference, and reactivation of a developmental arrest. Unpublished paper.

Van Gaard, T. (1968). Symposium: Acting out and its role in the psychoanalytic process. *International Journal of Psycho-Analysis* 49:206–211.

Waelder, R. (1936). The principle of multiple function. *Psychoanalytic Quarterly* 5:45–62.

Weiss, E. (1942). Emotional memories and acting out. *Psychoanalytic Quarterly* 11:477–492.

Zeligs, M. (1957). Acting in. *Journal of the American Psychoanalytic Association* 5:685–706.

5

On Countertransference Enactments

THEODORE J. JACOBS

This chapter focuses on the relation of countertransference to psychoanalytic technique, calling attention not to the more obvious forms of countertransference that have been commented on by previous writers on the subject, but to its subtler ones. Often well camouflaged within the framework of traditional, time-tested techniques, this aspect of countertransference may attach itself to our way of listening and thinking about patients, to our efforts at interpretation, to the process of working through, or to the complex issue of termination. Less recognizable than its more boisterous counterpart and in some respects less tangible, this side of the problem of countertransference is no less important. For it is precisely those subtle, often scarcely visible countertransference reactions, so easily rationalized as parts of our standard operating procedures and so easily overlooked, that may in the end have the greatest impact on our analytic work.

A colleague of some renown who, though large in reputation, was extremely small of stature, received a telephone call from a man who wanted a consultation. The appointment was made, and at the arranged time the new patient arrived. About to enter the waiting room to greet him, the analyst suddenly stopped at the threshold and, momentarily, stood transfixed. There in front of him was a Paul Bunyon of a figure, fully six feet, eight inches in height, weighing perhaps 260 pounds, and wearing cowboy boots and a ten-gallon hat. For several more seconds the analyst looked at him in silence. Then, with a shrug of his shoulders and a resigned gesture, he motioned toward his office. "Come on in, anyway," he said.

This opening phrase carried with it worlds of meaning for both analyst and patient. It highlights the well-known though sometimes overlooked fact that from the very outset of treatment, transferences are activated in the analyst as

well as in the patient. Whether overt or disguised, dramatic or barely perceptible, the analyst's transferences may exert a significant influence not only on
his perceptions and understanding, but on the particular form and manner in
which the patient's transferences emerge. Conveyed in tone and gesture as well
as in words, these reactions may be expressed in ways more subtle than obvious—in the barest of nods, the most minimal of smiles, the scarcely audible
grunt, or the slightest variation in words of greeting or of farewell.

The analyst's countertransference reactions, however—and I am using the
term here to refer to influences on his understanding and technique that stem
both from his transferences and from his emotional responses to the patient's
transferences—may be expressed in ways that are even more covert, as aspects of his well-accepted methods and procedures. When they take this form,
countertransference reactions are intricately intertwined with and embedded
within customary, and often unexamined, analytic techniques and the attitudes
and values that inform them.

The way in which we listen, our silences and neutrality, the emphasis we
place on transference phenomena and interpretation of the transference, our
ideas concerning working through, termination, and what constitutes a "correct" interpretation—these and many other facets of our daily clinical work may,
and not infrequently do, contain concealed countertransference elements.

It is on this aspect of countertransference that I shall focus in this chapter because it seems that our understanding of the phenomena of countertransference can be enhanced by consideration of some of its subtler as well
as its more obvious expressions.

It is the latter aspects, its noisier and often dramatic forms that, for the most
part, have received attention in the literature. Illustrative in this regard are some
of the statements made by Annie Reich (1966) who remarks that "countertransference pushes the analyst to act out in a positive or negative way." The
affects stirred up in him, she says, "carry the full charge of repressed impulses
suddenly bursting out from the depth. Thus they lead to real action, to over-strong
emotion or to the opposite, to rigid defenses or blank spots" (p. 352). She describes the not uncommon situation in which the analytic material touches on
some specific problem of the analyst, precipitating in him an inappropriately
strong response. "In all relevant situations," she states, "the intensity of conflict
interferes with understanding. Sublimation fails. Real action, over-strong emotion,
misunderstanding, blocking, and so forth occur. Where minimal amounts of
energy should lead to thought, that is to trial action, real action occurs" (p. 355).

Such responses on the part of the analyst are, of course, not rare. Much
that we call countertransference behavior can accurately be described in these
terms. Because reactions of this kind impinge directly on the analytic work and
constitute obvious sources of difficulty, it is understandable that when, in the

1950s, the problem of countertransference began to attract the attention of analysts, such phenomena became the focus of interest. Even today the idea of countertransference, for many colleagues, is synonymous with overt actions and with an identifiable piece of acting out on the part of the analyst.

Typical of the kind of material that one hears at case conferences, when the issue of countertransference is mentioned at all, is the revelation made recently by a colleague well known for his candor.

"By mistake I ended one session three minutes early," he reported, "and I became aware then of how intensely frustrated this patient was making me. In fact, I was in a fury. She reminded me of the stepsister I could never get along with. She is the same kind of controlling, manipulative woman. After I realized my error, I did a piece of self-analysis that has helped me avoid a repetition of this problem." "Now," he added with a grin, "I usually begin sessions a couple of minutes late."

While such reports are unquestionably valuable, they refer to only one aspect of countertransference, that characterized by overt and rather obvious actions on the part of the analyst. In this regard they may be compared to a view of acting out that includes in such behavior only gross motor actions. This perspective, as Boesky (chapter 4, this volume) has pointed out in the preceding chapter, constitutes a limited way of conceptualizing the highly complex and diverse behaviors that come under the heading of acting out. For some patients acting out will be expressed not in motion, but in immobility; not in words, but in silence. For others acting out may be conveyed in subtle vocal qualities: in the pitch, tone, and rhythms of speech as well as in syntax and phrasing. Boesky has used the term *actualization* for phenomena of this kind, to distinguish them from the more obvious kinds of motor actions that are commonly associated with the term *acting out*.

A similar distinction may be made with regard to countertransference phenomena. Often it is not his overt actions, including even troublesome lapses of control, that are the source of the analyst's greatest countertransference problems, but the covert, scarcely visible, yet persistent reactions that pervade his manner of listening and responding.

This idea is not new. To the contrary, a number of authors, writing from quite different perspectives, have focused on the manifold, and often subtle, ways in which countertransference reactions may influence the analytic process. Langs (1975), emphasizing the importance of the framework and boundaries of the therapeutic setting, points out that the way in which these ground rules are managed implicitly conveys to the patient a great deal about the analyst's intrapsychic state.

In another vein, Arlow (1984) discussed indicators of countertransference reactions. These include not only blind spots with regard to specific material and parapraxes concerning such matters as billing and appointments, but certain reactions of the analyst that occur outside the consultation room. Among these are recurrent thoughts about the patient, often accompanied by feelings of depression or other mood changes, a repetitive need to talk about the sessions, and the appearance of the patient in the manifest content of the analyst's dreams.

Stein (1981) has stressed the importance in analytic work of analyzing the positive, or so-called unobjectionable part of the transference. Not uncommonly, he points out, hidden behind this transference picture, there are powerful competitive and negative feelings as well as an idealization of the analyst. Uncritical acceptance of the old analytic maxim that the positive transference should not be interpreted unless it becomes a resistance may contain a well-rationalized countertransference reaction. Often it is the aim of such reactions both to sustain the hidden gratifications afforded the analyst by the patient's positive view of him and to avoid confrontation of the aggression that lies behind the surface attitude.

Focusing on the patient-analyst interactions that comprise the essence of analytic work, Sandler (Chapter 3, this volume) has pointed out that in analysis each party seeks to impose on the other an intrapsychic object relationship. Responding to the patient with spontaneous actions, affects, and associations, the analyst employs a *free-floating responsiveness* that complements his *free-floating attention*. Although invaluable in providing cues to nonverbally transmitted communications from the patient and the analyst's response to them, these reactions may also contain significant countertransference elements. Unless these are grasped by the analyst, he may find himself simply accepting the role imposed on him by the patient and joining him in a piece of mutual acting out.

Writing from a Kohutian perspective, Wolf (1979) has noted the regular occurrence in analysis of mini-countertransferences. These are inevitable failures of empathy and understanding on the part of the analyst based on momentary countertransference reactions. Although such reactions are the source of temporary disruptions in the established analytic process, in Wolf's view they also provide an opportunity for patient and analyst to gain insight into the precise nature of these disruptions and their transference meanings.

MacDougal (1979) has pointed out that the use of ordinary analytic technique with patients who have suffered traumatic experiences in the preverbal period and for whom silence and abstinence are experienced as fresh traumas not infrequently contains countertransference elements. She writes:

> Like all other human beings we as analysts have difficulty in hearing or perceiving what does not fit into our preestablished codes. Our own unresolved transference feelings here play a role since the garnering of analytic

knowledge has been accomplished and deeply impregnated with transference affect and thus tends to carry an in-built resistance of its own, making it difficult for us to hear all that is being transmitted. We tend to resent
the patient who does not progress in accordance with our expectations or
who reacts to our efforts to understand as though they were hostile attacks
upon him. These problems, added to our personal weaknesses, provide us
with a delicate task. [p. 301]

In what follows I shall also discuss the question of analytic technique and
the way in which countertransference elements may be concealed within our
standard, well-accepted, and quite correct procedures. In citing case examples,
however, my focus will not be on the severely traumatized patient or the more
disturbed one, but on patients whose symptoms and character problems make
psychoanalysis carried out in an unmodified way clearly the treatment of
choice.

Some years ago, after I had begun analytic work with a man of considerable artistic talent and ingenuity, I discovered in myself an unusual phenomenon. I noticed that despite having listened to Mr. K. for better than four months,
I had not missed a word he had spoken. This, I must confess, was for me a
situation worth reflecting on for I was aware of a tendency, when I was tired,
conflicted, or anxious, for my attention to drift in the direction of my own associations rather than those of the patient. This had not happened with Mr. K.,
and I was on the verge of considering myself cured when I gave some thought
to the way I had been listening to him. Then I realized that in listening so alertly,
so carefully, and with such rapt attention, I had done nothing more than trade
one symptom for another. My listening had taken on a special quality that I
now recognized as familiar. It contained something akin to awe, and I realized
that although I had missed nothing, neither had I offered much in the way of
interpretation.

I became aware, too, of a frequently recurring theme in my visual associations to Mr. K. This involved the depiction of an orator or public speaker
holding forth before an entranced audience. It did not take much more detective work for me to understand what had been happening. I had been listening
to Mr. K. as, for years, I had listened to my father holding forth at the dinner
table, expounding his personal view of world history. Long after dessert was
served, I would sit transfixed listening to him spin tales of biblical times and of
the *tsouris* experienced by Rabbi Joshua, later known by the name of Jesus. It
was his show, and if I spoke at all it was simply to ask for more details—the
equivalent of my interventions years later with my patient.

Mr. K.'s talent for storytelling and his transference wish for me to play the
role of appreciative audience had transported me back four decades. I was

listening as I had listened as a boy of 10—silently, intently, half-mesmerized. Only later did I realize that the particular way in which I listened was serving an old and familiar purpose: to keep from my awareness the negative and competitive feelings I was experiencing toward the performer on stage.

Like the rather extended silences that, in this case, I found myself slipping into, silence in the analyst not uncommonly contains elements of counter-transference. Familiar to all of us are the silences that reflect anger, boredom, depression, and fatigue. Familiar too are the silences of confusion, of retalia-tion, and of momentary identification. Less well recognized as a potential con-veyer of countertransference feelings is the kind of silence that, as analysts, we strive to achieve as part of our analytic instrument: the silence of empathic understanding. Precisely because this attitude is so important to us, so much emphasized, and so valuable in our work, countertransference elements that on occasion may be concealed within it are easily overlooked.

This was brought home to me in the course of analytic work with a middle-aged professional woman. During one session in particular I became aware in myself of unusually strong feelings of empathy. In that hour I was able to see what Mrs. A. saw, experience what she experienced, feel what she felt. It was with considerable surprise, after the patient had left the office, that I noted in myself some irritation with her and the thought that what she had told me was only one side of a complex story. This reaction caused me to reflect on the material of our hour and, with the patient out of the room, once again to asso-ciate to it. I then realized that the scene Mrs. A. had depicted was entirely familiar to me and that in my adolescence I had played one of the central char-acters. Distraught over an argument with her husband, Mrs. A. had been un-able to sleep. She waited up until her teenage son had come in from an evening out and then talked to him at some length of her distress. He had listened and been understanding as I had been when, under similar circumstances, my mother had confided in me her hurt and anger over my father's behavior.

As I listened to Mrs. A. and imagined the scene she was depicting I had, unconsciously, become again the son at the kitchen table listening to and shar-ing his mother's upset. I had become the good listener, the empathic listener, but also the listener who had to conceal from himself some feelings of resent-ment at what he was hearing. It was only after Mrs. A. was gone that I, like the adolescent who, when alone, can experience certain emotions that do not surface in a parent's presence, became aware that my responses during the hour were only one side of a complex countertransference reaction. The other side, the resentment I felt over Mrs. A.'s presenting herself as the helpless vic-tim and her husband as the brutish aggressor, had been defended against as similar emotions had been defended against years before: by the upsurge of the strongest feelings of empathy.

For many colleagues the experiences in childhood and adolescence of being an empathic listener to parents or other family members has played a role of importance in their choice of vocation. It is not a rare occurrence for the memories of these experiences to be evoked in the analytic situation. Then silently, outside of awareness, the analyst's usually valuable empathic responses may contain enactments of those memories—enactments that, subtly, can alter and distort his perceptions and understanding.

Neutrality, too, may become invested with countertransference reactions. The analytic idea of neutrality is a highly complex one. Not only does it involve a way of listening that receives with impartiality material deriving from each of the psychic agencies and a technical approach that eschews the resolution of conflict through influence in favor of interpretation, but it implies in the analyst a state of receptivity that can accomplish these goals. The proper use of neutrality as a technical measure requires a considerable degree of inner neutrality, that is, a state of mind in which ego functions necessary for analytic work are not impaired by conflict. The relation between these two forces of neutrality (its outer one, which is an integral aspect of analytic technique, and the inner one, which defines one of the psychological conditions for the employment of that technique) has not been focused on in discussions of the issue of neutrality. Tensions and disharmonies between these two aspects of the analyst's neutrality frequently underlie its countertransference distortions.

Such a situation developed during the analysis of a young attorney. This was a man of outward charm and inner rage. So well concealed was his anger, that he appeared to all the world to be a man of utmost graciousness and wit. To his qualities of keen intelligence and sophistication, was added a persuasive tongue, so that Mr. C. was known for his ability to attract clients. This talent he utilized in the analysis in playful, witty, and seemingly good-humored efforts to get me to render judgments on one or another of the fanciful, and invariably self-defeating, schemes and projects in which he was forever engaged.

In the face of Mr. C.'s charm and persuasiveness, I remained admirably neutral, or so I thought. Repeatedly, if not doggedly, I identified and interpreted his central inner conflicts, his obvious oedipal rivalry, and his unconscious guilt and preoedipal attachments—all with no effect whatever on him. Not for many months was I able to confront Mr. C. directly either with the destructive impact of his behavior on his personal and professional life or with his aggression in the analytic situation. The reason for this was simple. Aggression in Mr. C., though deep and pervasive, was so well concealed, so covertly expressed, that for some time I was not consciously aware either of its presence or of the strong counteraggression it was stimulating in me. In a vague and not easily definable way, I felt uncomfortable with him, and I began, therefore, to pay attention to my autonomic responses during sessions. With regularity, I found my heartbeat to be rapid, my mouth dry, and my guts tense and knotted. It became increasingly clear to me that these were signs of concealed anger occurring in response to the covert anger directed at me.

Due to this state of affairs, I was unable to attain a properly "neutral" (that is, relatively conflict-free) inner receptivity. Because I was not consciously aware of this situation, but perceived it intuitively, I unconsciously overemphasized the outer aspect of neutrality, its technical side. I became not only a neutral analyst, but a determinedly neutral one. Afraid in the face of Mr. C.'s persuasiveness, and the aggression that lay behind it, to lose my stance of neutrality, I lost what Sandler has termed the analyst's free-floating responsiveness. In this case that meant the ability to confront Mr. C. more directly with his behavior both within and outside the analytic situation.

Reflection on my responses to Mr. C. led me to a memory that helped clarify some of my countertransference reactions. As a youngster I had great admiration for an afterschool sports group leader who, for a time, became for me a father surrogate. Bright, witty, and ingenious, he was also something of a provocateur with his charges. In ways that were both humorous and vexing, he would tease the boys about aspects of their dress or behavior. Increasingly I became angry at this leader, but because he was emotionally important to me I concealed my feelings both from him and from myself. It was not until after I left the group that I realized how large a role aggression on both sides had played in our relationship. No doubt Mr. C.'s behavior in the analytic situation, which in many respects was similar to that of the group leader and other important figures of my childhood, aroused in me a familiar pattern of response. This response, with its emphasis on attempting to quiet an inner disturbance through greater emphasis on outer neutrality, led to its inappropriate use.

Central to the question of working through, all analysts would agree, is the matter of repetition. It is the repetition of interpretations, first in one situation, then in another, that permits a patient to take the necessary steps from insight to the resolution of conflicts. Scrutiny of the analyst's use of repetitions, however, and the patient's response to them may reveal an interaction between patient and therapist that is quite different from that taking place in the usually conceived process of working through. Not uncommonly, a familiar scenario has developed. The analyst offers an interpretation, which in one way or another is resisted. He or she interprets again, and once again the patient's resistance rises up to meet the intervention. Consciously aware of the need for repetition to foster working through, the analyst once more repeats the interpretation, only this time more insistently. Again the patient offers resistance, only this time more stubbornly. I need not go on to complete the picture. Within the framework of what appears to be a necessary, if painstaking, process of repetition and the gradual working through of resistance, a formidable, if un-

conscious, battle has been joined. As a result of the arousal of infantile conflicts in both parties, the process of repetition becomes a hammer blow against
an iron door. The result, unless this transference–countertransference interaction can be identified and effectively interpreted, is the kind of stalemate that
often characterizes such struggles in childhood.

Even in situations in which the process of working through takes place
gradually, the interaction between patient and analyst may bear the hallmarks
of similar parent–child relationships. The analyst interprets and the patient
accepts perhaps a fraction of his offering. Further interpretations may lead to
the acceptance of additional fractions. No doubt this is what is meant by frac-
tional discharge. Under favorable circumstances, this situation may continue
until the patient's mouth has opened wide enough for the analyst to slip in a
few spoonfuls of special nourishment.

Much has been written in the analytic literature on the process of termination and the complex emotional responses it evokes in analyst and patient
alike. Less discussed has been the issue of the decision to terminate and how
this decision is arrived at. Frequently the idea of terminating is first broached
by the patient. For some, this decision is reached when particular goals have
been met, motivation to continue has slackened, or a plateau has occurred in
the analysis. For others the idea of terminating has clear transference meanings and is related on the one hand to feelings of rejection, anger, disappointment, or frustration or, on the other, to anxiety over victory and success. Such
situations are well known and require no elaboration here. What has not been
studied with equal intensity are those situations in which the issue of termination arises as the result of covert, often unconsciously transmitted cues that
pass between the participants in the analytic situation. These cues are manifestations of subtle and easily overlooked, but critically important, transference–
countertransference interactions. The following examples may clarify the kind
of situation I have in mind.

For some years I had been working with Mr. R., a middle-aged business-
man whose deliberate and weighty verbal style was exceeded only by the
ponderousness of his thought processes. He was not an easy man to listen to
or to analyze, and at various times in the treatment I had the thought that in
the face of his rock-ribbed obsessional defenses my interventions were little
more than small-arms fire careening off a fortified concrete bunker. For more
than nine years I had persisted, partly out of stubbornness, partly out of pride,
but also because I detected each year grindingly slow but tangible progress in
the patient's self-understanding and in the mitigation of troublesome symptoms.

About halfway into the tenth year of treatment, Mr. R. suddenly brought
up the idea of termination. He had been thinking, he said, and he believed that
he had gone about as far as he could in his analysis. Although certain prob-

lems remained, he was much improved. Since, as far as he could tell, things were pretty much at a standstill, he doubted if he could expect many more gains by continuing.

I was surprised by this turn of events. To begin with, Mr. R. was not a man who usually took the initiative in making decisions. Passivity was deeply rooted in his character, and I had long been convinced that when it came time for termination, I would have to raise the issue. Furthermore, there was nothing in the recent material that suggested Mr. R. had been thinking about termination. It is true that the analysis was proceeding with the speed of a hippo moving upstream and in the past few weeks the resistances had been unusually tenacious, but this situation had existed before and I had not been thinking about termination. Or had I? I began to wonder.

I now gave much thought to the idea of ending and it seemed to me that Mr. R. was probably right. In all likelihood we had gone as far as we could. There was no question that in many ways Mr. R. was better; as for the rest, analysis had at least given him some tools to work with. I was on the verge of saying just that to my patient and setting a mutually acceptable termination date when something gave me pause. The rather abrupt way in which termination arose and my ready agreement with Mr. R. made me uneasy. I decided to wait a bit and to review the material of the week prior to Mr. R.'s raising the question.

As I did so I remembered one session in which I had been particularly frustrated. On the basis of what seemed to me to be clear-cut material, I had made an interpretation connecting certain aspects of Mr. R.'s behavior in the transference to ways in which his mother related to him. Not only did the patient refute the interpretation out of hand with a barrage of sarcastic rejoinders, but in that session he could accept nothing else I offered. I recalled feeling tense and angry. In the face of his assault, I had lapsed into silence. I recalled also that in that hour, and in a subsequent one, I had been aware of experiencing a fleeting visual memory that involved my former analyst. This memory centered on a case conference at our institute, which I had attended, and at which my former analyst was a discussant. Although when it arose I was aware that such a memory must constitute a meaningful response to the analytic material, I could make nothing of it and so let it pass.

Now I returned to that memory and let myself think freely about it. What came to mind was something I had forgotten. In connection with the case presented at the conference, a patient who had been in analysis for a number of years, my former analyst had made the remark, "If you have not broken through after nine years of analysis, perhaps you had better rethink the value of continuing." My memory of that meeting was clearly a shorthand reference to that statement. In the face of Mr. R.'s stubborn and frustrating resistances I was, in effect, telling myself, "Your own analyst would not continue in such a situation. He would advise you to quit. Perhaps you had better listen!"

How I managed to communicate to Mr. R. my feeling that we were at an impasse and that there was no point in continuing is in itself an intriguing question. I had said nothing to Mr. R. about ending, and consciously was not thinking in those terms. What I realized in reviewing the situation, though, was that in response to the powerful resistances I had recently encountered, despair had set in and I had begun to withdraw. I spoke less, and when I did my tone was somewhat muted. I was aware, too, that fatigue, if not exasperation, had crept into my voice.

Always sensitive to the slightest hint of rejection and by nature a counter-puncher, Mr. R. had reacted to these clues in characteristic fashion. He struck back by being the first to propose termination and, by that means, sought to reject me before I had a chance to send him away.

The analysis did not end at that point, but went on for another two years during which Mr. R. made more progress than he had in the previous nine. However, we had come within a hair's breadth of terminating the treatment. Had we done so, the decision to end would have seemed, on the surface, entirely reasonable. It would have been initiated by a patient who had been in analysis for nine years, who had made substantial progress in a number of areas, but whose treatment had now reached a plateau. And it would have been agreed to by his hard-working analyst who had taken him a fair distance and who now recognized on clinical grounds that further progress was unlikely. That a countertransference factor was, in fact, the determining one might well have gone unrecognized. How often, one wonders, does the decision to terminate come about in a similar manner?

Of primary importance in our technique is the matter of transference interpretation. The current well-accepted view that such interpretations are the only mutative ones has led in some instances to a way of listening that may be called listening *for* the transference. Although such a focus in listening may be most valuable in detecting what Gill (1982) has termed the experience of the relationship, it may also prove problematic. Not only may the analyst's listening processes be restricted and, in the extreme case, deformed by so narrow a focus, but the analyst's less than subtle reactions of transference material may lead to its more abundant appearance. It may happen, too, that there is formed between patient and therapist a defensive collusion that has as its unconscious purpose the exploitation of the transference so as to avoid the emergence of other anxiety laden material.

Such was the case with Mrs. G., a clever and sophisticated woman who oriented herself to others by picking up in them the slightest behavioral and verbal cues. During a difficult time in her life, when her husband had become acutely ill, she brought in material that contained within it detectable, though quite concealed, references to her analyst. Though it took a hawklike alertness to the barest hints of transference to dig out these nuggets, I did so and was rather pleased at being able to interpret certain transference feelings that had not surfaced previously. Only after this period had passed and Mrs. G.'s husband had recovered, did I become aware of how patient and analyst had utilized this transference material. Terrified that her husband would die and unable in the analysis to face this possibility, Mrs. G. had, unconsciously, made use of her knowledge that I invariably reacted with interest to transference material by feeding me bits and pieces of it as a decoy. For my part, Mr. G.'s life-threatening illness had reactivated some painful memories concerning personal losses, which I, too, was eager to suppress. By joining with my patient in a particular kind of detective game called "locate the transference," I had colluded with her in doing just that. At this time in the analysis the central issue was not the subtleties of the transference, as important as these were, but Mrs. G.'s inability to face the reality of death—a reality that her analyst was also quite willing to avoid.

Finally, I wish to discuss the issue of correct interpretations. Although one of our primary goals as analysts is to offer interpretations that are correct, the extent to which our interventions are, in fact, accurate is not always easy to assess. The commonly held view that a correct interpretation will regularly elicit in the patient material that confirms it requires some rethinking in light of contradictory clinical evidence.

Every analyst has had the experience of making interpretations which, although later proven correct, are initially met with responses that are not obviously corroborative. Familiar are the reactions of silence, of incredulity, of anger, of denial, of awe, of protest, of depression or, in some cases, reactions characterized by an increase of symptoms. This state of affairs suggests that we may need to inquire further as to what constitutes a correct interpretation. On what level of meaning is its correctness to be judged? Is it solely the cognitive-denotative level, the overt meaning of the analyst's intervention and the resonance of his words with the preconscious of the patient? Or must we include also the metacommunicational level, the covert message hidden behind and within the analyst's words? If this is the case, how do these two levels relate to one another and to the "correctness" of an interpretation? Can an interpretation be correct on one level and not on another? If so, will a patient experience the intervention as correct or must both levels resonate with the analogous ones in himself in order for the patient to have the inner experience of an interpretation being true? Clearly these are complex and relatively unexplored areas that will require further investigation. For the moment, however, I must limit myself to the briefest discussion of a patient's negative response to a "correct" interpretation.

When I first began to see her, Mrs. L. was a woman in her late thirties who, since the age of 4, had sought reparations for the sudden loss of her mother. Full of rage, she had clung to and tortured three husbands before taking on her analyst. In all these relationships she threatened repeatedly to leave the men in her life but never did so. Instead it was they who, weary and battle-scarred, threw in the towel.

Her threats to end the analysis were no less frequent. Quite regularly, after excoriating me for not getting her out of her present unhappy marital situation, she threatened to get rid of me too. Although for the most part I was able to maintain my equanimity in the face of Mrs. L.'s attacks, on occasion I found it difficult to do so. During one session in which, once again, she threatened to leave treatment, I offered an interpretation aimed at bringing to the fore one of the genetic determinants of the repetitive pattern in which she was engaged.

She was treating me, I said, the way she treated her husband, her husbands before him and, in childhood, her feared and hated stepmother. Although she had told me many times that she was leaving treatment, in fact she seemed very frightened to do so. She acted as though I were the only analyst in the city and, in this attitude, she was responding to me as though, in fact, I were her stepmother. With her mother gone, she could never follow through on her ever-present plan to leave her stepmother as this woman had become the only mother she had.

The patient's response lingers in memory. She became tearful and agitated, accused me of wanting to get rid of her, and felt totally hopeless. She sank into a depression that lasted for several weeks and, for some months thereafter, was wary of any interpretation I might offer.

The cause of Mrs. L.'s reaction was clear. She had understood her analyst's message correctly. The manifest interpretation was probably correct enough, but these were not the words that reached her. It was my true meaning. Responding with anger to her sustained provocations, I had reacted like her stepmother and her husbands; they had invited her to leave. Because this countertransference reaction was so unacceptable to me, so contrary to a helpful intervention, I had blocked it from conscious awareness. It found its way out not in the formally correct overt interpretation, but in the covert one that served as a vehicle for the expression of my countertransference feelings.

Reactions such as Mrs. L.'s raise interesting questions about patients' negative responses to interpretations. No doubt some of these responses constitute aspects of the classical syndrome of the negative therapeutic reaction in which the issue of unconscious guilt often plays a central role. Others may derive from quite different sources. Among these are negative responses that represent accurate and intuitive readings of the analyst's hidden communications. In such instances we have to be alert to the possibility that aspects of the very interpretive process itself may imperceptibly have become an enactment. It is just such subtle and well-concealed enactments on the part of the analyst that, in many cases, constitute the greatest source of countertransference difficulty.

REFERENCES

Arlow, J. (1984). Unpublished papers. Meeting of Regional Council of Psychoanalytic Societies, Princeton, NJ, June 7.

Gill, M. M. (1982). *Analysis of Transference Psychological Issues*, Monogr. 53. New York: International Universities Press.

Langs, R. (1975). The therapeutic relationship and deviations in technique. *International Journal of Psychoanalytical Psychotherapy* 4:106–141.

MacDougal, J. (1979). Primitive communication and the use of countertransference. In *Countertransference*, ed. L. Epstein and A. Feiner, pp. 267–303. New York: Jason Aronson.

Reich, A. (1966) Empathy and countertransference. In *Psychoanalytic Contributions*, pp. 344–360. New York: International Universities Press, 1973.

Stein, M. (1981). The unobjectionable part of the transference. *Journal of the American Psychoanalytical Association* 29:869–891.

Wolf, E. (1979). Countertransference in disorders of the self. In *Countertransference,* ed. L. Epstein and A. Feiner, pp. 445–469. New York: Jason Aronson.

mally present to some degree in all dialogue. The intensification takes place in the analytic situation for both parties because ordinary actions are forsworn and visual communication is curtailed.

Given the potential for regression in both parties induced by the deprivations inherent in the analytic situation, it is expectable that words, as the word enactment itself informs us, become acts, things: sticks and stones, hugs and holdings. This secondary process, which we cherish for its linearity and logic, becomes loaded with affective appeal and coercion, to be experienced by either or both parties as significant acts or incitement to action.

These charged words of the analytic dialogue are themselves embedded in and surcharged by a steady clamor of nonverbal communication between the pair, much of which is registered and processed, at times subliminally, by both parties.

Each had learned from infancy, long before the words were there for the saying, how to appeal, coerce, clarify, and dissimulate through the signals of body language, gestures, facial expression, and vocal qualities. And both went on to add to, not relinquish, these wordless capacities to influence and be influenced as they also gradually learned the supple power and diplomacy of words.

To appreciate the imperatives both members of the analytic dyad have in them and bring to the analytic work along with their full repertoire of evocative-coercive capabilities, it is helpful to draw on the perspective our concepts of transference afford us. Especially useful is the broad view of transference as an inherent human tendency to impose the organizing of prior perception of experience upon the present (Freud 1925, McLaughlin 1981, Stern 1977), and thus as fundamental to shaping our psychic reality.

Put differently, whether analyst or patient, our deepest hopes for what we may find the world to be, as well as our worst fears of what it will be, reflect our transference expectancies as shaped by our developmental past. We busy ourselves through life with words and actions aimed at obtaining some response in self and other, in keeping with these expectancies.

We are accustomed to expecting this to be so for the patient—that the patient brings the baggage of his or her expectations to the analytic relationship and tries to make them happen/keep them from happening/find some compromise. As words fail him, and they usually must before they eventually suffice, he intensifies his appeal and protest through increasingly nonverbal ways. In brief: the patient attempts to shape a happening, an enactment, in accord with his fears and hopes.

When the patient views the analyst's behavior as having fulfilled his expectations, we are accustomed from our standpoint to designate this experience as the *actualization of the transference* (Sandler 1976), a phrase that nicely captures the patient's sense of the reality of his experience. This can also be viewed as an enactment in the general sense, because, from the viewpoint of the patient, it is a happening he experiences as an expectable repetition. If the patient's subsequent behaviors, based on his conviction that he has experienced the real thing, lead him to such further action as to strain or break the analyst's boundaries and capacities for doing analytic work, it has been our custom to apply the label, somewhat pejorative, of *acting out*. This is accurate enough, as far as it goes, but it falls short because it reflects only the unilateral perspective of the analyst and his chosen assignment of meaning from his assumed position of higher objectivity and uninvolvement. This shortcoming is equally evident in many of our traditional designations: *countertransference*, *acting out*, and *projective identification*, among others.

What we have come to know about the shaping of the analyst, his work ego, and analytic competence has long since required of us that we see ourselves in our work as indeed adequate at times, but liable to lapse and shortfall for many reasons. Because we know the assets and limitations we brought to our choice of career, and the forces of conflict and compromise that shaped that choice, we know we are not so different from our patients, except as our own analytic experience and training have helped us to evolve a little further in our development and adaptation through analytic ways of knowing. We realize that what we have been trained to do and molded to think both expand and constrain us, and reflect our identifications made with and against those who educated us. We build upon and take refuge in what they put before us.

When at work we bumble, stumble, and get lost, we know we are into mixes of not yet knowing (our dumb spots), not being free to know because of acquired biases and preference for theory and technique (our hard spots), or having lost, for reasons of intrapsychic conflict, our hold on what we know or thought we knew (our blind spots).

Enactment as a Designation for Specific Shared Behaviors

From this view of the analyst as an involved and not invulnerable participant, I would suggest that we employ the term *analytic enactment* in a second and more specifying fashion: to refer to events occurring within the dyad that both parties experience as being the consequence of behavior in the other.

It is obvious that the sources in the analyst of his needs to enact, that is, to retreat from or assert some pressure on the patient, can come from any combination of dumb, hard, or blind spots, touched by the contributions of the patient. The emphasis in this presentation will be on the analyst's blind spots. These are his regressions to less evolved perceptiveness in consequence of the stirring in him of old and only partially mastered conflicts, now given fresh and specific intensities by the particular qualities of the patient's dynamics and transference concerns. I see this focus on the analyst's blind spots as one that can encompass the many defensive factors that contribute to selective ignorance (dumb spots) and theoretical-technical preference (hard spots) in the analyst.

Implicit in this perspective of enactment in the clinical situation is the expectation that close scrutiny of the interpersonal behaviors shaped between the pair will provide clues and cues leading to latent intrapsychic conflicts and residues of prior object relations that one has helped to stir into resonance in the other, and between them actualized for both. I hope the following clinical data exemplify this.

Clinical Vignette: The Case of Mrs. P.

Mrs. P. and I undertook her analysis in the mid-seventies, for reasons of her nearly lifelong tendency to withdraw into depressed isolation and her pervasive sense of never having been in charge of her life, of never having been able to achieve her reasonable potential or to enjoy the fruits of her efforts.

We began at a time when I was actively seeking technical alternatives to the accustomed ways of my analytic training and early aspirations, whereby I had come to expect that I was to accomplish my best analytic work through an objectifying and assessing stance that allowed me to see and convey to my patients my surer grasp of the reality of their situations. This latter I was to articulate with an interventive precision that could be expected to promote mutative growth in my patients. Some of the time and with some patients this approach seemed effective. Much of the time it did not. Mrs. P. provided a plethora of the latter.

Mrs. P.'s running monologues about her chronic frustrations as wife, mother, and career dropout were masterpieces of circumstantial ambiguity. She touched on painful times in her childhood and adolescent years, but only in fleeting fragments. Her steady, flat intoning warded off any but the most insistent interruption aimed at seeking to learn her viewpoint or opinion about what she was talking about. At these interventions she invariably became puzzled and unable to think, then tensely silent and obviously anxious.

I could surmise from her history that her wary defensiveness and refusal to take a stated position or attitude were linked to her continuing frustration in reaching out to a distant and work-preoccupied mother, and tension in fending off a sporadically attentive father whose genuine caring was expressed in an overriding style of critical solicitude and steering. Both parents had wanted this second child to be a boy. Instead, they had to settle for another little girl whom they pushed along to grow up quickly and twin with an older, docile sister. What they ended up with was a quietly sullen rebel who held everybody at a distance out of fear of showing shameful need and flaw, who gave little of herself to anyone, and expected/deserved even less for herself. She had been a depressed, joyless underachiever for as long as she could remember, except for a brief flair of boyish athleticism in latency.

In the early years of this prolonged analysis, I could make no intervention that seemed to help her feel less morose, futile, and self-castigating. I shall focus on this early phase of the work, when repetitious behaviors quietly occurred between us, which will serve to illustrate what I see as crucial to the shared nature of psychoanalytic enactments.

Mrs. P. had an unvarying "Yes-but . . . " response to my best interventions, heralding each time a lengthy detailing of additional information offsetting or refuting what she had said earlier and on which my intervening was based. I came to feel that her responses to my interventions not only destroyed the cogency of the points I had made, but went on to bury their cognitive remains beneath a mound of negation.

Her silences, shifts of topic, and endless justifications for not understanding or agreeing were defensive modes I felt I could understand. But gradually my curiosity and seeking to explore became dulled, as did my active wishes to help her to understand. In wasteland stretches of hours filled with repetitious recountings, I retreated to dogged silence and heavy resolve to wait for better data. And when occasionally I had a sense of finally seeing something useful and broke into her monologue to state my viewpoint, I did so with a declamatory insistence that bothered me even as I heard myself speaking. I knew I would soon hear her justifying counters presented in that flat and sullen monotone.

For example, I had listened, in long silence, to an extended account of the patient's obsessional seeking for just the right dresses for her toddler, hearing the pain behind her flat statements about wanting to give her little girl the right to choose her own clothing (implicitly that she not be made to wear always what Mother wanted, as my patient said had been her lot).

A (somewhat declaratively): So you want very much to be a good mother, to [daughter], not be the controlling mother you felt you had.

P: Yes, but she really did give me choices—in fact, I could get anything I wanted because she'd never go with me. I'd pick what I wanted by myself and it was never right—you've got it wrong (voice briefly sharp, then suddenly flat). Let me tell you about my trouble with getting the walls painted. . . .

A (voice more assertive): Your voice sounded angry then, and sounds angry now. Can you talk about what you are feeling?

P: No—feel confused—you've mixed me all up—I don't feel anything except wish I could be comfortable—things are getting worse at home—and here—I get afraid to say anything.

A: What I'm doing somehow makes you worse.

P: No—it's not you—I just can't think—it's the pot I think, getting to me—so much to worry about at home (rushes into tortured account of troubles with her decorator who fails to give her what she wants, tries to get her to accept what he thinks she should have).

A (feeling weary and somewhat irritated): You notice that you are talking of your decorator's forcing you to see things his way. I think you are experiencing me in this way—that I keep pressing you to consider matters I bring up.

P: Where do you make that connection? I didn't say it quite that way about Mr. H. He's trying to do his job. I just get tired and begin to doubt my own instincts—can't see any connection with what we were talking about earlier in the hour. What *were* we talking about at the beginning? I'm lost.

I too felt lost and baffled at moments like this. Even more bothersome was the expectation that I would soon hear of the worsening of her depression and further retreat into binges of overeating, pot-smoking, and uncontrolled outbursts of verbal rejection of one or other of her preschool daughters. I worried about her sensitivity to whatever I said, and about her potential for destructiveness toward herself and others she wished to love.

My distress for her and for my own helplessness to find ways to intervene effectively in the face of her stubborn provocativeness and volatility was ample warning to me that we were deeply involved in a relationship of stalemate that was mine to explore. Before I sketch the essentials of this exploration, I would like to discuss briefly an important question raised by a member of the panel (1992) audience (Roger Shapiro) concerning the relation between enactment and projective identification.

Projective Identification and Psychoanalytic Enactment

On the basis of the clinical data just described, the designation of projective identification could well apply to what had shaped between Mrs. P. and me. Her behaviors left me repeatedly in states of futility and bewilderment, doubting my capacities to see anything clearly about her or to articulate effectively. I took myself to task for my ineptitude and felt helpless and angry. These reactions of mine were implicitly very like her own qualities of distress so central to her experience. And her behaviors effectively pressured me to experience these affects as my own with an intensity I found unusually painful.

This composite would agree well enough with one of the more balanced descriptions of projective identification that I have found in the literature. Ogden (1979) identifies the inciting fantasies and pressuring behaviors of the patient as the eliciting cause of the analyst's reactions that so mirror the patient's. Yet he emphasizes that the analyst's responses are not "transplanted" but are his own, "elicited feelings . . . under pressure from . . . a different personality system with different strengths and weaknesses" (p. 360).

This is a more perceptive view of projective identification than that of others, like Bion (1959), who for so long have depicted the analyst as a container for the projected thoughts and feelings of the patient. Yet Ogden's viewpoint falls short in not acknowledging and exploring the specific inner experiences of the analyst, his wishes, affective states, and object representations as these transferential resonances are stirred in him in the course of what Kleinians choose to think of as projective identification.

I suspect that the cumulative effect of such traditional constructs as acting out, projective identification, and countertransference has added to the blurring of our vision in perceiving and integrating the full significance of the analyst's contribution to the analytic work (McLaughlin 1981).

It is here that the term enactment, although itself another analyst-imposed concept, could help us in our discourse while it is still relatively unencumbered, and its emphasis on a conjoint process of attempted mutual influence and persuasion could be used to invite exploration of the contributions of both patient and analyst.

Further details of the work with Mrs. P. may support this argument.

Continuation of Clinical Vignette:
The Analyst's Contributions to Enactment

My protracted silences and assertive sorties in pressing my interventions in the first year of the work with Mrs. P. were enactments of my making. I was distressed by their clear evidence of regressive trends in myself in the presence of Mrs. P.'s unfocused circumstantiality and her reducing to fragments my best efforts to see and make sense.

From Mrs. P.'s viewpoint her behaviors before and after my silences, so reminiscent of her mother's habitual unavailability and preoccupation with her own interests, were reasonable ways of warding off expected rejection or withdrawal from what she had to offer. And her defensiveness and obfuscation in response to my insistent interventions that overrode her defenses were as appropriate as were her old responses to her father's intrusiveness and shaming criticisms.

In groping for clues that might open ways to insight, I caught sight of a somewhat unusual mannerism I had drifted into as I sat behind her. I repeatedly removed my bifocals and gazed blankly for minutes on end at the blur of my patient on the couch or at the soft merging of color masses that the vase of flowers on the coffee table had become. In so doing I felt a sense of peaceful detachment and esthetic pleasure. It was with reluctance that I would pull myself back to observing Mrs. P. once more through my corrective lenses—and still not seeing what I needed.

Something further dawned on me later as I heard myself intensely recounting to friends an old and retold story of how my childhood visual impairment had been first discovered by a golfing uncle who asked me, as a 9-year-old, to caddy for him. When he found I had not a clue to where his drive had gone, and could not track it even when he posted me behind a bush on the fairway ahead and it whooshed close by, I was put behind glasses and into a clear world for the first time. The blurred world familiar to me through auditory learning and cautious peering was suddenly, so long as I wore my glasses, an expanse of immense distance and detail, there to be explored and mastered with delight and apprehension. There was much family lore about my attachment to my glasses and the expansive changes their magic made in me.

But another side of these times drifted into focus over the weeks that followed, recollections of what it had been like to be semi-blind and not know it. I could see how it had been comfortable for me to have less expected of me in my accustomed bumblings. But, there had been a down side of defeat and failure in my inability to assert my knowing in the hubbub of my family. Older sisters, a male cousin, and I would have been through the everyday experiences we shared in fishing boat, berry patch, back road, or pasture. I, like the rest, had exciting recollections burning to be told. But my vague and uncertain recountings, vivid only to me, stood no chance in the forum of the family, full of sharp sightings and the keen words to express them. I was readily outtalked in any version of our shared doings. The correction of my efforts by sisters and cousin was frequent and often funny. In my impaired visual state I had usually considered these as made not so much out of malice, but from the sheer delight of children asserting their sharpness of seeing. After I acquired my glasses, I could better recognize what was there of rivalry and put-down.

These inadequacies of seeing and knowing, while the others ahead of me were getting so good at it, had given me moments of pain and despair, with shamed bewilderment over what was lacking in me that was so blithely evident in the rest. I had turned in my nearsightedness even more to books to find an authority of meaning my own vague visual perceptions could not get quite right. Corrective lenses helped more than just my sightedness; yet the puzzlement and uncertainty of the prior years left their traces in my continuing need to be accurate and quick in seeing and saying it right, now that I had the chance and the responsibility to do so.

Years later, functioning as an analyst in the manner of my training of the late 1940s was for me a natural extension of this bent: to seek for and come upon the right interpretation or point of intervention, to articulate correctly my understanding of the patient, and to watch her reactions to my words. Obviously my seeking to be right through a clear and accurate analytic vision was amplified by all my needs to be an analyst in the first place, mainly those centered on ambivalence toward close family members and compensatory needs to repair and enhance. As this clinical instance attests, I was vulnerable to an excessive use of this basic analytic stance under times of particular threat to my sense of competence.

What I gradually came to see clearly enough and with fresh vividness was that my behavior with Mrs. P. reflected needs and concerns of my own, rooted in the vicissitudes of family relationships skewed for me in fairly specific ways by a visual defect (severe myopia and astigmatism), congenital or early acquired. I carried heightened sensitivities to extended attack on, or question of, my seeing and understanding. Mrs. P.'s particular ways of eliciting my efforts to reach out and provide understanding, then turning them topsy-turvy with defensive repudiation, contradiction, and trivialization brought me too close to my old pain of groping and failing. Anger and wary withdrawal into excessive silence as a defensive overuse of the classical analytic stance were signs that I was regressing from a more evolved and adaptive analytic position, and the lensless blur was finally a cue.

What I experienced was so very close to Mrs. P.'s distressful transference preoccupations as to place us for a while in a symmetry and simultaneity of wishes and fears, defensive postures, and affective tension. To ascribe all this to projective identification from patient to me would, as I see it, blur the perception of the individual internal forces in me that had led us into common resonance. From my side these intrapsychic pressures reflected the intensifying effects of the preceding months of effort to identify myself sufficiently with Mrs. P. to be able to make contact with her pain and with the intrapsychic processes in her that occasioned it. In the necessary openness of doing so, I had fallen into transferences I obviously had not sufficiently worked through and mastered in this particular context.

Somehow, in the enigmatic ways that lucky pieces of self-analysis sometimes work, I was able to tap fresh sidestreams of familiar transference sources and was able to feel the surprise of new understanding about old concerns I had thought well settled. I find that this is often the way it is—that work with a specific patient will bring into vivid focus an old conflict well known and dull in a generic sense, but now experienced in a particular variation that lights up yet another aspect to be recognized and settled as best I can.

I trust that it will be evident, however, that this vignette with its personal disclosures is not intended as any new assertion of the value of self-analysis, nor as any claim for unusual capacities in me for doing the necessary work of self-correction that analytic work asks of each of us. Rather, the data are provided to exemplify the rich concordance and complementarity in the dynamic states that will be found to have resonated in both patient and analyst when moments of enactment are explored adequately in both.

What gradually ensued between Mrs. P. and me was a quiet difference in how things got said: fewer silences on my part and a greater freedom to say what I needed in a fashion that did not feel defensive or declamatory. With less need to be right, I could float ideas and questions in a tentative, exploring way that was less intrusive or preempting, providing in words much that Mrs. P. could pick up or shoot down as she needed.

The following brief example shows the kind of exchange that came to denote our more effective and collaborative work in the next two years.

Mrs. P. had launched into a long and familiar lament on how hard she struggled to control her destructive tone and words of rejection toward her older daughter. As she went on, her voice grew high-pitched and strained, breaking off into silence with a squeak as she scratched her head vigorously with her right hand.

A: Sounds like you could be into more and more feeling?

P: Why? Why do you say that? What do you hear?

A: Think I hear your voice rising, getting more tense, maybe a hint of tears. Does it seem so to you?

P: I don't know, you have a way of hearing things I don't. But it *is* true—I *was* hearing my voice going up, but I don't know why you'd connect that with tears. That's just *your* view of it. Why should it be tears, my tears?

A: We could be hearing your voice differently—thought I heard it break as you became silent and began to run your fingers hard through your hair—made me think of strong feelings, maybe pain and anger, that you might not want to feel, or was I not hearing you right?

P (with sharp edge to voice): You *like* to be right, don't you! Oh, scratch that (voice softer). I know you're trying not to force ideas on me, and I appreciate that, at least some of the time. Right now (voice loud and declamatory) I *know* you are critical, right now I expect you to be critical even before I say anything—I've said enough! Too much like Father!

A: Are you saying no more, or there could be real trouble?

P: That's right! I don't mean I won't *ever* say; but right now I've said all I *can* say. I have to be *sure*.

As we parted I had the impression of her as less strained, that she had reacted with less defensiveness and some sense of relief in having her pain and anger recognized without her yet having to risk acknowledging these feelings as her own..

Gradually this became the main, but not exclusive, mode of our working together. When I could be active in putting into tentative, nonassigning words what Mrs. P.'s circumstantiality hinted at, she had words and ideas about the possible meanings of her experiences that she could discount, fend off, or cautiously acknowledge in a repetitious, grudging "I knew *that* all the time, so what's new?" fashion. This allowed us some access to the huge fear and stubborn withholding that lay behind her *not* saying what she consciously knew or felt, and then to her more affectively rich reworking of the transference origins of this defensive stance. Her style became one of disagreeing with the ways I had put things, then restating them in her fashion, which extended or deepened what I had put before her. I thought it a significant indication that she could now experience my interventions, so tentatively put, as less intrusive and possibly helpful, in that she gradually showed less regression to tight helplessness in the hours and less bent to impulsive aggression outside.

Implications for Enactment

In the context of enactment, my altered ways of interacting so as to minimize unnecessary affront and wounding of the patient could be seen logically as the analyst's sharing in an enactment of the patient's transference hope to find understanding and not criticism, with patient responding in a facilitating collaboration that extended her knowledge of herself. Because we lack an adequate vocabulary to designate many of the positive events in analytic work, or to help us better to define what *is* essentially analytic in what we do, I would regard such adjustments by the analyst to the patient's psychic reality, to her particular ways of experiencing the analyst, as indeed enactments of the sort usually attributed to analytic tact (Poland 1975) or, in Sandler's (Chapter 3, this volume) terms, instances of appropriate analytic role-responsiveness.

Because such corrections so often come about after the analyst recognizes that he and the patient have fallen into obstructive interaction, they can also be viewed as a restoration to a more evolved analytic stance of optimal neutrality and abstinence whereby such regressive enactments are avoided (Panel 1992).

I would like to carry the implications of this mode of close attunement to the patient's psychic reality to matters that lie beyond analytic tact and further than the responsibility of the analyst to repair his or her regressive lapses in technique.

In struggling to learn how I might work more effectively with patients like Mrs. P., for she was not that exceptional in her sensitivity to my ways of responding, I came to sense the rich analytic potential and yield that lay in steadily seeking out the patient's view of reality and doing all I could to facilitate the patient's voicing his or her experiencing of that reality (McLaughlin 1981). For me this became the essential significance of Freud's technical enjoinder that we begin at the surface, and it led me to the tentative, questioning, and non-declamatory mode detailed previously. Others have added large increments of understanding to this focus on patients' perceptions of their experiences (Gill and Hoffman 1982, Gray 1973, 1982, Schwaber 1983, 1986). From their different conceptual approaches, each has substantiated the value of a way of working that imposes fewer theoretical presumptions and less assertion of personal bias and steering. I have been increasingly struck by the aptness of Schwaber's (1986) technical and conceptual approach in furthering this quest through a mode of inquiry and listening that seeks always to ascertain and acknowledge the patient's reality view as reflected in his or her experiencing of the analyst's behaviors.

I stress the importance of this technical approach for the matter of enactment in order to express essential agreement with Schwaber's observation about many of the crises and complications in our analytic work, events we have been accustomed to designate as acting out, and may now designate as enactments. She sees these events as often being the patient's specific responses to our prior failures to seek and acknowledge the patient's viewpoint of our behaviors that he or she has found distressing. Schwaber notes the cumulative impact of the analyst's further failure to respond and help to articulate the patient's distress. Her data are impressive in pointing to the analyst's lapses as reflecting countertransference issues of conflict and avoidance, along with defensive needs to adhere excessively to theoretical-technical preferences.

The enactments that Mrs. P. and I shaped demonstrate these points rather well. When I was too long silent or too insistently declamatory, Mrs. P. gave strong indication of not being understood or acknowledged. Her distress mounted as she became more needy, rageful, and depressed. For quite a while I took refuge in my silences and found comfort in my declamatory sureness, for these were analytic modes I saw as consonant with my early training and technical knowledge.

We all can point to certain enactments that continued for some time before being discovered and repaired by analyst and patient (McLaughlin 1988). In such instances I have the strong impression that the period of tension and impasse and then the phase of discovery, reworking, and resolution combined to make for levels of affective intensity and an immediacy of actual experience that added appreciably to the clinical value of the experience for patient and analyst.

In the instance of Mrs. P., I did not have that conviction. Instead, I feel that the work could have moved into a more productive collaboration earlier had I not been impeded by both my idiosyncratic, regressive responses to her particular behaviors and the comfort I took in some of the stereotypes of my early training.

While I have been able to go beyond some of the limiting aspects of the latter, I ruefully rediscover the old truth in the former: that the transference ghosts of the past are never entirely laid to rest. In the intensity of new work with qualities unique and not yet known, they return in fresh shape to revive shades of significance I had long forgotten I knew. Enactments are my expectable lot.

There is comfort in knowing that it is possible and restoring, most of the time, to turn back to the slip and shortfall, to rework these closely through the eyes of the patient. And there is satisfaction in finding those lucky moments when the reflections from the patient stir the glimmer in one's own eye that allows vision to be restored.

The concept of enactment acknowledges this two-sidedness of the analytic relationship. It can thus facilitate the analyst's recognition of and reflection on his own contributions and foster a more comfortable stance toward his lapses and their transference roots. Given such internal easements, self-analysis and seeking help from colleague or group are more likely to occur and their findings to be assimilated.

REFERENCES

Bion, W. (1959). *Experiences in Groups*. New York: Basic Books.
Fenichel, O. (1945). *The Psychoanalytic Theory of Neurosis*. New York: Norton.
Freud, S. (1925). Negation. *Standard Edition* 19.
—— (1926). On the problem of lay analysis. *Standard Edition* 20.
Gill, M. M., and Hoffman, I. (1982). A method for studying the analysis of aspects of the patient's experience of the relationship in psychoanalysis and psychotherapy. *Journal of the American Psychoanalytic Association* 30:137–167.
Gray, P. (1973). Psychoanalytic technique: ego capacity to view intrapsychic activity. *Journal of the American Psychoanalytic Association* 21:474–494.
—— (1982). Developmental lag in the evolution of psychoanalytic technique. *Journal of the American Psychoanalytic Association* 30:621–655.
Guttman, S. (1980). *Concordance to the Standard Edition of the Complete Psychological Works of Sigmund Freud*. New York: International Universities Press.
McLaughlin, J. (1981). Transference, psychic reality, and countertransference. *Psychoanalytic Quarterly* 50:639–664.
—— (1987). The play of transference: some reflections on enactment in the psychoanalytic situation. *Journal of the American Psychoanalytic Association* 35:557–582.
—— (1988). The analyst's insights. *Psychoanalytic Quarterly* 47:370–389.
Mosher, P. W., ed. (1987). *Title Key Words and Author Index to Psychoanalytic Journals 1920–1986*. New York: American Psychoanalytic Association.
Ogden, T. (1979). On projective identification. *International Journal of Psycho-Analysis* 60:357–374.
Panel (1992). Enactments in psychoanalysis. M. Johan, reporter. *Journal of the American Psychoanalytic Association* 40:827–841.

Poland, W. (1975). Tact as a psychoanalytic function. *International Journal of Psycho-Analysis* 56:155–162.

Sandler, J. (1976). Actualization and object relationships. *Journal of the Philadelphia Association of Psychoanalysis* 3:59–70.

Schwaber, E. (1983). Psychoanalytic listening and psychic reality. *International Review of Psycho-Analysis* 10:379–392.

—— (1986). Reconstruction and perceptual experience. *Journal of the American Psychoanalytic Association* 34:911–932.

Stern, D. (1977). *The First Relationship: Infant and Mother*. Cambridge, MA: Harvard University Press.

a more evolved
analytic stance
of optimal neutrality
and abstinence
whereby (such)
regressive enactments
are avoided

7

The Evocative Power of Enactments

JUDITH FINGERT CHUSED

Although we think of words as the primary modality of communication in analysis, patients do more than talk to us. They also communicate with other forms of behavior—with actions, attempts at actualizations (Boesky, Chapter 4 this volume), and enactments. The role of these behaviors during an analysis, in particular the role of enactments, has provoked much discussion (Panel 1992). Most of the analysts who participated in that discussion, both panelists and members of the audience, agreed that enactments in analysis are inevitable. What remained unsettled was the question of whether and how enactments could beneficially contribute to the analytic process.

Enactments are symbolic interactions between analyst and patient that have unconscious meaning to *both*. During an analysis, they are usually initiated by the patient's actions or by the covert communication in the patient's words (Poland 1988). Enactments also may originate with the analyst (Jacobs, Chapter 5 this volume), although in these instances, it is often the analyst's countertransference response to the patient's material that leads to the enactment.

Throughout an analysis, patients engage in symbolic action (both verbal and nonverbal) that generates a corresponding impulse for action in the analyst. In the best of all possible worlds, an analyst is sensitive to the patient's transference, as expressed in either words or action, but does not act. Sympathetic with a patient's pitiful state, the analyst does not nurture; temporarily aroused by a patient's seductive attacks, the analyst does not counterattack. An analyst contains his impulses, examines them, and uses the information gained to enrich the interpretive work.

This best of all possible worlds is the ideal, something we strive for, but often fail to achieve. In the second best possible world, where most of us dwell, an analyst reacts to the patient, but catches himself in the act, so to speak, regains his analytic stance and, in observing himself and the patient, increases his understanding of the unconscious fantasies and conflicts in the patient and himself that have prompted him to action. As Sandler (Chapter 3 this volume) notes, the analyst will "tend to comply with the role demanded of him [but] may only become aware of it through observing his own behavior, responses, and attitudes, *after these have been carried over into action*" (p. 35).

It is written into our job description that in "doing analysis" we must contain ourselves yet still experience the impulse to action. But when actions are forbidden, often the experiencing of the impulse also feels forbidden. I believe at times it may be more useful for an analyst to act on an impulse, catch himself, and thereby learn about the impulse and its stimulus, than to be so constricted that he is never stimulated or so defended that he is not aware of his behavior. I do not think that enactments are therapeutic in themselves, and I do not advocate consciously gratifying a patient's wish for mutual enactment. However, unconsciously determined enactments, if observed, can inform the analyst in a new way.[1] They provide information as to the content of the fantasy, memory, or impulse that is being enacted, and they lead to affects that can enrich the analytic process. The value lies not in the enactments themselves, but in the observation, description, and eventual understanding of their transferential meaning.

The potential for enactments is omnipresent throughout an analysis. As soon as there are transference distortions of the analyst and the process, any exchange within the relationship may lead to an enactment. A patient who "imagines" that the analyst is critical or seductive has some distance from his experience, which permits the analyst to have distance from the experience. There is no such distance during an enactment. During an enactment, the patient has a conviction about the accuracy of his or her perceptions *and* behaves so as to induce behavior in the analyst that supports this conviction. Even if an analyst is neither angry nor critical, a patient's accusations can still induce

---

[1]Enactments have been used in support of various clinical theories. For example, Alexander (1950) presented a clinical vignette containing an enactment to support the therapeutic value of the "corrective emotional experience." He described a patient who *unconsciously* provoked his analyst into disliking him in order to reinforce a defensively distorted memory of his relationship with his father. In the discussion, Alexander noted, "The analyst's reaction was not calculated to be different from that of the patient's father. He simply lost, for a moment, the type of control which we consider so important in psychoanalytic therapy" (p. 491). In essence, Alexander *unconsciously participated* in an enactment of a defensively distorted object relationship. He makes clear that it was his subsequent awareness and articulation of this that enabled the patient to gain from the experience. Nonetheless, based on this observation, Alexander made a recommendation for a *consciously manipulated* experience for his patients.

guilt, defense, and retaliative anger. This is one aspect of the evocative power of enactments.

In addition, all object-related wishes and fantasies (including the wishes and fantasies of the analyst) are evocative of relationships with the primary objects. Both gratification and frustration contain a potential for regression, which exposes the individual to dormant internal conflicts and the possibility of maladaptive compromise formations. Every time a person has a wish within an object relationship—in this case, the therapist's wish to be of help to his patient—he exposes himself to the possibility that the interaction will evoke an earlier object relationship, that is, will become laden with transference. To want anything from patients, to want to cure, to help, even to be listened to or understood accurately, is to be vulnerable to the experience of one's own transference and thus be susceptible to an enactment.

Communication is always a two-person procedure; what is intended to be said is altered by the person and the context in which the information is received. When patients or analysts speak, the meaning and intent of the words are altered by how each hears the other, altered for the speaker as well as for the listener.

If an analyst accepts the inevitability of his contribution to enactments and analyzes them to separate his participation from the patient's understanding of his participation, to distinguish the determinants based on his psychology from those arising from the patient's, the work can only be enhanced. As illustration, I shall present material from the analysis of Debra, a latency-age girl. Much of the work with Debra can be related to work with adults. I find it useful to focus on her analysis because so much of a child's communication is through action, and so many of Debra's actions led to enactments.

Debra

Debra was 8 years old when she was referred for treatment. She was an exceptionally intelligent child who was working at that time with an educational consultant regarding school placement. Debra had already attended three private elementary schools but had been unhappy at each, ostensibly because they "failed to stimulate" her. She had applied to and was accepted at a fourth school, one of the best available in the city, but the consultant feared that without psychological help Debra would continue to be unhappy.

Before I had even seen her, the parents' pride-filled description of Debra created an image in my mind of a very talented, somewhat vulnerable child whose environment continually reinforced whatever grandiosity already existed. My expectation proved correct—as far as it went—for Debra was talented and grandiose. What I was not prepared for was the intensity of her rage, the totality of her isolation, and her utter contempt and lack of empathy for others.

On first meeting, Debra was a physically beautiful, totally self-absorbed, angry, sullen child. She had taken gymnastics since age 4, and as she posed gracefully and motionless in the chair opposite me, with no evidence of discomfort or anxious chatter, I felt as if I were part of the stage set for a movie of "Debra's visit to a psychiatrist's office." There was no apprehension in the gaze of this incredibly self-possessed child as she communicated that I, not she, was expected to perform. She did say she had no idea why her parents had wanted her to see me and that, as far as she was concerned, the whole idea of talking to someone about her private life was ridiculous— "After all, it's private, isn't it?" As I struggled to find some subject with which to engage her, I was impressed with the difficulty of my task and a sense of not wishing to expose myself or my thoughts to any more of her contempt than was absolutely necessary. This concern with self-protection set the stage for my participation in the first enactment: a guardedness in approaching Debra.

Debra was the oldest of three children. She had two younger brothers who were good athletes, on whom the father spent a great deal of time as coach for their soccer teams. Her parents were upper-class, concerned about social form and status, yet quite invested in all their children. The father was well-meaning, insecure, and totally dominated by his wife. She was an imposing woman whose enormous energies were devoted to furthering peace and fellowship in the world and to achieving an atmosphere of total psychological and physical sharing in her family. She also was given to emotional storms, which were made more dramatic by their unpredictability. During my weekly meetings with the parents I often found the mother intimidating, and I was more than relieved when, after a year of Debra's analysis, the mother accepted a recommendation for therapy for herself.

Debra's development during infancy was normal. However, from early on her precocious intellectual achievements were an important focus of her parents' lives, and she was subject to constant cognitive, physical, and psychological overstimulation. By the time Debra came to analysis her mother was sharing intimate details of her own emotional, sexual, and excretory functioning with her daughter and expected Debra to do likewise. In contrast, the father's wish to shut the door when he toileted was considered peculiar and prudish, and his "selfishness" was a family joke.

I recommended analysis reluctantly, although I believed that only an analytic experience could enable Debra to emerge from her narcissistic isolation and expose her conflictual impulses and unhappiness. Nonetheless, I felt that to engage Debra would be no easy task.

My reluctance proved fully justified. Debra began the work with her self-esteem further reduced by the recommendation for treatment, and she was enraged at me for "belittling" her. She made it clear that it was inconceivable that there would be any benefit from the treatment.

During the first hours Debra sat silently, noting only when I took a deep breath or seemed as if I wanted to speak. That was her signal that I was open to criticism and that it was time for her to begin an attack on my appearance, my smell, or my "rudeness." Rudeness was her name for my interest in talking with her and for my curiosity about her irritation, her anger, and her desire to be left alone. It was not lost on Debra that I made a deliberate effort not to ask too many questions and restricted my interventions to responses to her or clarifications of what I perceived to be happening between us. She said, with some satisfaction, that she knew she made it hard for me to speak. Debra's awareness of this first enactment—my self-esteem preserving caution in response to her message that I was persona non grata—made the situation all the more uncomfortable. I felt ridiculous trying to make myself inoffensive to an 8-year-old.

Although my self-esteem preserving caution and guardedness in approaching Debra was " . . . a *compromise* between [my] own tendencies and the role-relationship that the patient is unconsciously seeking to establish" (Sandler, Chapter 3 this volume, p. 36), I found no evidence that the elements in my life that gave rise to my participation in the enactment were relevant in understanding the significance of the enactment for her. The affect evoked in me did seem to complement hers, and I used that affect as a clue to her *current experience* within the transference. However, the *genetic determinants* for our participation in the enactment were quite different. I believe this is important, for had I assumed that the *unconscious meaning* of the enactment was the same for Debra and for me, it might have led to inaccurate interpretations, which would have further confused an already difficult situation.

I noted, in the midst of this first enactment, that I had ceased being neutral or abstinent, and instead was engaging in a counterenactment, that is, I was using clarifications as disguised directives. This realization, that through my words I was covertly trying to control Debra's behavior, led me to a beginning understanding of what was being enacted. And so, in the midst of her protests that I was a prying busybody, intent on sticking my nose into her business, I said she had told me that she knew her complaints and criticisms made it hard for me to speak. I wondered whether this made her feel more powerful than me, as if she could control me, and whether *she* had ever felt controlled. Much to my surprise (for I had begun to question whether there would ever be a nonadversarial exchange between us), Debra responded spontaneously that the kids "picked on" her at school, but she didn't care, she just ignored them. I then asked, "Are you trying to get me to ignore you?" To this she responded, "It probably won't work; my mother never ignores me when I want her to leave me alone."

My understanding and clarifying her use of complaints to try to control me seemed useful. For a brief period, Debra was less uptight, and a comfortable silence, alternating with talk about her mother and school (both of which displeased her), took over the sessions. Then the next set of enactments began.

Debra became very curious about me. At first she expressed her interest through casual questions about the sweaters I wore and whether I made them. But soon the questions escalated to a belligerent inquisition of relentless intensity. She quizzed me about my taste in clothing, perfume, hairstyles, and lipstick colors. She told me my furniture wasn't "fine," my toys were old-fashioned, and my waiting-room magazines were dull and, she was sorry to say, rather tacky. Worst of all were my other patients—they were disgusting. She was particularly interested in and censorial of the bathroom manners of the 5-year-old girl whose hour preceded hers. She talked at length about the smell, dirtiness, and habits of this other patient, watching carefully for my re-action. From my protective feelings for the other child, it was clear Debra's comments had gotten to me. However, I said nothing until she began to attack me directly. Focusing on my failure to join in her criticism, she said it was proof that I was as disgusting as the other child. I asked her, as she was shouting at me for being disgusting, whether she expected me to defend myself and shout back at her. She stopped short, then, smiling rather sheepishly, she said, "No, I guess I'm not giving you a chance. Do you think I sound like my mother when I yell?"

Debra's remarks and her finicky behavior when describing the disgust-ing habits of others were related to conflictual anal fantasies. Her haughty self-isolation expressed both a compromise between the wish and fear of intrusion and a defense against an awareness of this. Her anal fantasies had contributed to her low self-esteem, and during the course of the analysis, as they became less forbidden, she projected less and became able to speak about them more directly. The problem was, as with other children (and some adults) at this early stage of the treatment, that evidence of her unconscious conflicts and fantasies was clear long before she had any conscious awareness of them. This made it hard to talk about her internal world in a nonthreatening, nonintrusive way that did not bypass defense, that was experience-near and understand-able, and that at the same time was therapeutically useful. I found that with Debra enactments provided a ready, albeit not always welcome or comfortable ve-hicle for this, for they enabled the analytic process to be a joint venture. Her awareness that I could be touched by our interaction seemed to make me more available to her as an object for transference projections and externalizations.

In analysis (particularly in child analysis), the inequality of the doctor–patient (or adult–child) relationship often functions as a resistance to an inte-gration of the analyst's words with the analytic experience. The words become encrusted with authority because of the source and are discredited at the same time they are ostensibly accepted. Recognition of the potential for and occurrence of enactments, a shared experience, diminishes the authoritarian image of the doctor and the tendency of patients, particularly child patients, to fall into a submissive (iatrogenically induced) relationship with the doctor. It is not that the analyst "confesses" his participations in enactments, but his and his patient's awareness that the process has engaged them both enhances the sense of a collaborative effort and, to the extent the analyst is nondefensive, permits the patient greater freedom to give voice to his or her transference-based perceptions of the analyst.

In the beginning phase, all my attempts to explore the projection in Debra's comments had led to a heated denial and further isolation. However, Debra *could* talk about her behavior toward me and the interaction it produced. Her initial success in inhibiting me was clarified in a way that felt right to her and made Debra curious about herself in a new way. To be sure, everything that was condensed in the enactment, that contributed to it, was not explored. But from our talk she began to understand how her reaction to her peers was similar to her reaction to me, how anticipating discomfort in the contact with her classmates, she retreated from any real engagement and "turned them off" just as she tried to turn me off.

When Debra first quizzed and criticized me, I had worked hard not to withdraw or counterattack, but I *had* felt inhibited from commenting on the sadistic, intrusive aspect of her questioning. In my apprehension about stimulating rage in Debra, I had participated in the enactment of her fantasy that she could control me. Again, although it was my own early life experience that made me particularly vulnerable to the threat of her anger, I did not think the specifics of my experience informed me about hers. However, becoming aware of my overdetermined reaction and its origin enabled me to talk more easily about Debra's interaction with me, which led, in turn, to her first attempts to understand herself. Debra's self-scrutiny yielded only the explanation that her wish to control me was justified by my crudeness, my curiosity about things scatalogical. Nonetheless, her willingness to think about herself, even if only for a moment, did permit us to extend the area we talked about. Initially, in response to, "Oh, Dr. Chused, that dark-haired girl got pee on the floor again; you must be crazy to let her use your bathroom," I would simply say, "Debra, you're telling me that girl does disgusting things; are you also telling me that if *she* does something disgusting, *we* shouldn't have anything to do with her?" Now, I was able to make more exploratory comments such as, "You've said I'm interested in sex and bathroom stuff and that's disgusting, but it's not clear what it is about having sex or getting pee on the floor that's so awful." Sometimes she could follow me into this type of dialogue, but more often than not, as we began to approach her own impulses or defensive reaction formation, she would project, with remarks such as, "You're a strange grownup, always wanting to talk about sex with a kid." For a long time, no matter what I said, Debra heard guilt, defensiveness, or seduction in my response.

It was not that Debra could not understand the words, for, as Katan (1961, p. 185) has said, with analysis, "verbalization [increases] the possibility of distinguishing between wishes and fantasies on the one hand, and reality on the other," but rather that my speaking had accrued symbolic meaning. I thought I was trying hard to "say it right" because I was so invested in the work. Debra thought I was self-motivated and intrusive. My efforts to verbalize our interaction became, for a while, an enactment of her transference perception of me as intrusive. But here, too, the clarification of our differing perceptions of my talking was part of the working through and permitted us to better understand her attempts to control me as she had wanted to control both her mother *and* her own arousal.

Although Debra was engaged at this point, and her isolation had given way to greater responsiveness, the anal erotic fantasies that preoccupied her had not yet entered the sessions in a usable fashion. Then, after about eighteen months of analysis, Debra began to come into my office with her school uniform unbuttoned at the waist. She also started to wear her sweater under her skirt, with a leg in each sleeve and the neck hole over her perineum. She stated her legs were cold and it was important for a gymnast to wear warmers, but since her family was poor, she had to make do with her sweater. I resisted making any comment about the sweater until it became obvious, through her unbuttoned uniform and requests for safety pins, that she wanted me to notice the hole. When I stated this, she told me that she liked to have her body noticed, and described, in rather vivid detail, the tickly perineal sensations she had when she thought someone was looking at her. She went on to volunteer the fantasy she had of intercourse, of two Ferris wheels that rose up from a horizontal position on the ground to join together vertically, like two wheels fusing. But just as the holes in her clothing and her showing and my seeing her body were to lead to an enactment, the telling of her fantasies also became part of an enactment. The fantasies were not communicated to me as evidence of her inner life, shared so that together we could understand them better. Instead they were presented, like the hole over her perineum, to excite me and titillate her with the thought of my excitement. Speech serves many functions; affective appeal (Loewenstein 1956) rather than the communication of ideas was often the motive force behind Debra's words.

Debra's fantasies did indeed interest me. Having spent many hours with her, listening (as one must) to recitation of daily events, school activities, stuck-up friends, and mean parents, I was pleased when she began to reveal her inner life more directly. Trying to ferret out the significance of material expressed in displacement or through play is a difficult task. Direct verbal communication of a fantasy, wish, or fear always appeals. However, this was not the only reason for my heightened interest. My curiosity was also a response to the covert communication of excitement, a communication that contained critical information about Debra. I did not recognize this at first, but it soon became apparent (from the increased pressure in her speech and the associated gestures) that Debra's understanding of my increased attentiveness was not entirely the same as mine. It was through my self-scrutiny, the recognition and integration of what was stimulated in me with what I knew of Debra, that I began to understand what we had just enacted. And it was to this I directed our attention. I stated rather simply that my listening to her seemed to make her excited. With some pride and a bit of a giggle, she agreed she wanted to see how I would respond to her story about the Ferris wheels—she liked to think about it while she was in the bathroom. She went on to say, "I could tell you were interested. My mom also likes to hear me tell what I think about sex, about getting breasts and hair and all that stuff." She then asked, "Did you know I don't use the bathroom in school, only at home and now in here, while I wait for you?" Actually, during the past several months I had noted that she was always in the bathroom when I came into the waiting room to get her, but I had refrained from commenting on it (another enactment), apprehensive that a direct comment would anger her and lead to an attack. Now I said, "Was I supposed to notice? Maybe notice but not say anything?" Again she smiled slyly, then said, rather irritatedly, "But you always ruin things by talking about them." As if to prove her point, I went on to say that I thought not using the bathroom at school was like not playing with the kids—it was as if they would find out something private about her, something she wanted them to know and not know, something she wanted them to like but was afraid they would not, just as she did not like the little girl's pee on the floor. She made no response immediately, but then said, "In my family we all like to stay on the pot a long time, and we all fart a lot too; my father has the smelliest. We always talk and joke about it, but my father doesn't like that. He also doesn't like to kiss me on the lips, only on the cheek and the forehead. My mother always kisses me on the lips . . . and *she* talks about everything."

The enactment of her transference perception that I, like the mother, was sexually interested and aroused by her, but like her father, retreated from stimulating interactions, followed from my attentive silence. As we explored her understanding of my interest in her erotic fantasy and my noticing yet not saying anything about her exhibiting herself, she began to talk of her experiences with her mother (who, in regular baths with her daughter, intently examined Debra's body for evidence of pubertal development) as well as her disappointment that her father was not more involved with her physically.

There was an additional enactment that preceded Debra's acceptance of her disappointment in her father's unavailability. As Debra was explaining how she saw me, she said that even when I was silent, she knew I wanted to ask questions, that is, pursue her and intrude into her. In part Debra's perception was correct, for when she had begun to describe her interaction with her mother, I had reacted with a silence that was far from neutral. The extent of the overstimulation she described had made me uncomfortable, and I had withdrawn from the analytic process. This enactment, though initiated by Debra's attempt at transference gratification, was created by the interaction of her behavior *and* my response. My withdrawal, a countertransference response, appeared to Debra to parallel her father's, and she elaborated it into the same secret arousal she wanted to see in him. I do not know if the reaction formation of dismay that Debra's experiences aroused in me was similar to the father's reaction. I do know, however, that Debra chose to deny my withdrawal just as she denied her father's discomfort—and her own. It was the defensive denial that I addressed.

Debra's connection to her mother had been in yielding to her mother's persistent questioning about sexual and excretory functioning. This became part of the transference as did her denial of disappointment in the exciting yet unavailable father who kissed her on the forehead rather than on the lips and had the poor manners and selfishness to close the door when he was using the bathroom. Though she initially saw me as intrusive as her mother was and as she wished her father to be, the exploration of our enactments and her transference misperceptions enabled her to see both her parents more clearly, to separate her wishes from theirs, and to begin to behave more autonomously. In addition, her gradual awareness of her disappointment and sadness over her father's unavailability (which she had initially talked about only as a joke) marked the beginning appreciation of the extent of her longing for him.

Before I say more of Debra, I would like to elaborate on my understanding of enactments and how I differentiate them from acting out or repetitions. Terms such as acting out and repetition refer only to the patient's behavior; they imply that the analyst is an observer of the experience, not a participant in it. Even the term projective identification, while recognizing the analyst's responsiveness to the patient, does not acknowledge the contribution to the analytic experience, which is determined by the analyst's own psychology (McLaughlin, Chapter 6 this volume; Sandler, Chapter 3 this volume).

Enactments, distinguished by the unconsciously determined affective and behavioral involvement of the analyst, result from the patient's attempt to create an interactional representation of a wished-for object relationship. Through getting the analyst to enact with the patient, the latter achieves a measure of reality for his or her transference fantasies. *Enactments occur when an attempt to actualize a transference fantasy elicits a countertransference reaction.*

Many analysts today recognize that they are both observers and participants (to a greater or lesser extent) in the analytic process; however, this was
not always true (McLaughlin, Chapter 6 this volume). Even now, although there
is general agreement that threats or overtly seductive gestures stimulate responses in the analyst that affect his analyzing capacity, there is still a failure
to attend to the more subtle behavior, more ambiguous expressions of a
patient's affective state, which can wreak havoc with analytic abstinence and
neutrality and can lead to enactments.

There are several possible scenarios when a patient attempts *unsuccess-
fully* to evoke an enactment. The analyst may recognize what is transpiring and
may be able to usefully interpret the process to the patient. Or, with no reaction from the analyst, the unconscious intent of the patient's behavior may be
lost, to reemerge later in another form. If the patient has sufficient self-observing
capacities, he or she may become aware of frustrated wishes and begin to speak
of them, rather than enact them. Or the patient may continue to provoke until
the analyst is roused to action. So it was with Debra.

After disclosing a wish that her mother were less intrusive and her father
(and I) more involved, Debra stopped talking about her excitement with me,
and instead turned to the play materials. Within several weeks, she had begun
a repetitive game that continued for six months. Debra's pattern was not unique;
many latency children (Debra was then 10) dramatize their conflicts and wishes
in play rather than speaking about them directly. What made Debra's activity
interesting was that not only were her conflicts expressed through the content
of the play, but she also played to an audience (me), and the manner in which
she played was determined by the response she wished to elicit from me.

It began with a confession of masturbation, which occurred while Debra
was decorating a lamp in my office that is in the shape of a glass ball. She and
other children I analyze have discovered that this ball (lit by an interior light
bulb) melts any crayon pressed to its surface, and it has become a means for
them to draw, mess, and play out conflicts. The crayon melting for Debra began
as a distraction, intended, I believe, to draw off some of the motor tension she
was feeling as she told me of her masturbation. This had come in the midst of
discussing my prurient interests. Although *she* initiated the confession, she
began by saying there was something she did that she guessed *I* might be interested in since *I* was so nosy. Her tone made it clear she was being forced to
talk. Somewhat defiantly, then, as she melted a crayon, she said she sometimes
stuck her finger "in there" to see if she was clean.

At this point she became aware of a design left by another child, and with
competitive vigor, wiped off the other child's work and took over the lamp.
The next hour she returned to the lamp as soon as she entered the office, and

by the end of the week crayon melting was her only activity (other than speech). Within two weeks her crayon melting had assumed the characteristics of a ritual. It was performed in an identical manner each day; her absorption was total, her movements sensual and slow. At first she pretended that the melting crayons were men trying to cross over a barrier she had to keep clean. If they dribbled across the barrier before she could wipe them away, they would do evil. If she kept the barrier clean (and destroyed the dribbles), evil would be overcome. While her total absorption in the melting crayons made it appear she did not want me to "cross the barrier" surrounding her, her comments seemed designed to provoke me to penetrate her reserve. She spoke angrily of the other children who dared to touch the lamp. She also said she thought *I* was angry that she messed up the lamp and did not talk much (though I kept it hidden, she said, because I was supposed to "act" like a "good doctor"). Gradually her transference misperceptions and preoccupying sexual daydreams became interwoven, and she developed an erotic fantasy of my punishing her, spanking her again and again on her bottom for messing. She imagined that I would act in anger but claim, "It's for your own good."

Over time, as Debra began talking more directly of her fantasy, her interest in melting crayons decreased. Its function shifted from being a symbolic playing out within the transference of sadomasochistic anal fantasies (not only did she create an incredible mess on and around the lamp, but regardless of the colors other children used, after Debra's hour the lamp was always yellow-brown) to once again being a means to release enough of the affective tension associated with her aggressive and erotic fantasies to tolerate talking about them.

Of note is that during the lamp game, when I had expressed concern for the crayon splatters on the wall, Debra did not hear me as particularly angry. Her belief that I was angry or disgusted or aroused seemed to have no relation to my behavior or affect. During this time Debra was so caught up in the analysis that within her psychic reality I was a full participant in the transference, even when I was abstinent (Bird 1972). Though our interaction during much of the lamp game does not fit my definition of enactments, it served the same function. The major difference was that when I was not enacting I was able to understand the determinants of Debra's behavior sooner.

However, not long after the lamp game stopped, another enactment ensued. Debra by now had become more comfortable in school and had begun to take pleasure in describing her activities there. Nonetheless, talking about friends soon became conflictual (I believe because she felt that I, like the mother, would be jealous of her relationships with others), and she gradually slipped into her "actress mode," overdramatizing scenes and events. Once again I felt excluded and began to overtalk, chasing Debra with words. When

I became aware of how insistent I had become, I asked Debra if she noticed that the more I talked, the less she seemed to hear. Her response was, "You sound like me trying to talk to my mother," and she went on to speak of her helplessness in challenging her mother's opinions. Later this was elaborated into her feeling of being helpless yet excited by her mother's sexual intrusion and the sensations it stimulated.

There was one final enactment that heralded the onset of termination. Debra began to not understand my interpretations and clarifications. During the lamp game she had acknowledged that her withdrawal was motivated by a wish to have me ask questions, and together we had connected my questions with her genital "tickles" and her confused and troubled experiences with her parents. Now, over a year later, she again withdrew, ostensibly without any understanding of why. I began once more to work hard at teasing out the determinants of her behavior, as Debra, sensitive to my desire to be helpful, unconsciously manipulated me into "playing analyst." When I regained my self-observing capacity and asked her about this, she said, "Don't you like helping me understand myself?" I replied that I did, but then asked whether she was worried that I would not like her being able to understand without me. She nodded her head in agreement.

That enactment (our joint participation in the fantasy that she still needed me) was followed by a change in her behavior, not an enactment, but a clear nonverbal communication. Debra insisted that we play card games. She knew from past experience that I generally do not play card and board games (because of their tendency to degenerate into ritualized resistance), and over the years we had been together, she had grown to accept this, with some reluctance and irritation, but with eventual tolerance for my limitations. Now there was a new insistence, and when I would not join her, she played solitaire. I tried to clarify her behavior: she did not ignore my words, nor did she disagree, but she kept on playing cards. She then brought in yarn and began knitting in the chair opposite mine (she knew that I sometimes knit while listening to patients). Again I felt frustrated—not angry, but somewhat useless. It took me a while to recognize that Debra was telling me I *was* useless to her now, that it was time for our work to be over. Why did she tell me this way? I asked her that. Her reply was, "I don't know; I wasn't sure it was time to leave. I know I feel good, that I like school and the kids, but I also like coming here. And maybe I didn't want to hurt your feelings."

Thus began Debra's termination. This initially very vulnerable, defensively isolated child was experiencing what she had avoided for so long, that once you are engaged, it hurts to become disengaged. That she saw it in terms of *my* being hurt was not a bad beginning. We had lived with our joint participation in the analytic process, through enactments and other analytic interactions, for a long time. I was certain that if she thought I had feelings, she was aware she had them too.

Debra's analysis contained many enactments, not only because she was a child, but because she was a chronically overstimulated child whose capacity to organize and contain her impulses was less than other children's, and I was susceptible to the primitive, dramatic quality of her behavior. In addition, her isolation and hunger, as well as her previous discomfort and feeling of vulnerability in relationships, had intensified my importance to her and her susceptibility to transference misperceptions. Like other patients in analysis, when stimulated by significant regression, she attempted to actualize the transference through enactments.

Discussion

Given that enactments are inevitable during an analysis, the question remains, how can they be most effectively utilized? Words that name can reduce anxiety by organizing conflictual emotions. Enactments, in creating experience beyond words, engage the participants in a regressive experience that often *increases* anxiety and decreases ego mastery. Yet this regression can lead to a new depth of understanding of conflict, fantasy, and memory. Enactments also link current and past experiences with a vividness of affect and intersubjective relatedness that imparts enormous conviction. They are a concrete shared experience in which the opportunity for defensive denial, intellectualization, and distortion is diminished. If an analyst finds that he is unintentionally enacting with a patient, withdraws from the enactment, and then subjects his behavior and subjective sensations to analytic self-scrutiny, he often has additional information that was not available when he was not so fully engaged.

I believe enactments result from a communication via unconscious clues (Sandler, Chapter 3 this volume) that relies on an affective signaling similar to that used by (and with) very young children, before the capacity for abstraction and symbolization takes place. Both Stern (1985) and Emde et al. (1976), in their work on the affective mode of communication that antedates language, have demonstrated the appeal, clarity, and universality of such signals. However, that repressed conflictual fantasies and wishes find expression via a developmentally early mode of communication does not mean that the conflicts expressed are from a preverbal period of life—only that a more primitive channel of communication, reliant on affectively laden signals, is being called into play. Throughout our lives we all are attuned to the subtle clues contained in gesture, tone, facial expression, and rhythm. What makes analysis unique is not the analyst's reception of the clues, but his examination of them, and his effort to find the words to describe their message.

In any analytic search to understand the intrapsychic domain, much of the initial data come from the observation of interpersonal behavior; the problem during an enactment is that the analyst's power of observation is clouded. In addition, as unconscious conflicts lead to one's participation in the enactment, even after one becomes aware of the enactment, the analyst's resistance to full understanding will continue. There were times during my analysis of Debra when all I was aware of was my discomfort and a feeling that the work was nonproductive. Occasionally it required taking verbatim notes immediately after the session or discussing the process with a colleague for me to recognize when I was enacting.

Enactments do not necessarily offer an easier road to the unconscious determinants of behavior or a better way to communicate with patients. But as they occur, repeatedly, in the course of every analysis, an objectivity about them, a capacity to deal with them just as we deal with the associations or memories that are called forth by our patients' verbal communications can only increase our technical armamentarium. To continue to track is the work of analysis, whatever the mode of communication.

Even after one enactment is recognized and interpreted, others may ensue. When a defense or resistance, impulse or fantasy, is revealed in a patient's associations and interpreted, his or her psychic equilibrium will shift, often with new compromise formations and the expression of the conflict in a new form. Similarly, when an enactment is interpreted, the arena of enactment may also shift, with the patient's conflicts expressed in new behavior, which again tests the analyst's vulnerabilities.

For example, after an analyst has withdrawn from participation in an enactment and has integrated the experience with his cognitive understanding of the patient and the analytic process, he often wants to share his understanding of the enactment and its determinants with the patient. However, to a patient enmeshed in transference, the very act of intervening can become a vehicle for an enactment. Interpretations, heard as meaning that the analyst understands something that the patient does not, are denied. If the analyst tries harder to clarify the experience, he is heard as defensive or irritated, and his words become evidence of his authoritarian stance.

Or, after the analyst first interprets, the patient may begin to speak in such a way as to manipulate him to continue to interpret the *seemingly unconscious* connections. This too is an enactment. And though quite common, this use of words to stimulate the analyst to act like an analyst can be difficult to detect.

In the panel on enactments (1992), Boesky said, "Just about everything the patient feels, says, thinks, or does during the session is influenced by wishful tendencies which press for actualization." When we as analysts are conscious of this "press for actualization," we are able to interpret and, through our interpretations, increase our patients' awareness of their motivating impulses and fantasies. When we are not so aware, we enact. Enactments are often the first sign of a shift in a patient's transference, a shift that caught the analyst by surprise and made him a participant in an emerging transference paradigm he is not yet able to objectify and observe. The analyst does not consciously choose to enact; the analyst enacts and then thinks, "Why did I say (do) that?" It is his or her scrutiny of the enactment, not the enactment itself, which will lead to a new understanding of the transference.

In analysis we interpret more than words; we also explore and articulate the unconscious links between what is said at one moment and what is said at the next. That these links are revealed through the process of speaking has misled many of us into assuming that the content of verbal communications is the focus of our work. This is not true. Not that the content of the patient's material is not valuable. It is, for it leads to an awareness of unconscious connections and enriches the analyst's interpretations and makes them immediate, specific, and therefore real to the patient. But in the work of making the unconscious conscious, it is the determinants of the words and their sequence, rather than the conscious thought, that we attend to.

The same process of looking for unconscious determinants is at work when we examine enactments. We look beyond the conscious intent of behavior (both ours and the patient's) and examine it within the context of the analytic situation, hoping to uncover its relation, via the transference, to unconscious processes. Jacobs (Panel 1992) has suggested that enactments in analysis often reflect specific identifications and are essentially memories put into action—memories of actual events or events defensively distorted by the patient but retained in memory as enacted. This has not been my experience. I think that enactments, being a resultant of unconscious forces in *both* the analyst and the patient, are rarely so specific. However, I do agree with Jacobs that external behavior can sometimes communicate what thoughts and feelings do not quite capture. The determinants for the analyst's participation in an enactment will not be the same as for the patient, but the intrapsychic conflicts being stimulated may prove similar enough to provide a new source of empathically derived information which, when "made consonant with the patient's material according to disciplined, cognitive criteria" (Arlow 1979, pp. 204–205), can lead to an understanding that was not accessible through words alone.

Nonetheless, enactments are still seen as deterrents to analysis. Is this just because of the potential for gratification in enactments, or because they are tenacious resistances? Or is it also because our participation in enactments leads us, the analysts, to behave in ways that feel unanalytic?

Enactments will convey, from patient to analyst, knowledge of impulses and affect that may be impossible to communicate through verbal description.

But enactments will also convey to the patient the analyst's participation in the process. Unlike repetitions, in which it is the patient who repeats and the analyst who witnesses, in an enactment both analyst and patient are participants.

The communication of the analyst's involvement and his vulnerability to involvement, inadvertent though it be, will have important ramifications for the course of treatment. It is different from a deliberate act by the analyst, for the latter, be it classical abstinence or Kohutian mirroring, is under the control of the analyst and carries with it a sense of his authority. There are times during an analysis when the analyst's involvement can be an important fuel, motivating the patient to continue the work. At other times, even with the same patient, it can be a significant source of resistance, or a threat to the patient's comfort with the relationship. But all reactions to enactments, including these, are information to be explored and analyzed. Not to do so is to collude with the patient's resistance.

In summary, an enactment is a nonverbal communication (often cloaked in words) so subtly presented and so attuned to the receiver that it leads to his responding inadvertently in a manner that is experienced by the patient as an actualization of a transference perception, a realization of his fantasies. Although not therapeutic in itself, an enactment can provide invaluable information and an immediacy of experience that enrich the work. Viewed as yet another source of information, greeted with curiosity and not guilt, enactments can become part of the analytic process from which we all learn.

REFERENCES

Alexander, F. (1950). Analysis of the therapeutic factors in psychoanalytic treatment. *Psychoanalytic Quarterly* 19:482–500.

Arlow, J. A. (1979). The genesis of an interpretation. *Journal of the American Psychoanalytic Association* 27 (Suppl.): 193–207.

Bird, B. (1972). Notes on transference: universal phenomenon and hardest part of analysis. *Journal of the American Psychoanalytic Association* 20:267–301.

Emde, R., Gaensbauer, T. J., and Harmon, R. J. (1976). *Emotional Expression in Infancy. Psychological Issues*, Monogr. 37. New York: International Universities Press.

Katan, A. (1961). Some thoughts about the role of verbalization in early childhood. *Psychoanalytic Study of the Child* 16:184–188. New York: International Universities Press.

Loewenstein, R. M. (1956). Some remarks on the role of speech in psychoanalytic technique. *International Journal of Psycho-Analysis* 37:460–468.

Panel (1992). Enactments in psychoanalysis. M. Johan, reporter. *Journal of the American Psychoanalytic Association* 40:827–841.

Poland, W. (1988). Insight and the analytic dyad. *Psychoanalytic Quarterly* 57:341–369.

Stern, D. (1985). *The Interpersonal World of the Infant*. New York: Basic Books.

8

The Role of Countertransference Enactment in a Successful Clinical Psychoanalysis

OWEN RENIK

Enactment and Awareness

Few of us any longer regard the existence of an analyst's varied, even powerful, emotional responses to a patient in the clinical situation to be a hindrance to analytic work. On the contrary, *countertransference* (to use, for convenience's sake, the familiar and problematic term for an analyst's evoked experience) is by now generally considered a rich and crucially useful source of information.

Nor is it expected that an analyst will always be immediately conscious of his or her countertransference responses. A burgeoning literature concerning the analyst's self-analysis shows us how subtly countertransference can manifest itself in action, how easily countertransference enactment can be rationalized as appropriate technique, and how countertransference is often acted upon for some time before being recognized (e.g., Jacobs, Chapter 5 this volume). The contemporary analyst strives to be completely aware of his or her countertransference reactions but realizes that this is an ideal that can never, in practice, be achieved (Abend 1986). Furthermore, an analyst knows that it is often possible to turn a countertransferentially motivated technical error to good account, once it has been identified, by exploring the analysand's reaction to what has transpired (Panel 1986).

I think it is fair to summarize the current consensual view as follows: an analyst's *awareness* of his or her countertransference is an asset that contributes to analytic work, whereas expression of countertransference *in action* is a liability that limits analytic work. In other words, countertransference enactment is considered inevitable, and by no means disastrous, but not desirable per se.

How does an analyst become aware of countertransference? We usually assume it is best if a countertransferentially motivated *fantasy* claims the analyst's attention, that is, if the analyst imagines acting in relation to the analysand in some way. However, it is commonplace for an analyst first to become aware of some way that he or she has, in fact, been behaving in the clinical situation, and then, through consideration of what the analyst has been doing, to become conscious of a countertransference motivation. The sequence of events in which awareness follows enactment is generally conceptualized as less than optimal—though, of course, perfectly expectable, given human limitations.

I think we have maintained, without realizing it, an unsubstantiated theory that fantasy can become conscious without having been expressed at all in action. According to Freud's (1900) early reflex-arc model of mental function, motivations are envisioned as impulses that can take either one or two quite separate paths: the efferent, leading to motor activity, or the afferent, leading to fantasy formation via stimulation of the sensory apparatus from within. Every clinical analyst has had the opportunity to confirm Freud's later (1914a) observation that conscious awareness of an irrational fantasy and of the unrealistic motivations that produce it can put an end to enactment of the fantasy. But I know of no empirical validation for Freud's early protoneurological conceptualization of thought and action as mutually exclusive activities.

On the contrary, there is every reason to conceptualize thought and action on a continuum, thought being a form of trial action, based on a highly attenuated form of motor activity. Darwin pointed out—and Freud (1926) agreed with him—that a physical response lies at the core of every affect. The data of introspection favor William James' (1890) formulation that awareness of emotion arises from one's observation of one's actions.

It seems likely that if we could always closely examine the sequence of events by which an analyst becomes aware of his or her countertransference motivations, we would find that it *invariably* begins with the analyst noting how he or she has put them, sometimes almost imperceptibly, into action. We are familiar with finding ourselves able to profit in the clinical situation from post facto investigation of our countertransferentially motivated errors. We might ask ourselves whether such instances show us with unusual vividness what is regularly the case, whether these "errors" differ from the majority of our preliminary countertransference enactments only in that circumstances conspire to bring them explicitly and dramatically to our attention, making disavowal of them more difficult.

We have little difficulty regarding transference enactment as a necessary prelude to transference awareness for an analysand. We expect an analysand to begin by playing out his or her transferences within the treatment relationship, and eventually to become aware of what he is doing; it seems we find it difficult to suppose that the same is true for an analyst with respect to his or her countertranferences. At the same time, we regularly observe that successful analytic work unfolds via a process of continuous mutual active embroilment between analyst and analysand, and continuous effort on the part of both to become aware of and clarify the nature of the embroilment. Sandler (Chapter 3 this volume) speaks of the analyst's "free floating behavioral responsiveness" and the analyst's post facto awareness of its countertransference determinants. Boesky (1990), for example, has concluded: "If the analyst does not get emotionally involved sooner or later in a manner that he had not intended, the analysis will not proceed to a successful conclusion" (p. 573).

Countertransference Enactment
and the Psychoanalytic Theory of Technique

The self-observation that leads an analyst to awareness of his or her countertransference can be of behavior on the very finest scale of magnitude—a subtle kinesthetic tension. It is tempting to believe that such microactivity remains essentially private to the analyst and has no significant impact on the treatment relationship, so that, for all practical purposes, countertransference awareness sometimes occurs without being preceded by countertransference enactment. However, experience indicates otherwise. Even the slightest nuance of disposition influences how an analyst hears material, whether the analyst decides to be silent or to intervene, how the analyst expresses himself or herself if he does make a comment, and so forth, all of which is of the greatest importance, as we know. For example, Jacobs (Chapter 5 this volume) describes how his particularly rapt, silently attentive listening in a certain treatment was motivated by his admiration and hostility toward the patient, who reminded Jacobs of his father. This was an extremely consequential countertransference enactment, even though it did not involve grossly aberrant behavior by the analyst, and it went unnoticed—consciously, at least—by the analysand.

As it stands, our theory of technique indicates that an analyst should strive to minimize his countertransference enactments in order to maximize his countertransference awareness. However, if countertransference enactment is a prerequisite for countertransference awareness, then elimination of countertransference enactment is not only unattainable as a practical technical goal, but it is misconceived even as a technical ideal toward which the analyst should strive. Although countertransference satisfaction is clearly not an objective to be pursued, in and of itself, in making technical decisions, neither does the presence of countertransference motivation constitute a contraindication to a given course of action.

This would seem to be a point worth emphasizing because analysts tend to be quite conscientious, so that interferences with an analyst's functioning arise at least as frequently from constraining inhibitions and reaction formations designed to guard against enactment of countertransference urges (perhaps with eventual breakthrough) as from direct enactment of countertransference urges per se. In my experience, the technique of beginning analysts tends to suffer more from stiffness than from an excess of spontaneity.

We have come to realize that analytic work is not furthered by preventing a patient from acting out, but rather by helping the patient become as completely aware as possible of the various motivations for his or her actions. Similarly, analysts can aim at maximum awareness of the elements of countertransference enactment that motivate their technical conduct, without assuming that gratification of a countertransference urge in the clinical situation necessarily opposes the analytic process.

Transference–Countertransference Enactment

Having considered the idea that countertransference enactment contributes usefully to an analyst's participation in the psychoanalytic process, just as transference enactment does to an analysand's, I would like now to examine the interaction between transference and countertransference enactment.

Freud (1912) pointed out that the treatment relationship is the arena in which definitive learning about transference takes place: "For when all is said and done, it is impossible to destroy anyone *in absentia* or *in effigie*" (p. 105). This famous comment resonates with our clinical experience. Any number of investigators have noted that the analysis of transference requires actual engagement by the analytic couple. Bird (1972), for example, puts it this way: ". . . the analyst . . . must somehow enable the patient to extend his intrapsychic conflict to include the analyst. Whereupon the analyst becomes protagonist and the patient antagonist, or vice versa, in a *real* conflict within the analysis . . ." (p. 235, my italics).

How else does the authentic engagement Bird regards as a sine qua non take place but via the playing out *in action* of a transference–countertransference drama? Without the analytic text of transference–countertransference enactment, what of any immediacy would there be to analyze? In fact, Bird goes on to say, referring to the need for real conflict between analyst and analysand, "In order for this to happen, I am tempted to believe *the analyst's own transference involvement is necessary*" (p. 235, my italics).

Certainly, there is a distinction between the role of the analyst and the role of the analysand in the analytic process, but it is hard to see how that distinction can be made on the basis of the degree of either party's actual involvement, that is, the extent to which either one expresses emotional responses in action. Rather, it would seem that the difference between an analyst's participation and that of an analysand has to do with the agreed-upon purpose of the partnership (to increase the analysand's self-awareness) and the intentions of each in relation to it. Thus, for example, what is revealed to the analyst in the course of the work about his or her countertransference remains private to the analyst, whereas what is revealed about the analysand's transference is a matter for joint consideration. In addition, while the patient can and should strive to verbally express himself or herself as freely as possible, the verbal expressions of the analyst are limited by the analyst's need to keep the goals of the enterprise continuously in mind.

The proposition that transference–countertransference enactment forms the required text for clinical analysis leads to a very different conception of the psychoanalytic process than is implicit when the treatment relationship is spoken of as an "as if" or "transitional space" in which transferences emerge and are investigated. Far from being not quite real, the analysis of transference depends on a *very real* relationship, no different in its reality from any other, taking place within the protective limits provided by the agreed-upon ground rules of the analytic contract. This is the point, I believe, that Bird means to address in the passages I have cited and that Freud (1914b) had in mind when he emphasized that a patient's "transference love," though lacking the freedom of love occurring outside an analytic treatment relationship, is every bit as genuine. One of the most familiar and potent resistances to the analysis of transference is precisely when a patient maintains, sometimes quite subtly, the conviction that events taking place within the treatment situation are less than completely real.

The Corrective Emotional Experience

It may be a bit disconcerting for us to admit that an analyst's awareness of countertransference, like an analysand's of transference, is always retrospective, in the sense that it is preceded by an enactment of which the analyst has been unaware. But by this admission we gain a way of understanding how an analyst becomes sincerely involved in the emotionally charged encounter that is the substrate and text of every successful clinical analysis. Aside from the authenticity of the engagement between analyst and analysand, there is another aspect of the analytic encounter that we know to be crucially important: for an analysis to proceed, the interactions between analyst and analysand have to be such that the latter is able to recreate and master crucial pathogenic experiences. This observation brings up the vexing problem of the concept of *corrective emotional experience*. Is clinical psychoanalysis a corrective emotional experience? If so, how is this taken into account in our theory of technique?

Analysts who have studied the historical development of our thinking about technique (e.g., Friedman 1978, Lipton 1977) agree that one of the most important shaping trends of the last forty years has been a reaction against the technical innovations introduced by Alexander and French (1946). At the same time, I think there has been an awareness on the part of many that if we do not continue to try to understand the importance to the analytic process of non-interpretive aspects of the interaction between analyst and patient, which Alexander and French labeled corrective emotional experience and addressed, though ultimately in an unproductive way, then we will have thrown out the baby with the bath water. Thus, some theories of the analytic process suggest that the analyst is a new object, providing new experiences that permit development to go forward (e.g., Loewald 1960, Settlage 1989), others emphasize the mutative role of empathic responsiveness (Kohut 1971), others conceptualize the analyst as passing tests so as to disconfirm the patient's pathogenic beliefs (Weiss and Sampson 1986), and so on.

Our difficulty comes when we try to reconcile these formulations with our other ideas about analytic process and technique. If psychoanalysis is a corrective emotional experience, then a systematic theory of analytic technique should direct the analyst how best to provide a corrective emotional experience for the analysand. We immediately come up against, in one form or another, the very same problems raised by the recommendations of Alexander and French: What is incorrect? Of what should correction consist? And who decides these matters? It is presumptuous for an analyst to take it upon himself to decide where a patient's psychological development went astray and how the defect can be remedied. Furthermore, contrived role-playing within the treatment relationship is hypocritical. Such presumption and hypocrisy contradict what most of us understand to be the essence of the psychoanalytic clinical collaboration.

One effort to resolve this dilemma has been through the claim that ordinary psychoanalytic procedure, the neutrality of the analyst and the analyst's commitment to the investigative task, in itself provides the required corrective emotional experience (e.g., Chused 1982). It can be argued that by interpreting resistances, the analyst engenders a corrective emotional experience. This proposition captures an aspect of the truth. For example, some of our clinical concepts can guide us toward providing optimal frustration–gratification sequences for our analysands (Renik 1990). However, there are elements of an analyst's activity, through which the analyst provides the corrective emotional experience required for a successful clinical analysis, that are not included in our description of ordinary psychoanalytic procedure.

The interactive guidelines indicated by an analytic stance, as it is usually enunciated, are very wide. At a given moment, how does an analyst choose from among the many possibilities consistent with the concept of a neutral analytic investigation the one that will facilitate rather than impede analytic progress? What are our specific intentions when we use what we call analytic tact and timing? We invite our analysands to observe themselves in ways that we judge they will be able to tolerate. For example, Poland (1975) considers the need to avoid counterproductive injuries to an analysand's self-esteem. Poland emphasizes that analytic tact takes place within a two-person field. Inevitably, then, an analyst's tact involves an effort to be regarded for the moment in one way and not another—perhaps as respectful rather than intrusive, or as accepting rather than punitive, or as helpful rather than competitive. We are thrown back upon the problem that the analyst, as an aspect of good technique, seems to deliberately influence the way he or she is experienced by the analysand, which runs counter to our usual understanding.

Some theorists deal with the problem by sequestering all purposeful interactive aspects of the analytic relationship under the separate heading of the *treatment alliance*, or *therapeutic alliance*, maintenance of which by the analyst is distinguished from psychoanalytic technique per se. This theoretical isolation keeps the concept of psychoanalytic process free from contamination by the concept of a certain salutary, noninterpretative interaction between analyst and analysand. However, regardless of the categories we establish, we are left with clinical reality and the observation that it is necessary for corrective emotional experiences to occur if analysis is to proceed. How does the analyst arrange for them without deliberately manipulating the analysand?

The conclusion seems unavoidable to me that it is because an analyst's conduct in the clinical situation is partly determined by motivations *outside his conscious awareness*, that is, because countertransference enactment always precedes countertransference awareness, that it is possible for an analyst to participate in what could be called corrective emotional experiences, and to do so in a genuine and unpremeditated way. I would say, in other words, that aspects of effective analytic technique are inherently outside the conscious control of the analyst—that many of the most useful things we do, we do for reasons of which we *cannot* be aware at the time. Not only is every technical act inevitably a countertransference enactment, at least in part, but it is useful for this to be so. Newman (1988) suggests that an analyst makes himself into a "usable object" for an analysand by virtue of unconscious countertransference involvement and subsequent self-analysis.

If we think of countertransference enactment by the analyst, along with transference enactment by the analysand, as a regular and necessary aspect of the psychoanalytic process, we can see how inadvertent and authentic corrective emotional experiences occur. However, while this conceptualization solves one problem, it poses others. How are we to say where productive analytic technique leaves off and self-indulgent exploitation of the analytic situation by the analyst begins? In addition, how do we understand the difference between clinical psychoanalysis and psychotherapies in which the therapist participates in corrective emotional experiences without necessarily knowing about it? I think the nature of the analyst's conscience and the role it plays in the psychoanalytic process are the central issues raised by these questions; however, that subject might be easier to consider if we have an illustrative clinical vignette to use as a basis for discussion.

Clinical Example

The patient was a young man who was terribly hemmed in by obsessions and compulsions of all sorts. He spent the better part of every day preoccupied with intrusive nonsense thoughts or executing various rituals. After two years or so, our analytic work together had progressed to the point at which we were able to understand that these activities served to prevent him from being aware of violent, sadistic fantasies that would come to his mind and disturb him very much. This timid and inhibited man was inwardly boiling with rage, often in response to apparently trivial events. A female co-worker would close a window he had opened, and he would imagine grinding his heel into her face.

The question for us had become why he was so prone to fury, especially to fury at women, and here we were stuck. He had certain grievances toward his mother, and we had gone over these. Something in his attitude toward me seemed relevant, a demandingness that was only thinly covered over by ingratiation and compliance, but the transference elements involved remained elusive. We just had not made much headway in clarifying his chronic anger.

There were sometimes claustrophobic aspects to the situations that seemed to provoke him, and his associations suggested that resentment toward a younger sibling in utero might be playing an important genetic role in generating his sadistic fantasies. He had a dream in which he was swimming around in a pond, urinating, thus killing some young corn that was growing on the bottom. The dream, in particular, made quite an impression on him. He felt it confirmed the idea that he might have been hostile to the arrival of a younger sibling, and he ransacked his mind, with characteristic obsessive thoroughness, about his feelings toward his 6-year-younger sister, trying to dredge up memories of her birth, his mother's pregnancy, his reactions, and so forth. It all yielded very little.

This man had trouble sleeping and from time to time made use of a mild sedative perscribed by his internist. When he first described taking the pills, I made some comment about medicating his anxiety instead of analyzing it, such that he firmly associated me with the idea that renunciation was in order. In fact, he came to take the pills less and less and would look to me for approval about his progress in this regard. It was not a major point of investigation, but I did have the chance from time to time to remark that not using the pills seemed to be something he felt he was doing at least as much for me as for himself. Of course, I encouraged him to look into his fantasies about my investment in the matter.

On one such occasion he came in and announced that he had not taken any sleeping pills for a month. As usual, I did not congratulate him, and as usual he complained about this. In the course of exploring his reactions to this familiar situation, he moaned that it was like being weaned from the breast—I couldn't realize how difficult it was. I made the following comment to him: "It's as if you feel like the only person who was ever weaned from the breast."

Now I think the content of this interpretation was valid and, as I will describe in a moment, it had productive results. My interpretation called his attention to a particular fantasy, based on an implicit denial of the facts of life. It related to attitudes of entitlement and a sense of injustice that was a central feature of his transference to me. All of this was potentially useful information, and conveying it to the patient was consistent with good analytic technique.

However, I remember very clearly the state of my feelings at that moment. The general context was my frustration with the treatment seeming bogged down and my exacerbated impatience with this man's hyperintellectual style and underlying whiny complaints. I had been going to save him when many before me had failed. But now, after a successful initial phase of analytic work that confirmed our mutual idealizations, we were each feeling disappointed in the other. Against this general background of resentment toward the patient, I was feeling sorry for myself, and when he essentially claimed that nobody knew the trouble he felt, my reaction was to review some of the more difficult periods in my own past and to ask myself who this guy thought he was, telling *me* about suffering.

Out of this not very admirable set of sentiments what I said to him was not entirely kindly meant and therefore was not put as gently as it might have been. My empathy with him was harnessed to my own emotional needs at least as much as to my analytic functioning. Far from realizing that my own grandiose self-pity had been provoked by a similar state in the patient, and fashioning a constructive interpretation on the basis of self-analysis, I had competitively contended with him for first place in a suffering contest, although I did use truth as my weapon and I did remain within the realm of observation, both of which were important constraints.

The patient was *struck* by my interpretation (pun very definitely intended). He blinked and paused fractionally, obviously feeling the hostility I had expressed, but he did not verbalize any reaction to this aspect of my remark and I, out of continuing denial of my countertransference motivation, did not address his avoidance. Instead, what happened was that the patient took my interpretation at face value and began to associate to the content of it. He thought about the fact that his own son had been weaned from the breast some years earlier. Compliantly, the patient reflected that what I had said about his not being unique had been true.

However, despite the patient's effort to keep his sense of injury by me out of conscious awareness, and despite my tacit collusion with his effort, his warded-off reaction broke through, and in a form that made it possible to elucidate his transference even while consciousness of my countertransference enactment was being avoided by both of us. As he spoke about recognizing that others had, indeed, been weaned from the breast, the patient made a slip, substituting the name Gary for his son's name. When he claimed to know no one named Gary, I suggested it couldn't have come from nowhere and that he seemed reluctant to associate to the name Gary. He shook his head and said, "No, the only Gary I can think of is the younger brother my parents told me about who was still-born when I was a year and a half old." (!) He couldn't believe he had never mentioned it before. Obviously, it was relevant to so much that we had explicitly puzzled about together over two years of analysis. When he had been assiduously searching his memory for experiences about the birth of a sibling that might illuminate the origin of his sadistic preoccupations, his mother's pregnancy with Gary, and the subsequent stillbirth, had never come to mind.

From here, our work led to retrieval of early childhood memories that had not previously been consciously available to him. After the delivery of his still-born brother, his mother had suffered a severe postpartum depression. A dream revealed the patient's childhood understanding of his mother's depression. In the dream, his mother was squatting and had a miserable, dejected expression. Something was terribly wrong. A long lip of bleeding flesh drooped from between her legs. He had a strong urge to go toward her to help, but at the same time he dreaded touching her.

Fantasies about stillbirth, his mother's genitalia, and the loss of body products by excretion all had become confused and condensed in the child's mind into an impression that his mother was depressed because she had lost something important. This impression resulted in a conflict between the child's wish to substitute himself for what was missing in order to make his mother once more loving and lovable, and his fear of having to sacrifice himself to restore her loss. In fact, throughout our sessions he had been expressing this conflict in his reports of the many dreams in which he would be irresistibly drawn toward a boiling sea or into the eye of a storm. The conflict was revived during his latency when his mother would, for ill-defined reasons, join him in bed, and he could feel the warmth of her body close to his.

His mother's depression had been sufficiently severe that he had been sent away to live with an aunt for six months. Early experiences of rejection and abandonment had been eclipsed in his memory by positive images of the aunt in whose care he had been placed. There had been a kind of tacit collusion with the aunt throughout his childhood, beginning during the time his mother had been disabled. His aunt totally idealized him and was unconditionally accepting, in return for which he did not contradict her fantasy that he was actually her son. Part of the patient's transference to me was an expectation that he could recreate the kind of collusion he had experienced with his aunt. One aspect of his reaction to my interpretation, consciously passed over but revealing itself through the slip, was that I was refusing the deal. I was insisting on being an angry, rejecting mother instead of a gratifying aunt in order to punish him for the hostility and demands toward me that lurked beneath his surface good-patient pose. The childhood theory had been that his devastated mother had sent him away because his resentment of the frustrations he had to endure during her pregnancy and his jealous rage toward little Gary in utero had caused the stillbirth.

As these concerns emerged and their origins were clarified, the patient's attitude toward women changed. He became less angry, and his preoccupation with sadistic fantasies diminished correspondingly. He developed more comfort in his sexual life. For a time, he was tremendously excited by cunnilingus and, noticing this, realized that he was counterphobically overcoming a long-standing horror and disgust toward the female genitalia. Frank confusion about women's anatomy came to light. His sleep difficulty essentially disappeared, and he discontinued sedative use altogether.

Eventually, I did take up with the patient his disavowal of my real lapses and the way he avoided thinking about the possibility that I could be angry at him and act on that feeling. His need to cling to an idealizing transference fantasy of mutual uncritical adoration and his need to avoid conscious disappointment in me became significantly less driven, though the amelioration was somewhat limited by his fear of re-experiencing what must have been an overwhelming infantile rage and despair.

Dimensions of the Psychoanalytic Process

The foregoing clinical vignette portrays a characteristic sample of the psychoanalytic process. At the heart of it was an investigation of the patient's transferences to me, clarification of which had an impact not only upon our relationship, but upon the symptomatic way he had been leading his life in general, and upon his view of his own history. This is what we expect from a successful piece of analytic work. For purposes of discussion, I would like to identify three dimensions of the psychoanalytic process illustrated by the vignette and to consider the relations among them.

First, there was what could be called our investigation of the patient's mental life. By drawing his attention to specific obstacles that he placed in the way of his self-awareness, and by inquiring with him into his motivations, I assisted the patient in enlarging his capacity for self-observation. This aspect of our collaboration would be considered by some theorists to comprise the whole of the psychoanalytic process. It is certainly what we usually conceive of as the distinctive essence of psychoanalytic work and the aim of analytic technique. From the point of view of investigation of the patient's mental life, a successful intervention—the one on which I have focused—was the comment by which I exposed to the patient compelling evidence of his passionately held but unrealistic image of himself as especially put upon. As we continued to pull on this loose thread and follow its course, we learned a great deal about his past that he had been withholding from his own view, information that helped him understand and alter some important, long-standing attitudes and behaviors. Thus, interpretation led to insight and change.

A second dimension of the psychoanalytic process was the evolution of transference–countertransference enactment between the patient and me. Initially we duplicated in many ways, without realizing we were doing so, his childhood relationship with his aunt. He construed my patient attention and therapeutic optimism as evidence of an all-accepting love for him, and I, in turn, saw in his eager cooperation the promise that I would be allowed to succeed with him where all others had failed. An early phase of progress confirmed both our fantasies, but then, as the pace of psychological discovery and symptomatic improvement slowed, mutual disappointment set in. In this context, my angry reaction to his complaining, which I expressed pointedly via my interpretation of his grandiose self-pity over discontinuing sleeping pills, vividly evoked his rejection by his depressed mother.

Our enactment of transference and countertransference preceded our awareness of transference and countertransference at every step. When I made my deflating remark and the patient responded to it, neither of us recognized that he was experiencing me as punishing him in the same way and for the same reasons he thought his mother had punished him long ago. Later, this experience came into consciousness, and the analytic work that brought it into consciousness had, in turn, its own unperceived transference–countertransference meanings: by finding a way to see the patient's entitlement and self-importance in a sympathetic light, as the consequence of a previously repressed childhood trauma, we re-established the possibility for mutual idealization and quid pro quo. Every experienced analyst expects that today's authentic piece of analytic investigation will very likely tomorrow be revealed also to have been a transference–countertransference enactment that was unrecognized as it took place. Because each successful bit of analysis creates something new to be analyzed, the analysis of transference reminds me of Achilles' fabled effort to catch the tortoise—a project whose completion by its nature is impossible and can only be approached asymptotically.

I want to emphasize that the *countertransference* as well as the transference significance of my interpretation only came into my awareness after the fact. At the time I made my remark, I realized in a general way that I was annoyed at the patient. I knew that what I had to say would probably deflate him and that I would take some satisfaction in his discomfort, but I said it anyway, telling myself that it was true and he needed to hear it. It was not until later in the analysis that I acknowledged to myself my outrage at the patient for treating me as if his experience of deprivation were superior to my own. At that point I could more fully appreciate the hostility of my motivation, which made it clear to me that since I had made my intervention I had been colluding with the patient to avoid his perception that I could be angry with him and want to hurt him.

A third dimension of the psychoanalytic process consisted of a corrective emotional experience—a series of noninterpretative interactions that permitted the patient to change misconceptions that had arisen in his traumatic past and remained with him since. First I joined with the patient in a kind of mutual seduction; then, in reaction to my own disillusionment, I wounded him; and finally, we struggled together to a workable rapprochement. He had dealt with his traumatic childhood experience by longing for and pursuing a cherished idealization of his mutually seductive relationship with his aunt, while avoiding at all costs anything that might resemble his catastrophic, unbearable image of rejection by his mother. The sequence of clinical events described in my vignette corrected this schism by providing him with an opportunity to learn that disappointment can be tolerated emotionally and that two imperfect people who care about each other can manage to sustain their relationship in the face of mutual disappointment.

These three dimensions of the psychoanalytic process describe the view from three different angles of what, in nature, is a unitary phenomenon. For example, my intervention existed in all three dimensions. It was a countertransference enactment, it was part of a sequence that provided a corrective emotional experience for the patient, and it was a useful psychoanalytic interpretation that drew the patient's attention to a feature of his mental life that he had been overlooking.

Psychoanalytic theory tends to treat as separate phenomena what might better be conceptualized as three dimensions of a single psychoanalytic process. It would seem that the most complete, and therefore most accurate, picture of what actually transpires in clinical analysis has to take account of all three. Every productive technical choice is, in part, a countertransference enactment, and it involves the analyst in a spontaneously occurring corrective emotional experience, an authentic encounter that then forms the text for self-conscious investigation.

Having presented a clinical example illustrating this conception of the analytic process, I would now like to address the two problems I mentioned earlier: first, the distinction between analytic technique and exploitive self-indulgence, which requires a consideration of the analyst's conscience alongside the analyst's countertransference; and then the distinction between psychoanalysis and psychotherapy, which bears upon the relation between corrective emotional experience and analysis of transference.

Analytic Conscience

Even when my unconscious countertransference enactment was most prominent, other motivations played a part in determining my technique. For example, my interpretation represented a compromise formation in which conscientious urges had a role. At the same time as I indulged myself in expression of my own self-pity, competitiveness, and resentment, I felt a countervailing wish to be helpful and honest, so that, as I have already mentioned, even my hostile intervention took the form of conveying a potentially useful truth to the patient. Furthermore, I continued to do my job, remaining interested in the patient's thoughts and feelings, and this attitude on my part was crucial to our negotiation of a rapprochement. I think the many technical decisions that arose from my original therapeutic optimism, as well as from my subsequent disappointment were, similarly, compromise formations to which both countertransference and conscience contributed.

We handicap ourselves if we conceptualize countertransference enactment as an impediment to effective technique. Rather, it would be helpful for our theory of technique to focus on the analyst's superego. We need to develop a more exact picture of its content and modus operandi in the clinical situation, of how other aims join with countertransference to produce the analyst's contribution to a successful psychoanalytic process. In the clinical moment, analysis of countertransference is not always the analyst's immediate priority. Sometimes it is useful for an analyst to accept the need to act under the influence of countertransference motivations before they can be thoroughly investigated. How analytic conscience functions in that decision and how the operations of analytic conscience convert countertransference expressions into useful analytic interventions are precisely the areas we need to learn more about. Poland (1986) notes: "Evaluation of the patient's analyzing needs combines with the analyst's inner regressive signals to move the analyst to speak. Deeply rooted motivations for analyzing provide the driving force. Technical skill and self-knowledge shape the movement of that force" (p. 271).

In order to study the workings of the analyst's conscience in the clinical situation, it is helpful to see countertransference enactment as the ever-present raw material of productive analytic technique, rather than as a counterproductive alternative to technique. In Boesky's (1990) description of how resistances are "negotiated" between analyst and analysand, there is the suggestion that technique can be conceptualized as arising from an interaction between countertransference and other components of the analyst's psychology:

> We have, since the dawn of our science, learned so painfully that we must guard against the serious errors introduced by the countertransference that we have failed to appreciate that the conflict of the analyst can lead to adaptive and useful outcomes as well. As in any matter of conflict, it is a matter of degree, and the quantitative aspect will determine whether pathological countertransference or creative subjectivity will be the outcome. [p. 578]

My impression is that the concept of conscience and countertransference coming together to form analytic technique accords with what we can observe about analytic development. The veteran analyst becomes more comfortable and effective not so much because the analyst has diminished the degree to which he or she acts out of countertransference motivations, as because the analyst becomes less defensive about countertransference enactments and more confident that he or she will be able to investigate the patients' experiences of them.

The example I have presented focuses on how an analyst's hostile countertransference urge translated itself into a useful intervention. I thought it would be a particularly relevant instance, inasmuch as acting with hostility toward a patient is so completely at variance with what we usually consider professional behavior, let alone good technique. Obviously, all sorts of impulses (to sexually stimulate a patient, to reassure, to warn, and so forth) also can be expressed through technique. In our literature, we are beginning to see analysts point out that various countertransference enactments can contribute to an analytic process and therefore need not be automatically rejected by a well-functioning analytic conscience. An excellent example is Chused's (1987) careful discussion of the benefits, under some circumstances, of an analyst's acceptance of being idealized. Kris (1990) suggests that commitment to the method of free association, rather than abstinence, is the basis of analytic neutrality.

Psychoanalysis and Psychotherapy

All well-intentioned therapists, regardless of their theoretical orientations, tend to engage in countertransference enactment at the same time as they try conscientiously to be helpful to their patients, so that inadvertent, therapeutically beneficial corrective emotional experiences are provided in many forms of treatment. Thus, although the occurrence of corrective emotional experiences is an *essential* feature of the successful psychoanalytic process, it is not *unique* to the psychoanalytic process. What is unique to the psychoanalytic process is the way in which therapist and patient work together toward conscious insight into the corrective emotional experiences that do occur. In practice, clinical psychoanalysis depends upon commitment to a searching examination of the treatment relationship itself as the highest priority of the work. To the extent that conscious insight into corrective emotional experiences is achieved (that is, to the extent that successful analysis of transference takes place), the patient obtains a degree of self-awareness and autonomy, a pervasiveness and durability of benefit, that is generally not available, to my knowledge, from other therapeutic methods.

Psychoanalysis has always been at pains to distinguish itself from other treatments—at first from hypnosis, then from technical modifications of the type suggested by Alexander and French (1946), and most recently from a plethora of psychotherapies, psychoanalytically informed and otherwise. Unfortunately the effort to preserve a special identity has sometimes led psychoanalytic theorists to concentrate exclusively upon those aspects of the psychoanalytic process that are unique to it, and to neglect—even disclaim—aspects of the psychoanalytic process that can also be found in other therapeutic modalities. The result is a picture of analytic process and technique that is incomplete and therefore distorted—a picture in which the special, best-studied part is taken for the whole. I think we want to avoid the mistake of the blind man who feels the elephant's trunk and is convinced that colleagues who describe a foot or a tail, parts that are not unique to the elephant, must have hold of some other kind of animal entirely. It does not serve us well to say about a corrective emotional experience, "That's psychotherapy, not psychoanalysis," or "that belongs to the therapeutic alliance; it has to be there, but it isn't part of the psychoanalytic process itself."

Because transference–countertransference awareness follows enactment, we can conceptualize a successful *psychoanalytic process* as one in which a series of unpremeditated corrective emotional experiences comes to be examined and understood retrospectively (see Panel 1986, pp. 707–708), and a successful *psychotherapeutic process*, on the other hand, as one in which corrective emotional experiences take place but remain largely outside the patient's, and perhaps the therapist's, conscious awareness. (Cf. Gill's [1984] view that a clinical psychoanalysis and a psychoanalytic psychotherapy are best distinguished by the extent to which unwitting suggestion within the treatment relationship has been analyzed.) If a purely psychotherapeutic process at one pole and an ideally complete psychoanalytic process at the other define a spectrum, most analytic treatments certainly fall somewhere in between.

Conclusion

Wallerstein (1986) demonstrated by careful empirical investigation what many of us already suspected: that psychotherapy and psychoanalysis are not as different as we sometimes like to think. My main point of emphasis has been that no matter where on the spectrum of therapies we look, even if we examine a well-conducted clinical psychoanalysis, we find that a sequence of corrective emotional experiences based on transference–countertransference enactment forms the substrate of the treatment. I have the impression this was true in the case I have presented here. However, it should be stated explicitly that the kind of anecdotal account I have offered in the form of a clinical vignette is of negligible evidential value in support of my point of view. I intend it only as an illustration of an hypothesis that must be tested against more systematic observation if it is to be either accepted or rejected.

REFERENCES

Abend, S. (1986). Countertransference, empathy and the analytic ideal: the impact of life stresses on analytic capability. *Psychoanalytic Quarterly* 60:563–575.
Alexander, F., and French, R. (1946). *Psychoanalytic Psychotherapy.* New York: Ronald Press.
Bird, B. (1972). Notes on transference: universal phenomenon and hardest part of analysis. *Journal of the American Psychoanalytic Association* 20:267–301.
Boesky, D. (1990). The psychoanalytic process and its components. *Psychoanalytic Quarterly* 59:550–584.
Calef, V., and Weinshel, E. (1980). The analyst as the conscience of the analysis. *International Review of Psycho-Analysis* 8:279–290.
Chused, J. (1982). The role of analytic neutrality in the use of the child analyst as a new object. *Journal of the American Psychoanalytic Association* 30:3–28.
—— (1987). Idealization of the analyst by the young adult. *Journal of the American Psychoanalytic Association* 35:839–860.
Freud, S. (1900). The interpretation of dreams. *Standard Edition* 5.
—— (1912). The dynamics of transference. *Standard Edition* 12:99–108.
—— (1914a). Observations on transference love. *Standard Edition* 12:157–171.
—— (1914b). Remembering, repeating, and working-through. *Standard Edition* 12:145–156.
—— (1926). Inhibitions, symptoms, and anxiety. *Standard Edition* 20:75–174.
Friedman, L. (1978). Trends in the psychoanalytic theory of treatment. *Psychoanalytic Quarterly* 47:524–567.

Gill, M. (1984). Psychoanalysis and psychotherapy: a revision. *International Review of Psycho-Analysis* 11:161–180.

James, W. (1890). *The Principles of Psychology*. New York: Henry Holt.

Kohut, H. (1971). *The Analysis of the Self*. New York: International Universities Press.

Kris, A. (1990). The analyst's stance and the method of free association. *Psychoanalytic Study of the Child* 45:25–41. New Haven, CT: Yale University Press.

Lipton, S. (1977). The advantages of Freud's technique in the Rat Man case. *International Journal of Psycho-Analysis* 58:255–274.

Loewald, H. (1960). The therapeutic action of psychoanalysis. *International Journal of Psycho-Analysis* 41:16–33.

Newman, K. (1988). Countertransference: its role in facilitating the use of the object. *Annual of Psychoanalysis* 16:251–265.

Panel (1986). Countertransference in theory and practice. O. Renik, reporter. *Journal of the American Psychoanalytic Association* 34:699–708.

Poland, W. (1975). Tact as a psychoanalytic function. *International Journal of Psycho-Analysis* 56:155–162.

—— (1986). The analyst's words. *Psychoanalytic Quarterly* 55:244–272.

Renik, O. (1990). Comments on the clinical analysis of anxiety and depressive affect. *Psychoanalytic Quarterly* 59:226–248.

Settlage, C. (1989). The interplay of therapeutic and developmental process in the treatment of children. *Psychoanalytic Inquiry* 9:375–396.

Wallerstein, R. (1986). *Forty-two Lives in Treatment*. New York: Guilford.

Weiss, J., and Sampson, H. (1986). *The Psychoanalytic Process. Theory, Clinical Observation, and Empirical Research*. New York: Guilford.

9

Between the Scylla and Charybdis of Psychoanalytic Interaction: A Discussion of Owen Renik's Chapter

STANLEY GRAND

Owen Renik's stimulating and thought-provoking chapter takes as its point of departure a novel and provocative hypothesis about the role of counter-transference enactments in the psychoanalytic situation. For Dr. Renik, the basic substrate of change in psychoanalysis is the re-enactment, in the transference and countertransference exchanges between patient and analyst, of the core scenarios of past significant relationships. What this means for Dr. Renik is that enactments on the part of both the patient and the analyst constitute the key dynamism powering a therapeutically "corrective" emotional experience in psychoanalytic treatment. Enactments here include even those highly attenuated, almost imperceptible, forms of *kinesthetic tension* that emerge in the analyst's interactions with the patient.

Although our traditional psychoanalytic view of the process of change has always given great weight to the analysis of the re-enactments of the patient's core dynamics expressed in his or her transferential constructions of the analyst, what is both novel and provocative about Dr. Renik's hypothesis is that he extends this notion about the process of change to include the enactments of the analyst's countertransference constructions of the patient as well.

Dr. Renik supports his hypothesis by an empirical examination of his countertransference reactions to a patient of his own, and the way these reactions shaped a confrontational intervention, the patients' response to which was subsequently subjected to intense analytical scrutiny. He marshals support for his hypothesis from both the clinical and theoretical literature and elaborates upon a number of clinical and theoretical issues from his novel perspective along the way.

I will begin my discussion of Dr. Renik's chapter with a close look at his clinical example because it was clearly chosen as an exemplar for the kinds of experience that have led him to formulate his hypothesis. In addition, I think that it is here that Dr. Renik is most concretely, and perhaps most confidently, linked to it. After all, it was from the phenomena revealed by his own self-analytical work that the conceptual perspective he addresses emerged, and it was to support his clinical conviction that he turned to both the clinical and theoretical literature. This is, indeed, the way all empirical investigative work proceeds, and it has always been the method of choice for the clinical investigator. Dr. Renik's chapter gives us a clear view of how such hypothesis-generating work occurs.

In addition to his clinical example, I will also consider Dr. Renik's application of his novel perspective to a number of clinical and theoretical issues currently in contention in our literature: his view of the "real" relationship in the analytic situation; the principles of analytic neutrality and abstinence; the corrective emotional experience; the relation between thought and action; and the distinction between psychoanalysis and psychotherapy.[1] But first, I will consider the clinical example from which Dr. Renik's hypothesis derives.

The Clinical Vignette

Dr. Renik's clinical vignette presents us with an example of how a stalemate in treatment, related to a subtle and unanalyzed piece of transference material, could be overcome by an examination of the transference–countertransference dynamics that both patient and analyst had been collusively avoiding. Without reviewing the details of the excellent work that Dr. Renik and his patient did upon acknowledging what had been for so long disavowed by both, let me focus simply upon the confrontation that Renik made of his patient's intense feelings of entitlement and the underlying rage generated by the core conflictual issues surrounding his wish for closeness and his enormous fear of engulfment. Dr. Renik's confrontation that "it's as if you feel like the only person who was ever weaned from the breast" initiated a sequence of resistance and then analytic work, the understanding of which opened the patient to warded off material that ultimately could be integrated with relief of the analytic stalemate and improvement of the patient's heterosexual relations. The essential issue here for Dr. Renik is that the core confrontation was actually an expression, in large

---

[1] In a previous version of this chapter, Dr. Renik addressed several of these issues somewhat summarily. Although his treatment of these issues here has been more carefully modulated, as well as deepened, my comments are as relevant to the conclusions that he draws here as they were to the previous version.

measure, of his own irritation, resentment, and frustration with his patient, constrained only by the "truth" and a commitment to "remain within the realm of his observations." It is, for Dr. Renik, the re-enactment of such feelings, in constrained form, that provides, in Boesky's (1990) terms, the emotional involvement that brings conviction to the analytic work.

If we look more closely, however, at the sequence of events following the confrontation, we can see that its immediate effect on both the patient and the analyst was not an *increase* in emotional involvement but rather *a heightening of the denial of aggression*. On the patient's part there was an avoidance of the emotional significance of the aggression contained in Renik's confrontation, in the service of preserving the illusion of the "good object" (i.e., the patient's aunt) transferred onto the analyst. In the analyst there was an avoidance of pursuing the implications of his irritability over the stalemate. The stalemate was broken only when, following the patient's slip, the analyst was able to see the patient's feelings of entitlement and self-importance in a sympathetic light (i.e., able to bring his own angry feelings under self-analytic scrutiny and re-establish a more neutral analytic stance vis-à-vis the patient's resistance). Given this sequence in the material, the question at issue here for me, and parenthetically it is the technical point that Dr. Renik is addressing in his chapter, is (a) whether the clinical vignette that he provides to illustrate his hypothesis about transference–countertransference enactments more clearly supports his novel view that sees the countertransference enactment itself, albeit constrained by a well-developed analytic superego, as a ubiquitous and indeed essential part of every effective analytic encounter, or (b) whether the vignette more clearly supports a classical position that would see Renik's self-analytic scrutiny and control of the matrix of his unconscious hostile feelings as the necessary and effective agent for the unblocking of the analytic stalemate and the resumption of the analytic process.

A Conceptual Digression

Before addressing this question I would like to raise some important issues with respect to our understanding of the concept of countertransference. Tyson (1986), in a clarifying paper, has traced the evolution and broadening of this concept, in part from its original meaning as any act, feeling, or thought on the part of the analyst deriving from his own unconsciously determined transference to the patient, which interferes with the course of the analytic work, to the current broader definition, which includes a wide range of actions, conscious feelings, or thoughts directed toward the patient, including those that are provoked by the patient and may or may not impede the analytic work. Within this more modern definition of countertransference one can now specify a variety of countertransference enactments ranging from those idiosyncratic responses of the analyst deriving from his or her own transference to the patient, to those countertransference responses that are induced by the patient in the service of actualizing past significant relationships. Now these are important distinctions to keep clear in any discussion of countertransference interactions because each has very different implications for the treatment process, and each requires a different technical approach to working with it, points increasingly emphasized in our current literature on mutual enactment (Johan 1992). For example, it makes a difference whether countertransference enactments reflect the analyst's transference or represent a nonchronic reaction induced in the analyst by the patient's provocativeness. In the former case the analyst's first task is to self-analyze his own internal conflict and then help the patient become aware of his reaction to the analyst's enactment. The analytic task is somewhat different in the case of induced or nonchronic countertransference because here the analyst can use his induced reaction to show the patient how he attempts to repeat by provoking an earlier form of object-related scenario. Furthermore, with respect to the case of the analyst's transference to the patient, unless the analyst can become aware of, and bring under control, his transference feelings, it is most likely that these feelings will impede the analytic work, whereas in the case of induced or provoked countertransference reactions, this need not be so. The induced countertransference may simply reinforce or intensify the patient's transference struggle and may provide the analyst with the potential (via interpretation) for increasing the patient's awareness of and conviction that what he or she experiences in the transference is a repetition of earlier conflictful themes. The analyst has a better chance to become aware of and interpret countertransference reactions when they are nonchronic and induced by the patient than when they are motivated by his or her own internal struggle transferred to the patient. The implication of this last point is that under conditions of provocation the analyst's more ready awareness of countertransference reduces its potential for impeding the analytic work.

Enactment vs. Interpretation of Countertransference Reactions

Given these distinctions, I would like to return now to the reactions that both the patient and the analyst had to Dr. Renik's confrontation and see whether these distinctions help to clarify the question I posed earlier about Dr. Renik's novel hypothesis. The initial heightened defensiveness in the patient and the analyst suggests that Dr. Renik's frustration and anger itself induced an intensification of the resistance to the awareness of the transference–countertransference dynamic in both. That is, his confrontation and subsequent collusive denial of the aggression it contained initially impeded the analytic work of resolving the transference stalemate. Thus, in line with the distinctions I have already drawn, Dr. Renik's countertransference reaction, at this point in the sequence, would most likely reflect a strong component of his own transference struggles, since he was unable to overcome the need to collude with his patient's denial. It should be remembered that at the time of the confrontation Dr. Renik was aware of his irritation with his patient. Although he tells us he was irritated, and implies that his own personal issues became implicated in his reaction to his patient, he does not tell us to what extent his own issues were already actively intruding into the analytic work, relatively independent of his patient's provocative complaining. It would be useful to know this so that we might be better able to pinpoint the sources of the analytic stalemate and pin down Dr. Renik's hypothesis. Regardless, however, of whether the countertransference was chronic or induced, it was only later in the sequence, when the analyst was able to resume his analyzing function, that is, when he was more able to separate his own countertransference reaction from the patient's need to re-enact his early relationship scenario, that the analyst was able to help the patient analyze his own distortion and wish to preserve the "good object" of the aunt. It was only at this point that the stalemate was broken. Thus, it appears that although the countertransference enactment may have primed new material, *it was Dr. Renik's scrutiny of his enactment and not the enactment itself* that led him and his patient to a new understanding of this material. I think that this is an important distinction to make, as well as a caution, if we are to maintain an intrapsychic perspective on our clinical material. This is particularly important in light of the current emphasis in our technical literature on the subject of therapeutic interaction. I suspect that Dr. Renik would also subscribe to this distinction, although his emphasis in his chapter directs us toward the technical utility of the enactment itself.

Intrapsychic vs. Interpersonal Reality

It has been said that one person's empathy is another person's countertransference. I think that this comment is particularly cogent with respect to the complexities I have just drawn distinguishing chronic from induced countertransference enactments. And I think it underscores a major problem with the so-called "real" emotional involvement that Dr. Renik desires. How to distinguish what is induced by the patient from what the analyst brings to the analytic encounter, what is real for the analyst from what is transferentially distorted by him, becomes a serious problem in any emotional clinical interaction. Clearly, Dr. Renik wants to highlight the importance of the analyst's emotional involvement in the analytic encounter, and with this desire I am in total agreement. Emotionally flat analytic work, or work done for the intellectual pleasure alone, reflects countertransference enactments on the part of the analyst that themselves require much self-analytic work. However, while all counter-transference is emotionally involving, not all emotionally involving work is countertransference. Furthermore, while all emotionally involving work is actual, it may not all be "real" in the sense that Dr. Renik describes in his chapter. The pleasurable feelings, for example, generated during the analytic encounter, in which both analyst and patient seem at once to see the deeper emotional significance of a long-standing difficulty that has been repeatedly played out both inside and outside the transference, or the assertive confrontation of the patient who, in a provocative moment of sadomasochistic retributive behavior, attempts to destroy the analysis through self-destructive maneuvering are types of emotional encounter between analyst and patient that seem to be distinguishable from the sorts of countertransference enactment to which Dr. Renik refers in his chapter. They are both actual and real and yet they do not derive from the wellsprings of the analyst's unconscious conflicts. They derive from the analyst's sublimated capacity for objectivity and his work ego, and they form an important part of the analytic process largely independent, I think, of the countertransference.

In this regard, then, I believe that I have a somewhat different understanding of the meaning of "real" with respect to the analyst's engagement with his patient than does Dr. Renik, and this difference can be sharpened by considering the way that Dr. Renik and I disagree in our understanding of Brian Bird's (1972) view of real conflict within the analysis. Although Bird does indeed view transference as a projection of part of the patient's conflict onto the analyst, so that the analyst is viewed by the patient as an offending party, Bird does not mean by this that the analyst accepts or attempts to play the role that the patient assigns to him or her. For Bird, the analyst is placed, by the patient, in the position of the protagonist whether or not, in reality, he complies with the patient. An excellent example of how this occurs is given by Bird himself in the paper to which Renik refers. My sense is that Bird's argument is with those analysts who too quickly and too intellectually prevent the emergence of murderous rage in their patients out of fear that their own murderous rage will be activated. The analyst's defense, here, serves as a countertransference that impedes the analytic work. When Bird says that the analyst's own transference involvement is necessary for real conflict between patient and analyst, I believe he means that only when the analyst can tolerate his own aggression will he be capable of allowing the patient to express his completely. I do not believe that Bird is advocating a real enactment of the analyst's aggression, but rather, an awareness of it and a capacity to tolerate it in himself and the patient. Only then will the patient experience the depth and reality of his emotions in the transference encounter. This is as true for transference love as it is for transference hate. It seems that in his desire to conceptualize the analytic relationship as a deeply felt emotional encounter, Dr. Renik finds it necessary to view the analyst as a real part of the patient's conflict. But, in so doing, Dr. Renik runs the risk of shifting our frame of reference from an intrapsychic to an interpersonal one.

On the Distinction between Thought and Action

Clearly, countertransference is most often noted by the analyst following some degree of enactment. But the fact that this may frequently be the case does not mean that it is invariably the case, nor that it is the most effective basis for what Renik has termed a corrective emotional experience. I would like to emphasize here the point that Freud (1911) saw thought as experimental action, that is, as detour activity on the road to discharge of impulse into action in the real world. Clinically, he never conceived of thought as opposed to action, but simply as a constraint upon it in the service of economy, as well as protection from the danger toward which impulsive action might lead. Freud always viewed thoughtless activity as a danger to psychic as well as physical survival. To say, then, that an analyst's awareness of his or her countertransference is, like the patient's transference, always retrospective, that is, preceded by enactments, and that such enactments may be some of the most useful things we do as analysts, seems to me to reverse Freud's emphasis on the dangers of impulsive discharge and to turn the analytic situation into one in which, at least in part, both analyst and patient seem to be *blundering* toward success. This is certainly not Renik's intention. Rather, he suggests that such countertransference enactments provide an opportunity for the patient, via his alliance with the analytic task, to disconfirm his fears that derive from the distorted reconstructions of early pathogenic relationship scenarios. However, if the analyst, through his own transference, or the provocativeness of the patient, actually seduces or aggresses against the patient, no matter how subtly, do we not have a situation where the analytic relationship does indeed *repeat in reality* and thereby confirms and reinforces those early pathogenic relationship scenarios? How then can we expect the patient to distinguish intrapsychic reality from a *real interpersonal transgression*?[2] I think that Bird

---

[2]Renik's rationalization of the usefulness of the analyst's countertransference enactments on the basis of the "agreed-upon purpose of the partnership" (viz.: to increase the analysand's awareness) misses this point entirely. Furthermore, as we know, the analyst's conscious intent in relation to his goal is no guarantee that his less than ideal, and totally unconscious, goals are not being gratified as well. It is for this reason that Renik's position on countertransference enactments poses a serious and sometimes dangerous problem for the psychoanalytic work.

means something other than an enactment, on the part of the analyst, of the projected roles of malignant transference figures. I think that for him it is the fact of not repeating with the patient these pathogenic reaction expectations that gives the analyst the leverage (*as well as the right*) to demonstrate to the patient the effects of his intrapsychic distortion on the real relationship. This is the sort of thing that Freud (1914) referred to in his paper entitled "Remembering, Repeating, and Working-Through," where he spoke of providing the patient with *conviction* that his current feelings are misplaced. The fact that the patient can distinguish the analyst from an original object makes transference distortions palpable and real for him. Thus, not repeating in the countertransference provides a compelling *corrective reality experience* that is itself the basis for the sort of corrective emotional experience Dr. Renik is after. In our more classical view, when the analyst repeats, whether through provocation or his own transference, it makes the job of providing a corrective reality experience more difficult because it confuses *intrapsychic* with *interpersonal* perspectives.

Technical Neutrality and the Abstinence Principle

I have one final point to make about analytic tact and the concept of neutrality. Dr. Renik suggests that the analyst expends a great deal of effort in being tactful, that is, in his effort to be regarded by the patient in one way rather than another—respectful rather than intrusive, accepting rather than punitive, or helpful rather than competitive. He says, "We are thrown back upon the problem of the analyst, as an aspect of his technique, deliberately influencing the way he is experienced by the analysand." I have some concern about this way of viewing technique because for me it conflicts with my understanding of the concept of neutrality. If the analyst is truly neutral and capable of analyzing conflicts in a nonjudgmental way, then he will have no need to deliberately influence the way he is experienced by the analysand. A technically neutral stance is by definition a tactful one because it focuses upon the analytical understanding of the patient's productions and not upon enacting the transference–countertransference struggles with him. Even if it were that everything the analyst did was affected by his countertransference, it would be incumbent upon him to be sufficiently self-aware so that an effort to maintain technical neutrality could be made (regardless of his success in doing so). McLaughlin (Chapter 6 this volume) and Chused (Chapter 7 this volume) provided excellent examples of how such self-analytical work improved their technical ability to overcome stalemates with patients of their own.

In this regard it is important here to distinguish neutrality as an intrapsychic process (i.e., the way the analyst listens to and understands the patient's productions), from the abstinence principle (which prescribes the appropriate analytic response to such productions). What Renik refers to as influencing behavior actually falls under the abstinence principle, and it is important here only because Dr. Renik sees countertransference enactments playing so central a role in appropriate analytic technique. A neutral stance with respect to hearing and understanding the patient's productions already assumes that the analyst's countertransference is well within his personal awareness and control. The capacity to effect this state has a good deal to do with what Renik calls *analytic conscience*, but in addition, it also has much to do with the extent to which the analyst's inner struggles have been acknowledged and worked through. Indeed, it was a combination of Dr. Renik's own analytic conscience and his capacity to deal with his deeply rooted emotions that made his work with this patient so satisfying to both.

Psychoanalysis and Psychotherapy

I would like to pursue the matter of the abstinence principle just a little bit further, however, in order to sharpen the distinction that Renik raises between psychoanalysis and psychotherapy. I believe that the abstinence principle lies at the heart of this matter. From my own perspective, everything that I have discussed about psychoanalytic technique and understanding, up to this point, applies equally to a well-designed psychotherapy based upon psychoanalytic principles. However, in the area of abstinence a distinction can be drawn between psychoanalysis per se, as a specific therapeutic technique, and those psychotherapies based upon the psychoanalytic theory of technique. Whereas psychoanalytic technique holds itself fairly tightly to the principle of nongratification, in the sense that its model technique is interpretive, psychotherapies based upon the psychoanalytic theory have somewhat more freedom to utilize intervention strategies that hold this principle more lightly. That is, carefully designed psychotherapies have more freedom to utilize intentionally the analyst's relation to the patient in order to overcome inhibited growth and development. This assumes, of course, that such growth and development are indeed lacking. But this has little to do with whether the therapeutically valuable experiences of the patient or the analyst are allowed to remain outside of conscious experience for either. I believe that for both psychoanalysis and a well-designed psychotherapy, analytic (i.e., interpretive) attention to the transference–countertransference interaction is always important. I disagree, then, with Renik's conclusion that a successful psychotherapeutic process is one in which corrective emotional experiences take place largely outside the patient's, but more importantly, the therapist's, conscious awareness. Such a view is meaningful only within the perspective that Dr. Renik has proposed, that is, that enactments in the countertransference should take place, to a large extent, *inadvertently*. This ought not to be the case for either psychoanalysis or a psychoanalytic psychotherapy, and this is particularly the case for psychotherapies in which the conscious utilization of the therapist's relation to the patient needs to be so carefully designed to fit the patient's growth needs. Thus, while I agree with Dr. Renik's assessment that countertransference enactments form a common substrate of both psychoanalysis and psychotherapy, it is, in my view, not on the basis of their inadvertent use that the distinction between the two forms lay. Rather, it is upon the intentional use of the relationship to effect change that most psychoanalytical psychotherapies distinguish themselves from classical psychoanalysis (Grand 1995).

Having said all of this, I would like to thank Dr. Renik for providing me with an opportunity to consider a group of interesting and provocative ideas about countertransference enactment. I hope that the issues I have addressed will help clarify some of the difficulties that classical analysts have with the current debate over the role of interaction in the analytic situation.

REFERENCES

Bird, B. (1972). Notes on transference: universal phenomenon and hardest part of analysis. *Journal of the American Psychoanalytic Association* 20:267–301.
Boesky, D. (1990). The psychoanalytic process and its components. *Psychoanalytic Quarterly* 59:550–584.
Freud, S. (1911). Formulations on the two principles of mental functioning. *Standard Edition* 12:215–226.
—— (1914). Remembering, repeating, and working-through. *Standard Edition* 12:145–156.
Grand, S. (1995). A classic revisited: clinical and theoretical reflections on Stone's widening scope of indications for psychoanalysis. *Journal of the American Psychoanalytic Association* 43(3):741–764.
Johan, M. (1992). Enactments in psychoanalysis: report on a panel held at the annual meetings of the A.P.A., San Francisco, 1989. *Journal of the American Psychoanalytic Association* 40:827–841.
Tyson, R. (1986). Countertransference evolution in theory and practice. *Journal of the American Psychoanalytic Association* 34:251–274.

10

Enactment: What Is It and Whose Is It?*

HARRIET I. BASSECHES

Enactment is a word from common parlance that has slowly been adopted into psychoanalytic language until it has changed its identity from everyday usage into a technical term. The transition, however, has been relatively recent. As important a source as Laplanche and Pontalis' (1967) *The Language of Psycho-Analysis* does not include the term in its index. Freud may not have used the word at all, for there are no references to enactment in the subject index of the *Standard Edition*;[1] nevertheless, Freud certainly expressed ideas that seem to be evocative of something we could call enactment while discussing related terms, such as *acting out* (e.g., 1905, 1914, 1940). Laplanche and Pontalis (1967) say that acting out:

> . . . according to Freud, [is] action in which the subject, in the grip of his unconscious wishes and phantasies, relives these in the present with a sensation of immediacy which is heightened by his refusal to recognize their source and their repetitive character. Such action generally displays an impulsive aspect. . . . When it occurs in the course of analysis—whether during the actual session or not—acting out should be understood in its rela-

---

*A version of this paper was presented as part of Panel, *Enactment, A Closer Look: Clinical and Theoretical Aspects*, at the 1992 Spring Meeting of Division of Psychoanalysis, American Psychological Association, Philadelphia, April 3, 1992.

[1]McLaughlin (Chapter 6 this volume) mentions a reference by Freud to the term enactment, but to a meaning of the word antithetical to any of the uses for which it is being applied psychoanalytically. Freud discussed the enactment of the Austrian "quackery law." There, I believe, Freud is using a definition of enact in its legal sense: "To establish by legal and authoritative act; specifically: to make (as a bill) into law."

tionship to the transference, and often as a basic refusal to acknowledge
this transference. [p. 4]

Because of a pejorative association that has inadvertently become connected with the term acting out, some analysts have adopted the term action
rather than acting out as a way to view the communication aspect of the behavior and to avoid the suggestion of judgment. Of course, that shift also loses
the technical specificity of the term acting out in its relation to the transference.

Over time, as the term enactment has been used more and more frequently
and has entered the domain of technical language almost unnoticed, it has
appeared as if there were agreement or at least clarity of disagreement regarding its meaning. It seems possible that such an impression is inaccurate. This
chapter will attempt to demarcate those aspects of the term, as it has developed through usage, that seem to be problematic and those that do not.

As a novitiate in psychoanalysis, I came to understand enactment as expression in the form of action by the patient in the therapeutic setting that could
be understood as a "living," or perhaps more accurately a "re-living," of something unconscious, that is, unremembered, from childhood. Perhaps a better
term for this might be a re-enactment. The "something" that was being portrayed
might well be an unconscious fantasy, or to use Brenner's conceptualization
(1976), a compromise formation that had an unconscious fantasy or wish at its
core. As will be obvious to the reader, my training led to an understanding of
the term enactment that is close to if not indistinguishable from Freud's description of acting out.

The common language, nontechnical definition of enactment (*Random
House Unabridged Dictionary* 1986) emphasizes the idea of representing or
acting a role, as in a play on the stage. A play performed in the theater invites
the viewer to experience the portrayal, known to be "make-believe," as if he
or she were viewing something real.

That is not so unlike children's play. Neubauer (1987) defines play as
having three components: as expression of wishes and fantasies, as enactment
of those wishes in search of fulfillment and, most importantly, as action that is
"pretend." Child analysts, often concerned with children's play, write frequently
about enactments. By and large, child analysts coincide in describing enactments as the child's symbolic playing of a part from the past or the present
(e.g., "Psychoanalytic Views of Play" 1987, Sandler et al. 1980). Van Waning
(1991) makes an explicit effort to expound distinctions among the terms enactment, play, and acting out. She sees both play and acting out as "forms of enactment, of expressing in deeds" (p. 539). In adopting that stance, Van Waning
follows a definition proposed by Rangell (1986) who sees enactment simply as
thoughts or intentions expressed in actions of some kind. Rangell's delineation

leaves out not only allusion to the past, but also any implication that these actions might be a substitute for or an expression of something unconscious. Interestingly, his definition also leaves unspecified such details as the participant(s) in the enactment or the locus of the enactment, whether it occurs in or out of the therapeutic milieu. To return to Van Waning (1991), she, after Freud, assigns an unconscious component to the term acting out but not to the term enactment. She describes acting out as a *form* of enactment: "the transformation into behavior, outside or inside the analysis, of the still unconscious feeling that arises towards the analyst . . ." Acting out is specifically conceptualized as "resistance to the analytic process, in particular resistance to emergent transference feelings" (p. 540).[2]

To recapitulate, all definitions discussed thus far include the description of enactment as action behavior.[3] Beyond coinciding on the idea of action, however, definitions vary regarding characteristics that are reserved for a particular category of enactments called acting out or that are basic to all enactments. These elements include the following: a dynamic unconscious motivation; symbolic meaning; representation of the past and/or present; awareness of a quality of simulation versus a conviction of reality; location of the enactment within or outside of treatment; a functional relationship to the transference. Thinking about enactments exclusively in relationship to the transference brings the discussion to the central point of variance. Describers of enactments differ in their designation of whose enactment(s) are the focus of attention based on the therapeutic philosophy of the assessor. Three points along a continuum come to mind: at one end of the spectrum is the analyst whose orientation is exclusively intrapsychic; for that analyst, the psyche under consideration is that of the patient, and the enactment is a communication of that patient and belongs to that patient; and in that paradigm, the transference of the patient is attended. The analyst attends his or her own transference (i.e., the analyst's countertransference) attentively, but only as an important safeguard against its impingement on the process. The analyst's inner reactions to the patient's communications are distinguished from countertransference reactions and are thought of as the analyst's response to the transference.

---

[2]See Boesky (Chapter 4 this volume) for a thorough discussion of another point of view. In addition, see Steingart (1990) for a discussion of acting out as suspended self-observation.

[3]Again, it is important to remain aware of the complexity inherent even in this simple statement. For instance, note the paradoxical idea that a behavior may be considered as an "action," which by some standards might be thought of as quite the opposite of action, e.g., in the case of prolonged silence (Boesky, Chapter 4 this volume). Moreover, Renik (Chapter 8 this volume) reposes the idea that thought is a form of trial action.

At a central position on the spectrum, and perhaps the most universally accepted position currently, is that of the analyst who not only is interested in the intrapsychic phenomena of the patient, but is equally if not more interested in his or her own intrapsychic activity *as an avenue to the understanding of the patient*. For this analyst, countertransference is considered as *both* the analyst's own transference *and* a response to the patient's transference, and it requires a heightened self-analytic attitude. This analyst sees the enactment as a mutual event and, therefore, interpersonal factors as well as intrapsychic factors are important.

At the other extreme of the continuum are two kinds of positions. For one, the interpersonal and real relationship between analyst and patient is the focus; obviously, the enactment is seen as shared. For the other, which I call a countertransference essentialist position, the primary phenomena of attention are the analyst's own responses. Countertransference is, if not the exclusive subject matter, certainly the predominant focus of attention. From that vantage point, the enactment is shared, and attention is on the analyst, not on the patient, as the primary enactor for both partners.

These positions on the spectrum of analytic philosophy clearly differ with regard to the question of whose enactment is the focus of attention. Another way that these outlooks have been distinguished is by calling them one-person as compared to two-person psychologies (Aron 1990). According to Aron (1990), the classical psychoanalytic viewpoint can best be described as a one-person psychology, whereas relational theories envisage a two-person (or more) field.[4] The difficulty with that dichotomy, however, is that it seems to confuse or at least obfuscate the difference between inner representation and the *real* object. Indeed, the classical analyst would consider the intrapsychic world of the patient as peopled with a multitude of inner representations!

In referring to the real object, we come to still another important distinguishing concept, that of intersubjectivity (Stolorow et al. 1987). Here the idea is that all experience is intersubjective, the analytic situation being no exception and, therefore, a two-person event. The very act of analyzing has an influence on the intersubjective experience and is indivisibly connected so that neither party can ever be "outside" of the intersubjective experience. For the intersubjectivist, then, there can be no one-person psychology. This is an intriguing metaphor. It strikes at the heart of the notion that a participant in a situation could ever truly *step outside* of a situation to observe objectively. But there is a danger inherent in the intersubjective stand as well: taken to its ultimate implications, an intersubjective analysis can be a "hall of mirrors." As each element inevitably reverberates with another, no element could legiti-

---

[4]See also Sugarman and Wilson 1995.

mately be disentangled. No conclusion could be reached. Perhaps it would be better to apprise ourselves of the intersubjective concept without feeling obligated to discard the value of another metaphor, the imagery of a split between the experiencing ego function and the observing ego capacity (Sterba 1934).

Clinical Vignette

An illustration of an enactment exemplifying the analyst with the intrapsychic stance follows. The patient to be described, while prone to action, is also highly responsive to interpretation. He is an accomplished, even gifted, 24-year-old analysand who fails to pay for treatment at the agreed upon time explaining that his car was "booted" (an overdetermined expression in this patient's vernacular) because of unpaid traffic tickets and that he *has* to use the allotted money to reclaim his car. This young man comes from a family that seemed to him depriving, even neglectful. His parents divorced during his adolescence. He was the first-born of four children. He had long-standing grievances toward his parents for neglect and a later resentment directed particularly at his father because his father did not pay for college, only loaned him money for a graduate degree in mathematics, and would *not* loan him money for his treatment. Of course, these issues are built on earlier childhood frustrations and feelings of being left out. The withheld payment appears to reflect his wish to "borrow" from the analyst the money for his treatment. This symbolizes getting what he wanted from his parent. At the same time, it is a turning of passive into active and identification with the aggressor, because now he is doing to the analyst what he felt was done to him. It is also an expression of sadomasochistic object relational representation in which one member of the dyad withholds, i.e., "tortures," the other. The patient has a fantasy that the analyst will be so angry at him for not paying that he will be booted (the patient's word) out of the treatment. To get booted is also symbolic of a wish for the analyst to set limits—to be the attentive parent. And it is an overdetermined effort to sabotage the treatment, with the analyst to blame, not him. He recalls how many times his parents disappointed him and didn't give him what he wanted and needed. He especially recollects one Christmas in adolescence when he told his parents explicitly that he wanted boots (again, patient's word) as a present. When presents were unwrapped, he received presents, but no boots. He remembers buying his own boots sadly. Although it was a tribute to his ingenuity to be able to get for himself what he wanted, to him it meant only bitter deprivation.

Among the many analyst interventions that led to the emergence of the above material, a critical exchange seemed to be the following. The patient complained that the analyst wouldn't set limits on him, to which the analyst rejoined, "So then you set limits on me." "I hate it when you point out things like that to me," he replied. But then the patient seemed able to think more reflectively and began to look at his behavior in a new light. This example would fit the definition of a behavioral enactment by the patient fueled by his deepest wishful thinking, symbolizing a "living" of past conflicts in the present in the transference and encapsulating various compromise formations. The analyst is invited to participate in the enactment, to play a role assigned by the patient. The analyst attempts to understand the enactment, as with any other production by the patient, primarily through clarification and interpretation.

Were the analyst to discover herself acting in some way differently from her usual stance of interest and interpretation, she would be, in Kernberg's words, "out of role" (1987). Under the influence of her countertransference, she would be enacting in collusion with and, at some level, gratifying to the patient. For example, if the aforementioned patient, unmoved by interpretation, continued to enact the scenario and to build up an unpaid balance, the analyst might then feel compelled to act, such as demanding payment or perhaps remaining silent (i.e., passively tolerating the situation, for that too would be an action). I think that each of us could easily envision ourselves in such a situation rationalizing the necessity to enact. Nevertheless, that kind of reaction on the part of the analyst might still be evaluated in a variety of ways: primarily as an appropriate response to the patient's transference (i.e., countertransference, as considered in a broad definition of countertransference), or primarily as a countertransference response, in the sense of one's own archaic need to respond to that kind of pressure in a particular conflicted way (i.e., a neurotic countertransference response).

Judith Chused (Chapter 7 this volume) has described work with a child patient that portrays a series of *mutual* enactments. Dr. Chused appears to hold a view on the border between the exclusively intrapsychic and the intrapsychic/interpersonal stance. She contends that

> In the second best possible world, where most of us dwell, an analyst reacts to the patient, but catches himself in the act, so to speak, regains his analytic stance and, in observing himself and the patient, increases his understanding of the unconscious fantasies and conflicts in the patient and himself that have prompted him to action. [pp. 93–94]

Having acknowledged that enactments on the part of the analyst are less than ideal, Dr. Chused goes on to describe, possibly even glorify, the benefits and understanding engendered by these mutual enactments. Such a report, so admirably open and self-disclosing, does seem attractive. Aware of how sensitive we analysts are to our aptitude for accepting the role, that is, to be role-responsive (Sandler, Chapter 3 this volume), it is a great comfort to prize these moments rather than regret them. Often, we do "catch ourselves," and we do learn important things about our patients. Moreover, this form of knowing carries with it a sense of conviction that is particularly reassuring in treatment with a difficult or bewildering patient (Friedman 1988). Yet, questions remain unaddressed about the reliability of these responses of the analyst as consistent beacons of understanding about the patient: Do they drive each analysis in different directions depending on the inner life of that particular analyst, since countertransference (in the narrow sense) is so idiosyncratic to each analyst (Marill 1995)?

Another author advocating for the middle position of the spectrum is McLaughlin (Chapter 6 this volume). Acknowledging his intent to create his own definition, McLaughlin views an enactment as a shared event "occurring within the dyad that both parties experience as being the consequence of behavior in the other" (p. 80). McLaughlin, although maintaining the idea that "latent intrapsychic conflicts and residues of prior object relations" are present (p. 81), thinks enactment is "attempted mutual influence and persuasion" (p. 84). (Putting aside the emphasis on mutuality, that seems to be a pretty apt description of at least one, if not the major, function of transference.)

Renik (Chapter 8 this volume) argues for the inevitability of enactments to be considered mutual analyst–patient events. "Every experienced analyst expects that today's authentic piece of analytic investigation will very likely tomorrow be revealed also to have been a transference–countertransference enactment that was unrecognized . . ." (p. 155). And further, that "every productive technical choice . . . involves the analyst in a spontaneously occurring corrective emotional experience" (p. 157). He buttresses his point of view with a lovely vignette in which he reveals a complex web of personal associations and revelations. His work raises the question of whether it is possible to have an "authentic piece of analytic investigation" of an enactment exclusively organized around the patient's motivational core compromise formations and fueled by the patient's wishful thinking, with the analyst functioning in role (Kernberg 1987) and responding empathically to the transference, without arousing his or her personal countertransference (in the narrow sense).

My own view currently, as I review these issues, leans toward retaining a distinction between enactments primarily of the patient and those that are more mutual events. There are two points that lead me to continue to see important benefits in retaining a concept of enactments by the patient, no matter who the analyst might be, as separate from acknowledging the more inclusive term, mutual enactments. The first point centers on the value in preserving a focus on the enduring aspects of the patient, somewhat comparably to a focus on character or style. Obviously, an interaction that ensues will be influenced by the environmental response (i.e., the analyst's response), but the assumption here is that there is a core motivation for initiation of the enactment that is internal to and organized by that patient's compromise formations.

Secondly, the retaining of the concept of the patient's enactment is founded on the premise that the transferential role given to the analyst by the patient (representing some unique combination of self and/or other representations) is a projection of that patient's intrapsychic content and is a manifestation of an inner conflict (Bird 1972). In that sense of expressing an inner conflict of the patient, the interactive aspect of the enactment can be understood as an externalization of the intrapsychic life of that patient (Arlow 1993). Again, it is not to deny the interactive component or to ignore the analyst's valuable clues of countertransferential participation, but rather to re-emphasize the intrapsychic, conflict-laden motivational source of the event for the patient. I think that emphasis has the chance of getting lost in the enthusiasm to capture a more complex mutual flavor of analyses. The danger may then become a subtle tilt toward analyzing behavior and not conflicts.

The underlying supposition being considered here is whether five different analysts with the same patient would promote five *essentially* different enactments. Or would there be a basically similar enactment, no matter who the analyst, based on expression of some deeply held and particular wishful thinking on the part of the patient (Marill 1995)?

Notwithstanding plenty of evidence from my own experience of mutual transference–countertransference enactments, and the development of a real, interpersonal relationship between analyst and analysand, my concern centers on the continued dialogue about curative factors in the analytic situation. It seems that analysts differ in their beliefs—could we say, fantasies—about the source of that cure (Boesky 1990). As I have already stated, I find helpful the idea that a patient has core conflicts and attendant compromise formations to be understood, in a sense, irrespective of the analyzing partner. Moreover, I sometimes sense an attitude toward countertransference that seems almost idealizing: as if to understand the patient's inner structure and organization *requires* the analyst's idiosyncratic archaic conflicts; that without the analyst's conflicts corresponding to the patient's, there will be no resonance and therefore no understanding.

In conclusion, analysts' attitudes toward this matter of whose enactment is being displayed are informed by their broader psychoanalytic perspective. This broader perspective influences whether the analyst views his or her participation in a patient's enactment as a collusion and "out of role," or as a shared, mutual behavioral event reflective of the intrapsychic input of each participant, or as a shared mutual event about interpersonal communication between two people. I believe that the reason, in part, for these differences is that we each have the challenge of trying to conceptualize the vehicle for our understanding of the patient, that is, how we come to think we know what is going on for the patient. The proliferation of theories reflects the diversity of convictions of just how that process really works. The state of our perceptions inevitably colors our work with our patients and the work we describe to each other. Hopefully, the dialogue about our differing attitudes gives us an opportunity to listen to each other, as we continue to crystallize our own theories and test our long-held convictions.

REFERENCES

Arlow, J. A. (1993). Training for psychoanalysis and psychotherapy. *Psychoanalytic Review* 80: 183–197.

Aron, L. (1990). One person and two person psychologies and the method of psychoanalysis. *Psychoanalytic Psychology* 7:475–486.

Bird, B. (1972). Notes on transference: universal phenomenon and hardest part of analysis. *Journal of the American Psychoanalytic Association* 20:267–301.

Boesky, D. (1990). The psychoanalytic process and its components. *Psychoanalytic Quarterly* 59:550–584.

Brenner, C. (1976). *Psychoanalytic Technique and Psychic Conflict.* New York: International Universities Press.

Freud, S. (1905). Fragment of an analysis of a case of hysteria. *Standard Edition* 7:7–122.

—— (1914). Remembering, repeating, and working-through. *Standard Edition* 12:145–156.

—— (1940). An outline of psychoanalysis. *Standard Edition* 23:144–207.

Friedman, L. (1988). The clinical popularity of object relations concepts. *Psychoanalytic Quarterly* 57:667–691.

Kernberg, O. F. (1987). Projection and projective identification: developmental and clinical aspects. In *Projection, Identification, Projective Identification,* chap. 7, pp. 93–115, ed. J. Sandler. Madison, CT: International Universities Press.

Laplanche, J., and Pontalis, J.-B. (1967). *The Language of Psycho-Analysis,* trans. D. Nicholson-Smith. New York: Norton, 1973.

Marill, I. H. (1995). Personal communication.

Neubauer, P. B. (1987). The many meanings of play. *Psychoanalytic Study of the Child* 42:3–9. New Haven, CT: Yale University Press.

Psychoanalytic views of play (1987). Section of 12 papers. *Psychoanalytic Study of the Child* 42:3–219. New Haven, CT: Yale University Press.

Random House Unabridged Dictionary (1986). New York: Random House.

Rangell, L. (1986). In International Scientific Colloquium on repeating: enactment and verbalization in different stages of development. *Bulletin of the Hampstead Clinic* 9(2):79–152.

Sandler, J., Kennedy, H., and Tyson, R. L. (1980). *The Technique of Child Psychoanalysis, Discussions with Anna Freud.* Cambridge, MA: Harvard University Press.

Steingart, I. (1990). *Acting-out as play experience.* Paper presented to the New York Freudian Society, Washington, DC.

Sterba, R. F. (1934). The fate of the ego in analytic therapy. *International Journal of Psycho-Analysis* 15:117–126.

Stolorow, R.D., Brandchaft, B., and Atwood, G. E. (1987). *Psychoanalytic Treatment, An Intersubjective Approach.* Hillsdale, NJ: Analytic Press.

Sugarman, A., and Wilson, A., eds. (1995). Special section: contemporary structural psychoanalysis and relational psychoanalysis. *Psychoanalytic Psychology* 12(1):1–114.

Van Waning, A. (1991). "To be the best or not to be, that is the question. . . ." On enactment, play and acting out. *International Journal of Psycho-Analysis* 72:539–551.

11

Is Enactment a Useful Concept?*

PAULA L. ELLMAN

The more recent use of the term *enactment* appears to be part of a trend accompanying the growing development of object relations theory and technique. Here, an increased emphasis is placed on demonstrating the importance of the mutuality of interaction in psychoanalytic therapy. Sandler's (Chapter 3 this volume) writing on *role-responsiveness* set the stage for the concept of enactment. He wrote of the intrapsychic role relationship each party attempts to impose on the other. The patient attempts to impose an interaction between himself and the analyst, in order to actualize the transference. The analyst's acting out of this induced role is a compromise formation between his or her own tendencies and a reflexive acceptance of the role that the patient is forcing on the analyst. Both McLaughlin (Chapter 6 this volume) and Chused (Chapter 7 this volume) further developed the concept of enactment focusing on the interactive sphere of the analysis. According to McLaughlin, we should employ the term enactment "to refer to events occurring within the dyad that both parties experience as being the consequence of behavior in the other" (p. 80). There is an emphasis on a conjoint process of attempted mutual influence and persuasion in the analytic relationship.

For Chused (Chapter 7 this volume), "enactments are symbolic interactions between analyst and patient that have unconscious meaning to *both*" (p. 93). In the patient's transference distortion of the analysis, the patient loses distance from the experience and then has a feeling of conviction regarding the accuracy of his or her perceptions. The patient then behaves so as to induce behavior in the analyst that serves to support this conviction. Chused

---

*Presented at Division 39 Spring meeting, Philadelphia, April 1992.

believes the analyst's vulnerability to enactment has to do with the primary motivation for being an analyst. If a person has a wish in an object relationship, such as the therapist's wish to help the patient, there is then the exposure to the possibility that an interaction will evoke an earlier object relationship, that is, will become laden with transference. To want anything from a patient, even cure, is to be vulnerable to an experience of one's own transference and susceptible to an enactment. In focusing on the patient's behavior, Chused noted the contribution to the analytic experience determined by the analyst's own psychology, resulting from the patient's attempts to create an interactional representation of a wished-for object relationship. In getting the analyst to enact, the patient achieves a measure of reality for the transference fantasies. Enactments link current and past experiences with a vividness of affect and inter-objective relatedness; the great conviction tests the analyst's vulnerabilities.

In contrast to this approach to understanding the enacted interaction, the traditional concepts of transference, transference neurosis, and countertransference shift the emphasis of understanding. Here, instead, is the transference as a compromise formation reflecting the intrapsychic conflict. Freud (1920) first wrote of *transference neurosis*:

> The patient cannot remember the whole of what is repressed in him. . . . He is obliged to repeat the repressed material as a contemporary experience. These reproductions . . . always have as their subject some portion of infantile sexual life—of the oedipal complex, that is, and its derivatives and are invariably acted out in the sphere of the transference of the patient's relation to the physician. . . . Here the earlier neurosis has now been replaced by a fresh "transference neurosis." [p. 18]

For Brenner (1982) transference contains components of any conflict—drive derivative, defense, and superego functioning, so that it is a compromise formation; transference neurosis serves to specify the intense transference manifestation as indistinguishable from a neurotic symptom. And for Weinshel (1971), in analysis there is the mobilization of old conflicts and a recasting of them into symptoms, attitudes, and behavior that characterize the transference neurosis. The therapeutic action of analysis lies in the undoing of internal resistances. The transference neurosis becomes the vehicle of resistances and therefore is central to facilitating the undoing of repression.

Clinical Vignette

Mr. T. is a 32-year-old Middle Eastern man who has been in psychoanalysis for four years. He had lived his first five years in an underdeveloped country before his family immigrated to the United States. He was the second-born child and the first-born son, highly valued in his religious and cultural community. Mr. T. felt treasured, especially by his mother, until he was 2½ years old when his brother was born. (Two other children followed.) He then fell painfully from his pedestal. He was abruptly weaned with the help of his father applying pepper to his mother's nipples and was displaced by his infant brother from the special place he held with his mother. The ensuing years were turbulent with an abusive father and overworked mother. Memories of his early life are vivid and almost palpable for Mr. T. His adolescence and adulthood had involved drug and alcohol use. His relationships with men and women had been sadomasochistic, and those that had the potential for mutuality were not enduring. In addition, he had been consistently conflicted in his strivings both in school and in work.

In beginning his treatment, Mr. T. complained of having ended a relationship with a girlfriend because of religious differences, and he was left "hungry" for the strength he had gained when with her. He felt weak and associated this feeling with his having been hurtful to his previous girlfriend. His use of cocaine concerned him, and he complained of discomfort with being forthright in his work and personal relationships. Initially the analyst was moved by his disquieting anxiety and his being impeded in his realization of his life goals. From the start, the analyst's healing wishes were stirred. In the course of the analysis, it was these wishes, perhaps stirred by this particular patient but also having sources in the analyst's own internal life, that constituted her vulnerability to countertransference reactions to the patient's transference.

The initial period of the analysis can be characterized by Mr. T.'s complaints of being mistreated at work and in relationships. He insisted that he was deprived and conceived of his sacrifices as punishment for his gratifications. He was demeaning to himself, calling himself "no good, stupid, incompetent, and ugly." When these feelings were strong, he sought strength in the high of cocaine and then tearfully, pitifully, berated himself, which only served to create a yearning for the next episode of drug use. The analyst's interpretive effort was to attempt to uncover the guilt he was not aware of in his victim role. The next phase of the analysis involved his recreating and reliving his past suffering by his painful retelling of details of childhood physical abuse at the hands of his father. Although he presented himself as the helpless victim, it became clear that he provoked his father's attacks. His aggression and guilt were repressed and projected. He was the accuser of the aggressor who victimized him. His drug use continued, his gaining strength followed by self-punishment.

In the early phase of the analysis, the analyst's pregnancy stirred in the patient wishes to recapture the mother of his childhood. Accompanying memories of "having mother" were painful memories of death and of people killed in the street. This expressed punishment for wishes for his mother as well as repressed anger over unfulfilled wishes. An example of the transference manifestation of the wish coupled with the defense was Mr. T.'s request for the analyst to pass him the tissue box as he suffered with his memories. The analyst's reaction, feeling guilty that her analytic procedure was promoting such pain for her patient, prompted her to hand him the tissues. Realizing her countertransference reaction, when Mr. T. next requested tissues, the analyst spoke to the defensive nature of his request: that if she gave him the tissues, he could feel reassured and accepted by her rather than feel filled with guilt over his wishes to take from her. He responded, "I don't want to get up and have you see my terrible, ugly face. I need to feel good and accepted. I was so ugly, deformed, that my mother did not want to have anything to do with me." Mr. T. attempts to ward off his wants, for with them he is ugly. His tissue request was a defensive effort to seek protection from the guilt associated with his wants, which under the pressure of the analyst's own guilt she initially gratified but later interpreted to him.

In anticipation of the analyst's maternity leave, the patient repetitively insisted on his helplessness, asking her, "How can you leave me now?!" A childhood memory emerged: "I was at the beach, I swam far out across the reef. I slipped through a tube and went deep under water. I opened my eyes, and I was surrounded by a wonderful warm world. I thought of staying there but knew it would be death. I could almost hear my mother crying. It would hurt my mother, so I pushed up and I could breathe." In the transference and in genetic material, masochism was revealed; his suffering was both a self-punishment and a retaliation. The analyst commented: "You suffer not only to punish yourself but also as a way to get back at your mother and me." The memory suggests his longing to be the satiated fetus, protected, ever provided for. Mr. T.'s suffering relieves him of guilt over his rage. He justifies his aggression with being a victim and then can believe that his aggression is reactive. This fended off his primary aggression concerning his wishes to intrude and also the guilt over these wishes.

During these few months, Mr. T.'s cocaine use gradually stopped. With his new abstinence, Mr. T. associated the drug with his mother's breast. He stated that with drugs he felt invincible and could get what he wanted. He spoke of the "soothing, comfort zone" of nursing mother's milk. He feared his intrusiveness toward the analyst and commented on averting his eyes. He dreamed of the analyst referring him elsewhere because he was too pushy. What ensued were complaints that he was illiterate, no good, that he had no future, was hopeless at work, was discontented in his relationship with his girlfriend, and was getting nothing from his treatment. He wanted the analyst to provide her "soothing voice" to him.

The analyst reacted this time with guilt. Her initial response was to think that she was retreating too much into an analytic silent listening and not giving him sufficient help. She became more actively interpretive, more persistently pointing out to the patient his "victim role" in his life and questioning his motivation for his role—this was her effort to heal his suffering. His response was an exacerbation of the dynamic; he stepped up his self-blame. He must really be a terrible person, the one who is at fault for all his difficulties especially since his failings, his discontents, are attributable to his unconscious motivation to be a victim. When the analyst took note that her increased analytic persistence served only to produce masochistic reactions, she looked to her own feelings, her guilt, as a guide in formulating an interpretation of the transference. She interpreted that he was showing her how neglectful she was. She pointed out how he injured himself in order to accuse her (mother) and so that he might feel entitled to his anger. He commented with seeming satisfaction "when I don't do well, you then feel you're not doing your job."

In the course of the next year and a half, Mr. T. elaborated on an unconscious fantasy of a hostile introject—a demon that can be unleashed and damaging to the object. He associated this demon with any libidinal or aggressive pursuit of his. Mr. T.'s fear of his unconscious fantasy served to inhibit him in his career and in his pursuit of a viable love object. A pursuit was no different from a rape. He had the hope that he would meet the woman of his dreams accidentally so that there would be no pursuit and no monster unleashed. And he was "impotent" in the analytic work. "It would be hurtful to take knowledge from you. Like I'd be too greedy and would be sucking the life out of you. You'd discover the animal that kills in me."

With the gradual uncovering of the derivatives of an organizing fantasy came amelioration of his masochism and greater acceptance of his assertiveness in his career, in working toward a more realistic relationship with his girlfriend, and in allowing himself more freedom and pleasure with material acquisitions.

More recently, Mr. T. was struggling with mourning the loss of a fantasied childhood Garden of Eden. As he complained of how poorly he felt, he reiterated the idea that "you have it all, you hold the power, and you are holding out on me." He spoke of his wishes to induce guilt/sympathy to get the analyst to provide, without his having to then feel that he was coercive. Mr. T. was not aware that his efforts to induce guilt could, in fact, have a coercive effect and, as a result, provoke a reaction that would be far from caretaking of him. The analyst's annoyance with the coercive effect of the guilt induced in her prompted her to say, "You seem to wish for no limits." His response was, "If I have my mother, I'll have the whole world in my palm." No limits was equivalent to the fulfillment of incestuous wishes, and he insisted, "There's nothing wrong with being nursed all the time." The analyst replied that he was acting on the belief that his wishes for his mother could be realized. "You lead me to give up my goals. You're shaving away at them" was his rejoinder. The analyst realized that because of her wishes to help him, she was being exhortative and he then was tempted to oppose her with his continued pursuit of gratification. The analyst attempted to become more interpretive: "You seek more, more good, more pleasure, in your effort to neutralize the evil demon you believe is in you." It seemed that his pursuit of an illusory state of perpetual fulfillment was serving to replace work toward real gratification with an object in order to protect himself against his rage at acknowledging limitations.

To view this analyst–patient dynamic as an enactment would entail a substantial loss of clarity and understanding. As an enactment, the emphasis is on what Chused (Chapter 7 this volume) termed an "interactional representation of a wished-for object relationship" (p. 102). Applied to this case, it would follow that the patient used cocaine in order to gratify a wish to return to a perpetual nursing state. That this wish had become directed toward the analyst is demonstrated when the patient stopped his use of cocaine and attempted to get the analyst to give more to him through his guilt-inducing self-punitiveness. The analyst repeatedly was tempted to "enact" a series of symbolic gratifications with the patient. Viewing this material as a transference, or transference neurosis, accompanied by countertransference, brings to the material a subtle but important shift in emphasis. Reed (1990) wrote:

> . . . because (transference neurosis) is seen as a result of the transforming work of transference and as a midstation that will need to be dismantled, not an end of the cure, it defines psychoanalysis as a therapy that utilizes symbolic transformation in its process and aspires to the analyst's and the patient's understanding of the patient's reexperiencing of that internal symbolic transformation to effect change. [p. 447]

Psychoanalytic cure is a reorganization of structures, not a process of annihilation based on personal suggestion. Using the more classical terms of transference, transference neurosis, and countertransference can be more productive than using the concept of enactment in facilitating the analytic process. Rather than an interactional representation of an object relationship or wished-for object relationship, what is seen is an interactional representation of an intrapsychic conflict.

Mr. T.'s pursuit of a nursed state, of a cocaine high, of a transference gratification, is not his effort to satiate his oral drive, which would characterize the enactment with the analyst. Rather, the patient's demands, his pursuit, is the symptom—a compromise formation. There is always the return of the repressed contained in the symptom expression. The symptom also contains the defense. Mr. T.'s pursuit, his drivenness to be gratified, is his effort to defend against the anxiety of the awareness of his rage, that is, the fantasied demon in him that he believes would destroy if not gratified. It is this symptom that the patient brought into the analysis as a transference neurosis. The analyst's vulnerability to his wishes was a reaction due to a "wish to heal." In addition, this was the guilt that was repressed and projected in the patient's symptom, that of his masochistically pursuing gratification. (He said that he must pursue gratification to not feel bad, for any anger he feels, he takes as evidence of the demon.) In considering the material in the context of a transference neurosis and countertransference, one sees that the countertransference becomes a guide toward an interpretation of conflict: the symptom of anxiety, the masochistic defense, and the further working through of the unconscious fantasy. If the patient were solely enacting a wished-for object relationship of oral gratification, there would be no interpretation, only an exhortation to relinquish his unrealistic infantile pursuit. The treatment would be, as Reed (1990) maintains, one of personal suggestion, of annihilation of a wish. With an understanding based on transference neurosis and countertransference, the patient's analysis involved the working through of defenses against differentiating fantastic thoughts from the reality of emotions, so that derivatives of unconscious fantasy came increasingly under ego control.

REFERENCES

Brenner, C. (1982). *The Mind in Conflict.* New York: International Universities Press.
Freud, S. (1920). Beyond the pleasure principle. *Standard Edition* 18:7–64.
Reed, G. (1990). The transference neurosis in Freud's writings. *Journal of the American Psychoanalytic Association* 38:423–450.
Weinshel, E. (1971). The transference neurosis: a survey of the literature. *Journal of the American Psychoanalytic Association* 19:67–88.

12

Enactments Leading to Insight for Patient, Therapist, and Supervisor

FONYA LORD HELM

A few days before Valentine's Day, a chef brought his therapist a cake he had made and presented it to his therapist in a tentative fashion. As the therapist accepted the cake, the therapist had the thought that it was poisoned. The cake, however, was eaten later and shared with other therapists in the office, and everyone survived. The next year the chef brought a cake again, and the therapist noticed the same thought and felt somewhat apprehensive, even though everything had been fine the year before. The therapist proceeded to eat the cake. The third year the chef brought another cake and presented it to the therapist, who noticed the absence of the fantasy and wondered about it. During the session, the chef talked about his fantasy that he would poison the therapist with the cake. At the point that the chef was able to put his thoughts into words, it was no longer necessary to present the cake in a tentative, guilty, and hesitant way that communicated a fantasy of poison. It was no longer necessary to communicate that fantasy by enactment.

In this example, both patient and therapist are engaged in transference–countertransference enactments. An enactment is any action occurring during psychotherapy or psychoanalysis that repeats an earlier similar experience or fantasy and communicates feeling from such an experience or fantasy by nonverbal means in a way that will draw the therapist or analyst into a nonverbal communication. The patient induces the therapist to take on a role by setting up a situation in which the therapist will experience "role-responsiveness" (Sandler, Chapter 3 this volume). Enactments express something different than the verbal material presented by the patient, and they are the way to understanding those aspects of the patient that cannot yet be communicated in words. Enactment is defined by McLaughlin (Chapter 6 this volume) as an act intended strongly to influence, persuade, or force another to react. He also states that enactment "can be construed in all the behaviors of both parties in the analytic relationship" (p. 78), because during analysis the appeal or manipulative intent of our words and silences is intensified. Our words become acts or things, and the secondary process becomes loaded with affective appeal and coercion. He notes that these charged words are themselves embedded in a steady clamor of nonverbal communication between the pair, much of which is registered and processed unconsciously by both parties.

These definitions of enactment include both transference and countertransference enactment and projective identification and counteridentification. Enactments are both intrapsychic and interpersonal, and they are created primarily by communications that are not verbal. These nonverbal communications include facial expression, movements and positions of the body, and tone of voice. These communications are especially useful and important as carriers of affects, both conscious and unconscious, in addition to whatever unconscious ideas they may convey. Through enactment, the patient is capable of stimulating in the analyst or therapist conscious and unconscious affects and fantasies, even though the underlying unconscious fantasies and their genetic determinants will be different from those of the patient.

Smith (1995) has observed that the analyst characteristically discovers enactments with a feeling of shock or surprise. The enactments appear singular or discontinuous when viewed in retrospect, but they are not, and this very singularity can be used defensively to keep the analyst from realizing that he or she is involved in ongoing enactments. Enactments are ubiquitous and are intrinsic to the work. They occur in all human relationships, but in psychoanalysis and in psychotherapy they are analyzable.

This chapter illustrates ways that the communicative aspect of enactments can be used creatively in treatment to lead to insight and self-discovery for the patient, as well as for the analyst or therapist, and the supervisor. I emphasize the communicative aspect of enactment, and the search for meanings is primary. The fantasy or affect generated in the analyst or therapist by the enactment is an opportunity to tune into the patient's unconscious. Five clinical vignettes illustrate these nonverbal communications: two describe the patient–therapist dyad, and three describe the patient–therapist–supervisor triad.

In the past, enactments often were considered to be mistakes or errors in technique. Chused and Raphling (1992) have written about how difficult it is to accept mistakes as an inevitable part of the work in spite of the fact that most of us acknowledge that technical lapses occur during every hour. They point out that the unpleasant affects that accompany awareness of mistakes often lead the analyst away from a close examination of the errors. They argue that it is extremely useful to look at the mistakes of the competent analyst as a manifestation of the psychoanalytic process due to the unavoidable interactive influence of one person on the other in the dyad.

In the first of the following vignettes, the nonverbal communication that eventually became conscious for both therapist and patient made it possible for the therapist to tune into the patient's fear and excitement concerning exposure. In the second vignette, the therapist was able to recover an old memory of his own as a result of the analysis of an enactment that took place in the psychotherapy.

Clinical Vignette 1

A female patient was talking to her male therapist about how she had felt exposed and naked in past sessions and how she was not going to "get naked" again that day. Later in the hour she took off an earring, and the therapist had the idea that she was undressing. Then the patient said she felt as if she was undressing when she took off her earring, adding that she had had the same feeling before in the therapy when she had taken off an earring. She had never mentioned her feeling before because she thought her therapist didn't know. This time she decided to say something, because she thought he knew. She was correct about her therapist's perception. In this example, the enactment conveyed its unconscious meaning of undressing to the therapist. The way she removed her earring and the therapist's accompanying facial expression were both undoubtedly important, and were noticed by both patient and therapist, but neither had verbalized the perception. Both patient and therapist probably were unaware of registering the nonverbal communication, especially early in the course of this enactment that had developed over several months. The only verbal aspect remembered by the therapist was the patient's beginning the hour by saying that she did not want to feel exposed or naked. This was the hour in which the patient became aware of some of the therapist's nonverbal communications in that she thought he knew what she was thinking and feeling.

Clinical Vignette 2

A therapist learned of an important aspect of his own history as a direct result of an enactment that took place in psychotherapy. His patient was feeling very anxious and was expressing a sense of fragmentation of her body, to which she associated memories of early separations from her mother. During her description of these memories, the therapist also began to feel very anxious and experienced a sense of a part of his body as insubstantial, as if a solid object could fall through it. Later that day the therapist, in his own therapy, recovered memories of an early separation from a parent, memories that he had been unaware of before.

In these vignettes, the nonverbal communication that eventually became conscious for therapist and patient led to important insights for both. In addition, these vignettes emphasize the interaction between patient and therapist, a model that includes the therapist as a participant, rather than a model that portrays the therapist as a blank screen, a nonparticipant. The model of the therapist as an objective observer who works with the patient's observing ego to analyze an unfolding transference emphasizes a narrow definition of countertransference limited to the unconscious conflicts of the therapist. Over the years, many psychoanalysts and psychotherapists have accepted a broader definition of countertransference that includes everything the therapist thinks and feels about the patient, conscious or not. In these examples of enactment, the broad and narrow definitions of countertransference can be seen to occur at the same time. Whatever is communicated by the patient will be experienced by the therapist in his or her own way and will be filtered through the memories and fantasies of the individual therapist. Each therapist–patient pair will be different, and although the patient's core conflicts as seen in the transference are analyzable by different therapists, the way the material unfolds in the patient's associations will be influenced differently by each therapist.

When a supervisor is added, the communications then occur among three people, and enactments will be seen in the supervisory sessions. The analyst or therapist presents the case material in a way that creates affects in the supervisor. Factors that tend to create such affects are: the manner in which the patient's fantasies and historical events are presented by the supervisee, the order and selection of material to be presented, and the supervisee's voice tone and cadence. The communication seen in the relationship with the patient and therapist appears routinely in the supervision, and the same kinds of pressure that are put on the therapist are in turn put on the supervisor. This parallel process has been described by Ekstein and Wallerstein (1958) and by Gediman and Wolkenfeld (1980) as a triadic phenomenon, occurring among the patient, analyst, and supervisor. Gediman and Wolkenfeld point out that parallel enactments run the full range from normal to pathological and are a communication process in which the complex patterns that occur in one dyadic situation, such as therapy, show up in the other dyadic system, such as supervision. They note that this phenomenon occurs with both neophyte and experienced therapists, and even in supervision of supervisors. The parallel process is also multidirectional with no clear point of origin.

Often, the parallel process is so comfortable for patient, therapist, and supervisor that it is never discussed. For example, the mild positive transference that furthers the work of therapy can appear in the supervision as a "learning alliance" (Fleming and Benedek 1966), and the supervisor may feel gratified. The parallel process also may be so subtle that it goes unnoticed. It becomes most noticeable when the affects that are communicated are unpleasant, such as those of a negative transference, or when the patient characteristically relies heavily on enactments in the psychoanalysis or psychotherapy.

As a general rule, the more enactments there are in the psychotherapy, the more enactments there will be in the supervision. The beginning of an enactment in the supervision by the therapist often happens when the patient's affect is deeply repressed. When the affect is repressed in this way, the supervisor is able to understand the patient's communication only if it is enacted by the therapist, since the therapist will not be able to articulate it. The supervisor is also in a position to begin enactments that affect the supervisory relationship, and these enactments may be passed on by the therapist, who enacts them in the relationship with the patient. The supervisor is most likely to begin a noticeable enactment when the patient relies heavily on enactments and the material is confusing and chaotic. In a triadic system, it is often hard to tell who started the enactment. A tendency toward action in any of the three participants will increase the number of enactments, but the tendency of the patient to rely on enactments is the major variable.

Three vignettes of enactments in both therapy and supervision follow. The first, Vignette 3, gives the clearest example of the parallel process, as the stare of the patient is repeated in the supervision. The second, Vignette 4, concerns repressed aggression in the patient and how it was communicated through the therapist to the supervisor, even though the therapist herself was unaware of it at first. The aggression was eventually understood by all three participants, but it became conscious in the supervisor first. It is included as an example of parallel process because the aggression was present in all three participants, even though it was initially beneath awareness for two of them. The third example, Vignette 5, describes a protracted enactment that only gradually yielded to analysis and was repeated in supervision with two supervisors.

Clinical Vignette 3

The patient had begun to look longingly at the therapist in the psychotherapy, and very soon in the work the supervisor began to notice the therapist staring at her in the supervision. The supervisor felt somewhat uncomfortable with this stare, as did the therapist when his patient stared at him. The patient's stare began immediately and was at first understood by the therapist as good eye contact and a positive sign. A few weeks later, the therapist noted that the patient seemed vigilant and guarded. By the third month of the therapy, the patient had a pleading look that the therapist interpreted as, "Please do it for me." After a year, the therapist felt intensely uncomfortable, almost trapped, as if to turn his eyes away was forbidden by her. The therapist decided not to interpret this nonverbal communication for a long time, but contained and observed it, and often felt a peculiar anxiety. Eventually the patient had the idea that in her romantic relationships, she would beg with her eyes. The therapist asked what her eyes would say, and she replied, "Please don't go away. I want to be with you." The patient said she felt a panicky thumping in her chest, and while the therapist empathized with the panic, he felt it in his own characteristic way, in an urge to leave. Later the patient described eye contact as a sign that she was loved by a person, and when it did not occur, she felt deprived. She realized that when an important person looked away, her reaction was, "How dare you pull away from me?" This idea occurred just before the therapist's vacation. When the therapist pointed out that the patient was looking longingly at him then, she insisted that this feeling only applied to romantic relationships. Later in the treatment, this look became a useful signal with the patient sometimes asking if she was staring. She often said that it meant, "Don't disconnect from me," or "Do you still like me?"

The supervisor noticed the staring in the first few months and, interestingly, experienced a challenge in the therapist's look that was different from the therapist's initial experience of the patient's stare. Here the therapist's use of his eyes and a serious facial expression, along with a rather erect position in his chair, were instrumental in creating the impression of a beginning challenge and a hint of aggression. Often a supervisor becomes aware of aggressive aspects of enactments in the parallel process before the therapist becomes fully aware of them.

In this vignette, the patient was demanding the therapist's full attention at all times by her stare, so that the therapist felt constrained. The therapist, however, was not consciously aware of a more direct hostile aspect of this enactment. This lack of awareness served a useful purpose in the work, because the patient's aggression was not yet conscious enough to be in working position and the patient would have been unable to understand an intervention directed at the aggressive aspect at that time. Both the therapist and supervisor agreed that this patient could leave treatment abruptly if the therapist spoke to the aggression.

Both therapist and supervisor became conscious of the enactment fairly quickly, because of the discomfort the underlying aggression engendered. The result of their awareness was that the therapist and supervisor could begin considering ways to understand this enactment and eventually ways to show the patient its meaning. At the same time both therapist and supervisor contained the feeling, that is, they endured the discomfort of the staring. This enactment is unusual in that it was noticed quickly by both therapist and supervisor. Many enactments take much longer to be noticed, and many remain inchoate.

Clinical Vignette 4

This vignette is an example of an enactment that took longer to notice. It involved a patient with a characterological isolation of affect. He had had great difficulty experiencing his feelings as far back as he could remember. As the therapeutic process began to unfold, his anger began to leak into the transference in subtle ways that were outside his awareness. As his anger began to come into the transference in this way, the therapist's presentation in supervision became somewhat boring, because she presented the material in an affectless way. This therapist was an unusually good storyteller, so the supervisor quickly noticed the difference from the usual way she presented supervisory material. The therapist was unaware of the patient's aggression and consciously did not experience irritation in the countertransference. The superviser said he thought the patient was struggling with repressed anger unconsciously and asked if the supervisee thought the patient was expressing any opposition in the therapy. She had noticed a hint of stubbornness and eventually, as the patient became more aware of his anger and was able to communicate it in a nonverbal way, the supervisee became conscious of the anger it stirred up in herself. During this time period, the supervisor contained the affect in the supervision in that he noticed the material was boring at times but did not say anything. When the therapist was able to experience the affect consciously, the issue seemed to be in working position. The supervisor took note of the enactments and only mentioned the possibility of the existence of enactments and affects in the patient. The rest of the work was done by the supervisee.

In this vignette, the affects were preconscious or even unconscious in both the patient and the therapist and were only conscious in the supervisor. This experiencing of boredom, and consequent relating it to the patient's material, was the only way that the supervisor could have learned about the activation of the patient's aggression in the transference because nothing aggressive was being reported in words. Similar examples of this kind of awareness of the supervisor to repressed anger or other affects in the patient before the therapist becomes aware occur often in supervision, and they are part of the nonverbal communication process.

Clinical Vignette 5

This example describes a protracted enactment in the treatment of a male patient, whose major resistance involved silences. Many contributions to his enactment were uncovered over a period of years, and the silences were always a factor in the work, being particularly noticeable when the patient was under the stress of strong emotion. The patient consciously felt sadness and depression, alternating with resentment, and often threatened to stop treatment. An interesting aspect of this case was that the therapist had two supervisors, in succession, and a similar parallel process appeared with both supervisors. In both supervisions, the therapist had little material to present about this silent patient who wasn't "doing it right" and who was having extreme difficulty in associating. Feelings of frustration and annoyance were experienced by the therapist toward both supervisors, who also felt frustration and irritation. The therapist's countertransference toward the patient took the form of bewilderment about the silences, alternating with concern that the patient would stop treatment. The silences had different qualities, and many times there was a stony, resentful quality to the silence that generated considerable anxiety in the therapist. The therapist, also concerned about arriving at the supervisory sessions with no material, worried constantly that the patient would quit.

This transference–countertransference enactment between the patient and therapist appeared in the supervision as a parallel process. The therapist was unable to "do it right," that is, unable to provide the usual kind of material for the supervisory session, just as the patient was unable to "do it right," that is, unable to associate in the treatment. At this time, the patient consciously felt frustrated, hopeless, and misunderstood, and the therapist consciously felt bewildered and unsure of how to proceed. The therapist felt resentment toward the supervisors, just as the patient felt resentment toward the therapist. No conscious resentment was felt by the therapist toward the patient at the time, however. All resentment was displaced onto the supervisors, both of whom were aware of the enacted resentment in the supervision. This resentment was communicated by nonverbal means by the therapist, who, while aware of the resentment, was trying hard not to communicate it and hoped the supervisors would not notice it.

In this vignette, similar enactments and parallel processes were observed with both supervisors. Although alterations of technique were necessary, in the view of both the therapist and supervisors, the tension and frustration involved mirrored the tension and frustration that occurred in the psychotherapy, as the patient enacted the silent resistance. Both therapist and supervisors succeeded in containing the frustration, however, despite the fact that the intensity of the feelings was notable compared to the intensity of those found in the supervision of therapists of patients who do not rely heavily on enactments. Supervision should be expected to contain unpleasant affects when the patient relies heavily on such enactments or, in more verbal patients, when split-off or repressed affect begins to move into the transference.

Discussion

The patient, therapist, and supervisor function as a triadic system of non-verbal communication, with transference and countertransference enactments and parallel processes. This kind of communication was called the reflection process by Searles (1955) because the relationship between the patient and therapist was often reflected in the relationship between the therapist and supervisor. He thought that the reflection process comprised only a small proportion of the events that transpire in supervision, however, and he distinguished the reflection process from a classical countertransference, that is, a countertransference caused by unconscious conflict in the supervisor.

From today's vantage point, however, the therapy and supervision can be seen to be comprised of nonverbal communications that operate constantly and, at times, get the attention of the therapist or supervisor. Sometimes the patient notices the enactments first by becoming aware of his or her attempts to manipulate the therapist. Whatever is done by the supervisee can be used in the supervision to illustrate the conflicts of the patient. In addition, the supervisee as well as the supervisor will have a classical countertransference in the narrow sense of unresolved conflicts. These classical countertransferences will be embedded in the enactments and are indistinguishable from them. The counter-transferences provide the metaphor and affect that the therapist and supervisor need to understand and to translate the communication.

At times, the supervisor may think that conflicts of the therapist need further analysis. Although the supervisor may be correct, he or she may not always find it useful to advise the supervisee to take it to his or her treatment. Often these unresolved conflicts are not yet conscious enough to be workable, so that such advice only will promote intellectual compliance. What works better is to engage the supervisee in understanding how the patient feels and what the patient is enacting. Then the analyst or therapist can become creative in thinking about what interventions might work. He or she will begin to move away from the idea of a "mistake," which can be accompanied by unproductive shame or guilt. If the therapist or analyst is encouraged to consider the unexpected enactment as something interesting, he or she will become ready to work on the counter-transference aspects that relate to his or her own conflicts.

Can enactments be avoided? No. A skillful practitioner's attempt to analyze them and resist participating in the enactment can be seen in Etchegoyen's (1991) comments on a patient's silence. He stated that when a patient is suddenly quiet, the analyst has two alternatives, which are both mistaken. The first is to speak, in order to avoid the silence. Here, the words operate suggestively as a corrective emotional experience, and the coping with the silence and the understanding of the need for silence are delayed. The second alternative is to remain silent in the hope that the patient will overcome the silence and the frustration. This position, however, is coercive, and the patient feels pushed to overcome the frustration. A third possibility is to interpret the patient's silence as a desire to see whether the analyst understands his or her conflict and will be able to say something that will be helpful or useful. This interpretation is directed toward the conflict and attempts to avoid participation in the enactment by the analyst.

An analyst tried this intervention with a patient who often used silence as an enactment. Although the patient found it interesting, the effect did not last long and the silences began again. The occasional use over time of this intervention was useful but, again, it affected the silences only for a short time. Patients who have characterological resistances that take the form of enactments will not respond quickly to any intervention. Such patients continue to communicate by enactment and rely heavily on modes of communication that are not verbal. Articles that report a particular intervention as successful may be confusing the effect of that intervention with the working through that has taken place in an inchoate way over time.

Despite the unlikelihood that any particular intervention will cause a patient to stop using a particular enactment, analysts and therapists need to keep trying new interventions with their patients who communicate by enactment and who use it unconsciously but automatically as their resistance of choice. The effort itself is useful in helping the patients keep a sense of perspective, so that the patients become better able to remember that their therapists or analysts care about them, are on their side, and are working hard to be useful.

The effort also works against the development of a psychotic transference, a risk in the work with the kinds of patients who rely heavily on enactments. They are more vulnerable to being overwhelmed by their emotions to the point of losing their sense of perspective. Increased activity on the part of the therapist can distract them from believing their feelings too much. The analyst or therapist at times even may need to remind them that the analyst's activity indicates dedication to the work and is evidence of the analyst/therapist's effort and good will.

Summary

The enactments presented here illustrate ways of communication that are not verbal. The vignettes have shown how enactments can lead to increased insight for the patient, analyst or therapist, and supervisor. Enactments are expectable in psychoanalytic work. They provide useful information as they repeat earlier experiences and communicate affect from those experiences in a nonverbal way. Often the patient begins the enactments in the developing transference, and the nonverbal communications put pressure on the analyst or therapist to enact a role in the countertransference. Usually, the therapist discovers the enactment before the patient, but not always. In either case, however, the discovery of the enactment offers a unique opportunity to learn for both participants in the treatment dyad. Although the emphasis is on the patient's learning, the therapist continues to learn and at times can even uncover memories relating to his or her own history, as in the example of the therapist who identified with the patient's feeling of bodily fragmentation and fears of separation.

When a supervisor is added, the system becomes triadic. Parallel processes occur routinely in all supervision as the nonverbal communications among patient, analyst or therapist, and supervisor. As a general rule, the more enactments there are in the psychotherapy, the more enactments there will be in the supervision. Enactments may be initiated by any of the three participants, but most are begun by the patient as part of the unfolding therapeutic process. When the affect of the patient is deeply repressed, however, the therapist communicates in an unconscious nonverbal way in the supervision. The supervisor then is likely to notice it. Although the supervisor is least likely to begin an enactment, he or she may do so occasionally when the patient's material is chaotic or is presented in a chaotic way by the therapist. The enactments that appear in the parallel process are more likely to be noticed by the participants during those times in the therapy when the patient's transference is negative, when the patient is unable to describe his or her experience in words and relies heavily on actions, and when the patient is beginning to derepress split-off affects rather than doing the working through that comes later.

REFERENCES

Chused, J. F., and Raphling, D. L. (1992). The analyst's mistakes. *Journal of the American Psychoanalytic Association* 40:89–116.
Ekstein, R., and Wallerstein, R. S. (1958). *The Teaching and Learning of Psychotherapy*. New York: Basic Books.
Etchegoyen, R. H. (1991). *The Fundamentals of Psychoanalytic Technique*. London/New York: Karnac.
Fleming, J., and Benedek, T. F. (1966). *Psychoanalytic Supervision: A Method of Clinical Teaching*. New York: Grune & Stratton.
Gediman, H. K., and Wolkenfeld, F. (1980). The parallelism phenomenon in psychoanalysis and supervision: its reconsideration as a triadic system. *Psychoanalytic Quarterly* 49:234–255.
Searles, H. (1955). The informational value of the supervisor's emotional experiences. In *Collected Papers on Schizophrenia and Related Subjects*, pp. 157–176. New York: International Universities Press, 1965.
Smith, H. F. (1995). Analytic listening and the experience of surprise. *International Journal of Psycho-Analysis* 76:67–78.

13

The Fixity of Action
in Character Enactments:
Finding a Developmental Regression

NANCY R. GOODMAN

Introduction

Action is a central feature of the enactment process through which analysands bring their psychic realities to sessions. Enactments occurring in psychoanalysis are unconsciously motivated to bring to life scenes and role assignments between analyst and analysand that relate to fantasy and/or recreation of elements of childhood experience (see Chapters 3, 6, 10 this volume). Analysands bring their inner life to analysis with verbalizations of fantasies, wishes, and fears as well as frequent orchestration of "scenes" with the analyst. Patients with character problems are particularly likely to use nonverbal behavior sequences to enact features of their character organizations. In 1914 Freud connected acting out and character as he conceptualized ideas about the repetition compulsion.

> We have learnt that the patient repeats instead of remembering and repeats under the conditions of resistance. We may now ask what it is that he in fact repeats or acts out. The answer is that he repeats everything that has already made its way from the sources of the repressed into his manifest personality—his inhibitions and unserviceable attitudes and his pathological character traits. [p. 151]

This chapter brings together thinking about character and action by defining a category of enactments to be referred to as character enactments. Character enactments refer to action patterns expressive of the character structure of certain individuals who repeatedly create problems in their love life and/or professional life (Abend 1983, Moore and Fine 1990, Reich 1933). Their action patterns impact on others and often appeal to others to respond in specific ways. Some analysands reveal segments of their psychic realities through continual enactments that are intimately related to style and tone of their character experienced as central to their identity. A quality of *fixity* marks the nonverbal action sequences of such character enactments. Patients cling to these defining features of who they are.

This chapter explores the hypothesis that a developmental regression accounts for the fixity of the place of action that has found its way into a rigid defensive system. Regression is listed as one of the major defenses in *The Ego and the Mechanisms of Defense* (A. Freud 1936). It involves the return to an earlier mode of functioning to defend against the intrapsychic conflict of the present, such as the oedipal conflict. Ego regression may appear only at certain times when one is under stress from specific intrapsychic demands and may "affect only the ego functions involved in the conflict" (Moore and Fine 1990, p. 164). The developmental regression related to character enactments is made up of representations of action patterns involved with separation-individuation issues. The regression is not in form, that is, to be a toddler again; the regression is in function, that is, to rely on reworked ego representation of action equivalents now being used to defend against anxiety. In particular rapprochement-phase adaptations (occuring between about 15 and 22 months of age) involve motility and the beginnings of identity (Mahler 1972) and are represented in action schemata useful for regulation of anxiety. These schemata are now intertwined with an array of unconscious fantasies and intrapsychic conflict. The developmental regression is now being used defensively to ensure the holding back of knowledge about, and ultimate relinquishment of, infantile resolutions of frightening preoedipal and oedipal dilemmas.

Although the character enactments are utilized in the defenses, they also reveal compromise formations, which are present in the traits, styles, mannerisms, and so forth of the enactor. This chapter describes character enactments and resultant transference–countertransference configurations that hold the key for opening the way to understanding these enactments. As the analytic dyad works with character enactments, an alienation of purpose takes place. Analyst and analysand appear to be in an endless struggle over whether the manifestations of character in the sessions are available to analytic impact. Attending to the separation of analyst and analysand that is being enacted brings into view the regressive use of the developmental schemata and its moment-to-moment intrapsychic functioning.

Character Enactments

Character enactments consist of the continual playing out of repetitive patterns that are felt to be compulsive, out of conscious control, and very much a part of the way a person sees himself or herself. Both in and out of treatment, action is the modality for presenting sets of unconscious conflictual fantasies. There is something in the style of the person or something about the way he or she interacts that gets the person in the same type of trouble over and over again. In analysis the pattern, which may be omnipresent in significant object relations, appears in the transference through creation and repetition of particular interactions (Baudry 1983).

Core compromise formation fantasies are brought into treatment via style of behaving and interacting. Character enactments are presented through the manner in which a dream, wish, or fantasy is told and worked with rather than through the latent content of the material. The repetition of ways of pulling the analyst into interactions of communication and behavior provides the information base for character enactments. Patterns are seen over and over again and ultimately, after much else has been understood, take center stage. The analyst articulates the pain involved in these repetitions while the patient claims his or her helplessness and inability to behave in any other way. A knot exists in the fabric of character that invites recognition yet refuses to be unraveled.

Character enactments strongly resist psychoanalytic interventions because of the place of action in their revelation and because of the gratification and familiarity involved in the acting out. The action sequences include brief fulfillments of both forbidden wishes and feared punishments for such pleasure and present as set compromise formations. The action of continual re-creations both reveals and obfuscates the intrapsychic representations of conflict. The person has found a way to remember through repeating while simultaneously forgetting through action (Freud 1914). Full comprehension (i.e., with affect, vivid imagery, and conviction) is avoided and is replaced by a numbing of affects and a loss of the ego's capacity to observe. Knowing, which would arouse intense anxiety, is eluded by doing. The enactor has compromised memory.

Lifting the unconscious elements of these fantasies to consciousness is extremely difficult precisely because the action is being used as a powerful anesthetic to put the observing ego to sleep. In turn, the spot of ego blindness maintains the fixity of the enactments. One might wonder if the ego paralysis to fully recognize and acknowledge the pain of enactments is a modern-day version of the hysterical symptom, which by definition is spoken of by the sufferer with "la belle indifference" (Breuer and Freud 1893–1895, Freud 1905). Like hysterical symptoms, the enactments contain warded off and displaced conflicts. Until they are in working position for analysis, character enactments provide a protective shield preventing mutative analytic penetration of powerful core unconscious beliefs.

Clinical Vignette 1

Mr. E. is a 32-year-old man in his second year of analysis. He is constantly concerned with the possibility of failing at work and in relationships and for good reasons. He enacts conflicts over wishes for success by producing painful failures in business and in his intimate relationships. The display of inadequacies gets him in trouble with bosses and women and arouses intense shame and guilt. In analytic sessions, enactments of this repetitive pattern take the following form. Mr. E. tells a part of a dream and goes on to lament how he cannot remember the whole dream and will likely fail, arouse my pity, and leave us both feeling inadequate. He hopes I will understand his helplessness, feel how he needs me, and keep him as my incurable patient as long as possible—maybe forever. Mr. E. is also involved with doing and undoing in regard to the way he manages, or mismanages, his finances. He makes and loses money over and over again, recreating situations of impending disaster. His analysis is often at risk due to lack of monetary resources and piling up of debts elsewhere. The wish for pleasure at demonstrating a capacity to remember a dream, to earn and keep an income, and to enjoy a sense of accomplishment in his analysis is too fraught with danger.

Clinical Vignette 2

Ms. M. is a 30-year-old attractive woman in her fourth year of analysis who is now quite aware of a particular pattern in her life that has come to light in the analytic work. Ms. M. has begun a myriad of romantic involvements with a sense of excitement, pleasure, and hope that this person will be the one. Each new man is unable to arouse and sustain her love and passion. In a fairly short time, the relationship becomes agonizing and full of tormenting ambivalence. The object of involvement is continually on the brink of being so thoroughly devalued that the only choice is to end the relationship. Her professional commitments fare somewhat better but also are experienced over time as more and more drab and potentially leaveable. Over the first two years of her analysis, her activity in sessions produced equivalents of the hope and let-down experience in almost every analytic session. When I articulated a yearned-for analytic offering that she hoped would help, she often locked on to what my offering was not. By rejecting what was presented, Ms. M. returned continually to feeling lonely, helplessly enraged, and ashamed about not having the right fit with anyone, including her analyst.

Clinical Vignette 3

Mr. B. is a 42-year-old single male in his fourth year of analysis. Over time his enactments of a variety of "almost overexciting" dramas in and out of the analytic consulting room have generally lessened. He has managed to be in a profession that produces pressure to meet deadlines and invariably squeaks through by pulling all-nighters. With three different long-term relationships with women, he has created such tension that each has left before deciding to get married. As these relations become more intimate, he begins dramatizing a pattern of moving between feelings and behaviors demonstrating adoration and seductiveness and feelings and behaviors indicating anger and devaluing. His hostility threatens to win the day and lose the relationship. In a present relationship his increasing consciousness about this pattern has helped to keep it in check, but he continues to delight in informing his analyst through word and deed that he cannot change his style. He wards off insight as if it were a death blow to his autonomy. He repeats to his analyst his understanding of her analytic offerings with excellent recall; but alas, he adds, "insight cannot change me." A sadomasochistic struggle is set in stone, is familiar, and can be depended on.

Discussion of Clinical Illustrations

All these patients demonstrate features of character enactments that are closely tied to a conscious sense of self and ward off analysis of a set of conflicts contained in the repetitious syndrome. These patterns function as a basic glue holding together compromise formations and giving structure to the patient's sense of identity. The repetitive patterns of the enactments of Mr. E., Ms. M., and Mr. B. illustrate the *fixity* of the action sequences involved in character enactments. Each feels compelled to bring about a theme of failure with numerous variations being played out. Their intrapsychic and interpersonal elements of enactments are derivatives of unconscious sexual and aggressive drives and resultant fears unfolding in the representation of a particular object relation image.

Interpersonally, character enactments are compelling and draw others, often unwittingly, into the drama. A person acting out impulse, affects, and denial is pulling for particular affects and interactions from the recipients of their behavior. Two roles must be present to complete the drama (Sandler, Chapter 3 this volume). These patients demand that their drama be performed in the analytic room as well. For extended periods of time the analyst is the only one clarifying the presence of and identifying the problems with these sometimes grand and sometimes minuscule events that the patient experiences as ego-syntonic. Mr. E., Ms. M., and Mr. B. create their stories with the analyst while simultaneously denying responsibility or control and demanding that these patterns be off analytic limits. Just by being there, the psychoanalyst becomes a part of the drama, not symbolically as in a fantasy or a dream, but in the actual interactive system of the analytic situation.

Character enactments bring the patient's psychic reality to light by commanding that a performance of a familiar scene take place between analyst and analysand. Indeed it is the realization that one has gotten "into the act" that allows the analyst to learn about the patient's instinctual motivational system. A variety of analytic work has addressed how enactments inform the analytic process by reflecting on something that the analyst has just done or said that was unexpected. Research on the working mind of the psychoanalyst has uncovered a continual feedback loop by which the analyst is surprised at aspects of the ongoing analytic work; this then alerts the analyst to emerging unconscious processes (Goodman et al. 1993). Renik (1993) refers to the irreducible subjectivity of the analyst, which responds to the analysand's communication through enactment and becomes knowledgeable about the enactment and its dynamics after the fact: "Everything I know about my work and that of my colleagues leads me to the conclusion that an analyst's awareness of his or her emotional responses as they arise in the course of an analysis *necessarily* follows translation of these responses into action—i.e., awareness of countertransference is always retrospective, preceded by countertransference enactment" (p. 556). The analyst is often informed about the intrapsychic demands of the analysand when reflecting on "mistakes" (Chused and Raphling 1992). Patients enact their character conflicts and the analyst's unconscious receives the information and shows it through action to the analyst, who can then reflect on it.

Transference/Countertransference Sequelae of Character Enactments

It is my experience that character enactments lead to particular tensions between analyst and analysand that help the analyst identify the driving forces spurring them on. Experience near descriptions of transference/countertransference phenomena that result from character enactments help bring these elements into focus.

As discussed previously, analytic work with character pathology often moves from identifying the pull on the analyst to assume a role after the analyst notices how he or she has taken the role. A feel of impasse often occurs around the repetitive enactments that express tightly held character compromises. Analysand and analyst become engaged in a struggle. It is precisely this creation of being at odds analytically that holds the code for understanding how to move on.

The three analysands described in this section considered the character enactments to be their signature or modus operandi. A powerful sense of identity belonged to the character enactments and proved to be quite resistant to change. For example, when enactments were identified by his analyst, Mr. E. flaunted his lack of responsibility and announced proudly, "Well, this is what I do, this is me." Affects accompanying recognition of his maladaptive but clearly felt "me" experience were a mixture of shame, sheepishness, and a kind of narcissistic pleasure at showing off. Ms. M. demonstrated a similar tendency in regard to repetitive disappointments in her love life and with her analyst. She spoke of the failure in intimate relationships with a mixture of sadness and arrogance. "This is what always happens. It is never right. Maybe I just have not met the right man (or right analyst)." Over and over she justified the view that others had proven themselves to be inadequate. Her determination to hold on to failure took shape in the analysis by the absolute belief that this was the stamp on her life and her analyst could not effectively touch the problems of her love life.

Mr. B. also had numerous ways of bringing what he thought to be his defining incurable characteristics to his analyst. He appeared as a blind man who could not see what his analyst could see. He did not notice the mud on his feet. He did not notice the wrong date on his check. He used detailed descriptions of the ways he humiliated and degraded his girlfriend to demonstrate how his analyst and her analytic interventions were impotent to help him. He was king of the mountain and felt most alive when struggling with his analyst.

These examples appear fueled by motivations to feel safe with a solid sense of identity rather than to experience a fragmented feeling from overwhelming affects. As the drama is played out, there is an alienation of purpose between analyst and analysand. The actions of the enactments push the analyst out of a major aspect of the analysand's life while inviting the analyst to participate in a sadomasochistic struggle for the contents held within the enactments. Unconscious aggression propels the patient's psyche to attempt to produce a rift by creating a distancing of purpose with the analyst. The analyst attempts to bring action into the analytic dialogue and to unravel the meaning wound up in the repetitions. The patient continues to act and to deny directorship of the story contained in the action. Disparity between the analyst's view and the patient's view holds potential to be the grand enactment in the form of a negative therapeutic reaction. The analyst's curiosity about the patient's action can be felt as a seduction. The analyst's determination to free the patient from compulsive behaviors may feel like anal assault. The analyst's unveiling of the ego-dystonic aspects of the patient's enactments may come to be felt as a threat of castration. Analysis of such fantasy derivatives becomes necessary to keep the patient from enacting the wish to create permanent separation due to fears of loss of autonomy. The patient seems to beg for analytic failure rather than to give up the sense of identity arising from the enactments. Perhaps the primary wish being represented in the action of these character enactments is the creation of this alienation—a state in which analysand and analyst are clearly separate.

The Hypothesis of a Developmental Regression

Attention to the passionate desire to distance from the analyst helped advance the hypothesis that a developmental regression is involved in the enactment process utilized by analysands with character problems. Specifically, unconscious psychic representations of action schemata involved with separation-individuation issues are being lived out in the action of the enactments. Until the wishes and fears that relate to their makeup become conscious, they will continue to be fixed psychic maneuvers. This hypothesis grows out of daily analytic life with patients, observations of the object relation components contained in character enactments, and patient revelations of genetic material related to regulation of closeness.

As the theme of regulating separateness was made more and more conscious, patients articulated sets of behavior images that could be considered making up a cognitive schema of the action of separating and returning. Psychic representations and fantasies about getting both very close and involved and about getting away from and uninvolved are part of the makeup of the character enactments. The action itself functions as a protection against wishes for merger with a totally gratifying love object and wishes and fears concerning active aggressive aims to separate and be autonomous. The regression to use of action patterns connected with regulation of separateness, and the narcissistic pleasure contained within them, functioned to remove the patients from both terrifying preoedipal and oedipal material.

Although these transference–countertransference formations are compelling and convincing in themselves, each patient also presented genetic material similar to what they produced in the sessions. Each spoke of pleasures received at thwarting a type of involvement with mother, father, and other caregivers, and now a type of involvement with me. All patients expressed a pure sense of joy at getting away from significant early objects through physical movement. Mr. E. reported frequently running from mother and making her call for him. He would often return to her for love when feeling ill or having been hurt while at play. Ms. M. went to her room, feigning deafness and dumbness with her mother who would then beg her to speak. Mr. B. defied parental demands with bouts of overactivity and inattentiveness often provoking father's rage. Each patient viewed at least one parent as both too removed at times and too seductive, overstimulating, and intrusive at other times.

These patients used the action involved in the developmental regression as a defense against their fantasies about the aggression needed to separate and proclaim an independent identity. Aggression in the service of autonomy brought up fantasies about annihilation of self or others. In their discussion of the toddler's rapprochement crisis, Mahler et al. (1975) state: "Throughout the whole course of separation-individuation, one of the most important developmental tasks of the evolving ego is that of coping with the aggressive drive in the face of the gradually increasing awareness of separateness" (p. 226). The fixed defense of enacting a stubbornness of separateness of purpose with the analyst is intimately involved with saving the patient from fears of destroying the object. Furthermore, proclaiming separateness and individuation also brings up the specter of experiencing and coming to terms with libidinal oedipal strivings. The separate person has drives and, with representations of autonomy, these drives are more available and stir up anxiety. Vicissitudes of aggression and libido throw patients back into action schema representatives woven into their character and expressed through their character enactments.

I want to clarify what I am saying by explaining what I am not saying. I am not saying that the patient is working out a developmental problem by practicing with the analyst. Action sequences related to separation-individuation issues have mental representations and equivalents in the psyche. As with other patterns of adaptation, these representations are held within the ego to be used in defensive organization and, like all bits of reality, can attract id and superego fantasy material (Arlow 1969). These action sequences, presented through character trait, are laden with derivatives from all phases of libidinal development. Some patients develop character problems and character enactments as ways to help structure autonomous functioning and to defend against states of overwhelming affect. Action and its psychic representations are effective ways to self-regulate, discharge frustration, and experience a separate identity. Clarifying the presence of a developmental phase as a core factor in the person's mental life offers the ability to see how it functions intrapsychically, much as it did historically, to create equilibrium.

How a Developmental Issue Comes to Function Intrapsychically

As so often happens in the development of psychoanalytic thinking, we move back and forth between clinical observations and theory building and invariably discover that research of one question brings us up against another. The uncovering of a developmental piece in the defensive system leads to a further question: How does a developmental issue from toddlerhood enter a primary role in intrapsychic functioning? Images of action sequences associated with processes of separating and individuating have attracted derivatives of instinctual wishes and fears from stages of preoedipal and oedipal development.

For example, the image of running toward and away from mother while regulating autonomy can be seen as a magnet attracting sexual and aggressive drive derivatives. It seems likely that the toddler navigating through the individuation process forms representations of this journey. In turn, these representations become intertwined with instinctual conflicts, thus claiming a place in the drive/defense system. Mr. E.'s image of turning away from his mother and returning to her with ills and hurts carries with it the activity of rapprochement and the activity of anal and phallic phases. Ms. M.'s continual attempts to engage people in a chase as she withholds love contains a desperate attempt to protect autonomy as well as a wish for seduction and conquest and a fear of reprisals for winning the oedipal victory. The movement of an action sequence contains wishes and fears and the defense against their comprehension.

In research on the separation-individuation process, Mahler (1972) repeatedly observes that during rapprochement: "Oral, anal, and early genital pressures and conflicts meet and accumulate at this important landmark in personality development" (p. 147). She also reports observations that the rapprochement subphase, particularly during rapprochement crisis, is a crossroads for anxieties about object loss, loss of love, and castration anxiety. We might say that rapprochement schemata and their portrayals in character have become libidinized and aggressivized as part of the psychic system of fantasies and representations of self and others. Character enactments thus play out intrapsychic conflict collected from preoedipal and oedipal dilemmas and are narcissistically valued as major ego adaptations.

The following vignette illustrates this intertwining of separation-individuation action schemata and derivatives of instinctual life.

Clinical Vignette 4

Mr. B. has an extensive history of producing distance from others by getting them annoyed with him over the way he does not live up to what he promises in love and at work. Before analysis he appeared to career between exciting seductions and terrible states of being let down when he disappointed the expectations of others. Over three years of analytic work dedicated to identification of the presence of these patterns in the analytic dialogue, he enacted less often with others and with his analyst, and with less intensity. The loosening of the character enactments has allowed fantasy derivatives to come more into view in the analytic sessions. Now in his fourth year of analysis, Mr. B. is more able to speak about and associate to images of action rather than to only enact action with his analyst. A recent session contains both action enactments and articulation of emerging affect and experiences of self.

Mr. B. describes his state of exhilaration at having rushed from errand to errand that resulted in arriving ten minutes late to the session. "I feel bad for being late, guilty too. I've done it again . . . no control, but I feel like I can accomplish anything. I command time. I have the idea that I can expand time to meet my needs. It is grandiose I know. But sometimes it works that way. If there are no red lights, I'll get here on time." He goes on to describe how his mind and body feel in the session. "I am so glad I am here, talking . . . like I am drawing you into the experience with me. This is important, even though I cut off our time. My thinking is so alert, formed, on target. I see clearly. My body feels all in one piece . . . sensitive and energetic. You could take the couch away and I'd still be here . . . sort of rigid and fixed. I know I'm the penis not letting you near. What if I never come down from this state. I'll just stay this way. But I always do come down and feel exhausted afterward."

This is a particularly clear description of a type of experience produced by the process of bringing forth character through the action of enacting. In this vignette, derivatives of fantasies related to oral, anal, and phallic phases abound with transference implications. The action of Mr. B.'s movements away from the analytic object and the return to the analytic object (both the person of his analyst and analytic reflection) carry his intrapsychic story. For all patients who bring character enactments to analysis, the interpersonal sequences produced have intrapsychic function.

Summary

Character enactments involve repetitive patterns of action sequences related to the style of a person, which appear nonverbally and impact others to often respond to role demands. The patient clings to this nodule of psychic life and wants to use it as a central identifying mark. The character signature cannot be given up until both the wish to separate and to be autonomous no longer threaten the existence of the needed object and until the character enactments no longer function as defenses against fearful aggressive and libidinal drives. There is a fixity to the pattern that can appear to defy analytic intervention until the patterns enter transference/countertransference interactions that are palpable to both members of the analytic pair and thus receptive to analytic interventions. For patients who demonstrate this type of fixity of enacting, the action of enactments is ubiquitous and highly out of consciousness.

Indeed, as with hysterical symptoms described by Freud, there is a paralysis, now in the ego, blocking consideration of these actions as ego-dystonic and preventing reflection.

The hypothesis is put forth that the fixity of character enactments relates to the defensive use, in the form of regression, of developmental action schemata related to separation-individuation processes. The regression is used psychically to defend against unraveling of aggression and libido, which are considered too dangerous. In particular, navigation through the rapprochement phase has left its mark on the sense of self involved in character enactments. The motility useful for negotiating movement away from and back to love objects is used in enactments to maintain equilibrium of identity and equilibrium between id and superego pressures. Equivalents of these action schema appear in character and in the action of character enactments that now defend against breakthrough of feared affects and strivings.

It is further speculated that the developmental schema has been able to attain this role of last defense because it carries derivatives of preoedipal and oedipal issues; that is, it has been imbued with component instincts related to each erotogenic zone. In the analytic dyad, the patient acts to create an impasse with the analyst over the analyzability of the enactments. Clarifying the action of creating and maintaining separateness and individuation in the enactments allows the analyst and analysand to understand the importance of this action for the patient, the pain involved in giving it up, and the fears of moving on to a truly greater experience of autonomy and individuation. Bringing these representations into the analytic sessions and into consciousness allows a loosening of the character knot and the further emergence and working through of the affects and fantasies that were locked into the action.

REFERENCES

Abend, S. M. (1983). Theory of character. *Journal of the American Psychoanalytic Association* 31:211–224.
Arlow, J. (1969). Fantasy, memory, and reality testing. *Psychoanalytic Quarterly* 38:28–51.
Baudry, F. (1983). The evolution of the concept of character in Freud's writings. *Journal of the American Psychoanalytic Association* 31:3–32.
Breuer, J., and Freud, S. (1893–1895). Studies on hysteria. *Standard Edition* 2:1–306.
Chused, J. F., and Raphling, D. L. (1992). The analyst's mistakes. *Journal of the American Psychoanalytic Association* 40:89–116.
Freud, A. (1936). *The Ego and the Mechanisms of Defense.* New York: International Universities Press.
Freud, S. (1905). Fragment of an analysis of a case of hysteria. *Standard Edition* 7:1–122.
—— (1914). Remembering, repeating, and working-through. *Standard Edition* 12:145–156.
Goodman, N. R., Basseches, H., Ellman, P., et al. (1993). *In the mind of the psychoanalyst: capturing the moment before speaking.* The 38th Congress of the IPA, Amsterdam.

Mahler, M. S. (1972). Rapprochement subphase of the separation-individuation process. In *The Selected Papers of Margaret S. Mahler*, vol. 2. New York: Jason Aronson.

Mahler, M. S., Pine, F., and Bergman, A. (1975). *The Psychological Birth of the Human Infant.* New York: Basic Books.

Moore, B. E., and Fine, B. D., eds. (1990). *Psychoanalytic Terms and Concepts.* New Haven, CT and London: American Psychoanalytic Association and Yale University Press.

Reich, W. (1933). *Character Analysis.* New York: Orgone, 1949.

Renik, O. (1993). Analytic interaction: conceptualizing technique in light of the analyst's irreducible subjectivity. *Psychoanalytic Quarterly* 62:553–571.

14

Enactment, Transference, and Analytic Trust

STEVEN J. ELLMAN

The term *enactment* follows a long psychoanalytic tradition in being an important concept with no agreed upon definition. This may present an even greater confusion today than in the past, because the hegemony of the Freudian-classical position has ended in the United States. Thus the term enactment means different things within and across different theoretical positions. For one theoretical position enactment may be considered a transference–countertransference difficulty, whereas another orientation may view enactments as desired interventions. Despite the difficulties of providing a "universal" definition, I will attempt this task. One might conceive of my attempts as in part an answer to Paula Ellman's assertion (Chapter 11 this volume) that the concept of enactment has not added to analytic understanding or to the clarity of analytic conceptualizations.

Initial Assumptions

I will distinguish between analyst-induced enactments and patient (analysand)-induced enactments. In making this distinction I am positing that at times it is possible to understand the origins of an enactment and to place it mainly within one of the participants of the analysis. However, in this view an enactment implies an interaction, and both parties are affected to some extent by any (or at least most) enactments. At times it will not be possible to specify whether an enactment is induced by either the analyst or analysand. Following McLaughlin (Chapter 6 this volume), this type of enactment will be labeled as a mutual enactment. In this type of enactment both patient and analyst see the nature of the difficulty residing in the other, and this perception continues for some time.

Preliminary Definitions

Before stating my views, I will discuss a definition offered by Chused (Chapter 7 this volume) in which we can see some of the difficulties in defining the concept. She maintains that "enactments are symbolic interactions between analyst and patient that have unconscious meaning to both" (p. 93). This definition, while interesting, could apply to almost all, and perhaps all, interactions in analysis. For example, transference manifestations are usually symbolic interactions that by definition have unconscious meaning to the patient and usually, if not always, stimulate the unconscious of the analyst. Does the existence of transference imply that an enactment has or will take place? This is a central question, for this assertion (Renik, Chapter 8 this volume) would demand a new theory of transference and enactments. It would imply that all interactions should be understood as enactments. This, however, is not Chused's view for she states:

> In the best of all possible worlds, an analyst is sensitive to the patient's transference, as expressed in either words or action, but does not act. Sympathetic with a patient's pitiful state, the analyst does not nurture; temporarily aroused by a patient's seductive attacks, the analyst does not counterattack. An analyst contains his impulses, examines them, and uses the information gained to enrich the interpretive work. This best of all possible worlds is the ideal, something we strive for, but often fail to achieve. . . . As Sandler (Chapter 3 this volume) notes, the analyst will "tend to comply with the role demanded of him, [but] may only become aware of it through observing his own behavior, responses, and attitudes, *after these have been carried over into action*" (p. 35). . . . The potential for enactments is omnipresent throughout an analysis. As soon as there are transference distortions of the analyst and the process, any exchange within the relationship may lead to an enactment. A patient who "imagines" that the analyst is critical or seductive has some distance from his experience, which permits the analyst to have distance from the experience. There is no such distance during an enactment. During an enactment, the patient has a conviction about the accuracy of his or her perceptions *and* behaves so as to induce behavior in the analyst that supports this conviction. Even if the analyst is neither angry nor critical, a patient's accusations can still induce guilt, defense, and retaliative anger. This is one aspect of the evocative power of enactments. [pp. 93–95 this volume]

The analyst in this formulation is always susceptible for:

> Every time a person has a wish within an object relationship—in this case, the therapist's wish to be of help to his patient—he exposes himself to the

possibility that the interaction will evoke an earlier object relationship, that is, will become laden with transference. To want anything from patients, to want to cure, to help, even to be listened to or understood accurately, is to be vulnerable to the experience of one's own transference and thus be susceptible to an enactment. [p. 95 this volume]

If we look at Chused's commentary, we can say that although it may be ideal not to respond to transference, it hardly seems possible for the analyst not to respond with transference reactions of his or her own (countertransference). To not respond would require that the analyst be in a position of wishing nothing for himself within the analytic relationship. This condition does not seem possible to attain. Even if the analyst wishes only to be helpful, the fact that the analyst wishes anything raises the possibility of an enactment. Further, every patient will at some point in the analysis "believe their perceptions" and will for some time be unable to self-reflect. Chused maintains that frequently (most often) this is compelling to the analyst. Enactments then are inevitable.

In examining Chused's commentary and definitions about enactment we might ask what is present in her ideas that was not contained in Freud's ideas about actions of the patient (acting in, acting out). We might similarly ask if she has included anything new about the dangers of an analyst losing control in the analytic situation. A patient who loses the ability to self-reflect is more likely to do what Freud called acting out and what most analysts following Freud called acting in (Ellman 1991). An analyst who is unable to control his responses to a patient's reactions would be considered to be in the midst of a countertransference reaction. These concepts were present certainly in the 1950s if not before. What then is new in Chused's description? The answer to this is an idea that by 1991 was at least implicitly accepted; the analyst is continuously susceptible to being affected by the patient's reactions and affected to the extent of putting these feelings into action within the analysis. There is continuous and bidirectional interaction taking place between patient and analyst. Thus in the statements quoted from Chused we can say that what she adds to the discussion of analytic process is the acceptance of the continuous bidirectional nature of interactions between analyst and analysand. This assumption is implicitly or explicitly accepted by most of the writers in this volume from Sandler (Chapter 3) and Boesky (Chapter 4) to Jacobs, McLaughlin, and Renik (Chapters 5, 6, and 8). The question that remains is the extent to which one can differentiate the contributions of analyst and analysand.

Thus when we talk about patient-centered enactments we certainly do not mean this in absolute terms. If we were to be more careful in our statements we should say that most analysts would respond to the type of enactment that certain patients display. The extent of the analyst's response would also, in this more precise world, have to be put in relativistic terms. Because at present we have no empirical basis for this type of statistically based terminology, I will simply state that there are some patients who are more likely to evoke responses from analysts than other patients. In a similar manner I would state that there are some analysts who are more likely to evoke responses from patients leading to analyst-centered enactments.

To restate, a patient-induced enactment would be an activity without self-reflection that is likely to induce reactions in the analyst. Thus the patient would see his or her action(s) or reactions as *only* reflecting a reality in the analytic situation and would be unable to understand that action as part of their psychic reality. In Freedman's (1994) terms, the patient at that point in time would be unable to see his or her behavior as having symbolic meaning. An analyst-induced enactment is an activity that is performed without self-reflection and is likely to induce reactions in the analysand. Thus the analyst would *only* be able to see his actions in terms of a present reality in the treatment situation. At this point in time the analyst's ability to understand the symbolic value of his own behavior is inoperative or at least impaired. Both definitions are put forward without commenting on the therapeutic efficacy of enactments. That is, it may be possible that enactments under some conditions are beneficial for an analysis, detrimental to an analysis, and/or crucial for the success of an analysis. Mutual enactments occur during times when the analysis is stalemated, and both patient and analyst see the other as the cause of the stalemate. Here it is harder to determine that a mutual enactment is beneficial to an analysis, but it certainly may be that some patients need to be able to withstand a mutual enactment before they can trust the analytic process. (In my experience this is particularly true of patients who have undergone early trauma.)

Although these definitions seem easy to put forth, in reality all analysts know that an ongoing treatment involves a series of interactions and that unraveling these interactions is not an easy task. Despite this considerable complication (determining where an enactment starts), it still seems possible to make reasonable statements about whether an enactment is patient- or analyst-induced or a mutual enactment. It is important to note that although I believe there are virtually always interactions taking place in an analysis, the analysand's conflicts are still accorded an existential reality not accepted by some extreme intersubjective versions of analysis, which seem to imply that it is not possible to sort out the difference between analyst- and patient-induced enactments.

Given these definitions of enactment, what are the conditions that lead to enactments on the part of either patient or analyst? A related question is, if enactments are so common why did it remain for contemporary analysts to begin to discuss the topic, particularly analyst-induced enactments? The answers to these questions are the topics of the rest of this chapter.

Analytic Trust

I would like to offer a particular view of enactments and how I have come to understand this concept. The rationale that I present is one based on the concept of analytic trust that I have introduced in other publications (Ellman 1991, 1997a). It is my view that patient-induced enactments occur when analytic trust either has been disrupted or has not yet been firmly established. Although I have first introduced the concept of analytic trust as a concept describing an accomplishment of the patient's, it is now my view that analytic trust is bidirectional. Thus analytic trust has to occur within both analyst and analysand to have a successful analysis.

The first task in analysis is to help the patient begin to create a new reality in the therapeutic situation (Ellman 1991, 1997a,b). This new reality is one where the patient is understood in a different way than has occurred in the past. A necessary condition for this understanding is that the patient must penetrate the analyst's psychological world, and the analyst must allow this penetration to be gradually perceptible to the patient. This process is at the heart of analytic trust. Analytic trust then can be defined as the patient's realistic view of the analyst understanding his or her subjective world. This understanding is communicated not only in intellectual terms but also by the analyst feeling the intensity of the patient's responses and being able to communicate this to the patient. In this view the interpenetration is a necessary and usually sufficient condition of the patient feeling held. This experience of holding and a subsequent experience of containment are necessary concomitants of trust being built in the analytic situation. Analytic trust is not synonymous with the concept of therapeutic alliance. Therapeutic alliance refers to the patient being allied to the analyst's way of proceeding in the analytic situation. The patient complies with analytic instructions and, as Brenner (1976, 1982) has stated, this compliance is related to the patient's transference state. Analytic trust may be established whether or not the patient is willing to comply with the analyst's instructions. It involves a penetration of subjective states and a communication of this interpenetration. This trust is conceived as allowing the analyst to help the patient understand characterological transference responses. In other terms, it moves transference reactions into the realm of interpretable or understandable transference manifestations. Undoubtedly, analysts can communicate this understanding in different ways and through different theoretical lenses. In what follows I offer one pathway to the establishment of analytic trust.

A patient enters a treatment and complains of not being able to utilize her mind. As soon as she feels she understands something it changes.
She is anxious if the weather changes or if her employer seems to be looking at her in a different way (positive or negative). This woman has just
left a treatment where her analyst terminated the treatment. This occurred
after she had left various phone messages over a period of months saying
that she felt there was something wrong with the treatment. In a phone
message he finally agreed with her and suggested that she see another
therapist who could also provide her with help through medication. After
weeks of reflecting her bewilderment about these changes, including the
change in her analyst (who was initially confident of being able to help
her), we begin to understand that she wants me to remain the same whatever she may say to me or do in our sessions. She wants to be able to
change and have me remain the same. The next two years are spent in
my remaining relatively consistent and stable while she attempts in various ways to provoke me and destroy my stability. If I attempt to interpret
her provocations, she becomes irate and tells me in one form or another
that she can't stand me in this position (an interpretative position). Gradually she includes me in the thoughts that she shares with me and at first
relates that I hate people and that I am an analyst because I can secretly
be contemptuous of her difficulties. It is only when she can consider and
feel that there may be more to me than the hatred she has put in me, that
her transference has reached an interpretable form. Before that I can only
reflect her pain at having to "bare her soul" to someone who secretly is
contemptuous of her plight.

In this example there had to be sufficient holding and then containment
before her transference manifestations were in interpretable form. During the
period of stability I was limited to reflecting her frightening, horrifying states.
During the period of containment (of course, these periods are largely overlapping) I could reflect to her how dangerous it must be for her to be in a situation where she was in a constant position of feeling ridiculed and humiliated.
I was in a self-object position until she began gradually to tolerate the other
becoming another and she could allow complicated[1] objects into her repre-
sentational world. If one conceives of transference as either a projection or a
displacement into transitional space, then in the above example transitional
space had to be created before this projection could take place. Alternatively,
when the analysand projects into the analyst, transference is no longer seen

---

[1]By complicated I mean a representation that can provide more than one valence during a given
period of time. Thus she could tolerate ambivalent reactions to me and gradually others in her
life.

as a part illusory phenomenon but rather as a real occurrence. It is not as if the analyst hates people but rather that the analyst in fact hates people. In this situation interpretations are seen as defensive actions by the analyst rather than as potentially helpful interventions. Consistent interpretative efforts would lead to rounds of mutual enactments where patient and analyst would see the other as either unanalyzable or unable to helpfully analyze.

Countertransference and Analytic Trust

What are the typical difficulties that are faced during this initial phase of treatment? For the analysand I have tried to describe the process of analytic trust and the interpenetration that is necessary for the establishment of this initial phase of analytic trust. What are the difficulties that the analyst faces during this phase of treatment? One could describe this process in a number of ways. Surely it is a substantial task to try to feel another's subjective states and to gradually attempt to reflect, synthesize, and contain another's feelings in a manner that demonstrates that interpenetration has occurred. The difficulties in these tasks that I will focus on are issues of narcissistic equilibrium. The use of this term is not meant to imply that the analyst is narcissistic but rather that issues of self-continuity, self-esteem, and self-expression are continuously present in the analytic situation for the analyst as well as the analysand. Thus it was not surprising that when I presented a version of this approach, an analyst who was attempting to be conciliatory commented that some of us are more active and some of us wait and are willing to do nothing for a period of time. His impression of my approach in building analytic trust was that the analyst did nothing. In a similar vein (although from a different perspective), a Kleinian analyst commented that I was *only* concentrating on conscious phenomena. My view is that the analyst is quite active in listening and in offering the type of interventions that allow patients to be able to consistently tolerate, disclose, and feel their subjective states. Moreover my version of containment includes the analyst putting feelings back into the patient that the patient usually wants to get rid of as quickly as possible. Thus containment, synthesis, and reflection are active processes that allow the patient to utilize the analyst while beginning to explore the subjective world. The Kleinian analyst saw this as doing nothing. I suspect this is his view because there was little new that the analyst was adding to the patient's cognitive understanding of himself, and there was no particular area the analyst was helping the patient traverse. It is not that the analyst is not concerned with unconscious fantasy, but rather it is not the prime focus until the patient can tolerate another.

During the initial phase of analytic trust the analyst allows himself to be utilized by the analysand. For some analysts this may be a difficult state for they are in effect excluding aspects of themselves as analysts. It may be that analysts will feel they are not doing anything or are not really doing analytic work during this phase of treatment. Thus an analyst might offer an interpretation that the patient is not able to use or might confront the patient about aspects of his or her functioning in a way that the patient does not see as useful. This is the type of analyst-induced enactment that occurs when analysts feel some narcissistic disequilibrium, when they experience not being included in the analysis as full partners or as real analysts.

There are, of course, some analysts who achieve analytic trust and begin to interpret right from the beginning of a treatment. From my theoretical perspective there are two possible ways of understanding this different approach. The first is an oft-repeated statement of treating certain types of nonclassical patients; when asked what they remembered about interpretations, the patient mentions the rhythm or the timber of the analyst's voice or some other aspect of the physical characteristics of the analyst's movements. These patients often immediately rid themselves of the content of the interpretation and hear only a soothing voice or an authoritative stance on the part of the analyst that the patient feels is comforting and there for her or his benefit. In short, it is not the content of the interpretation but rather some other characteristic of the analyst that leads to analytic trust.

The second way in which patients can process interpretations early in the analysis is if in the interpretations the analyst demonstrates that he is able both to feel the patient's subjective world and to include the adaptive perspective (Rapaport and Gill 1959). In other terms, the analyst is able to show why, from the patient's point of view, the way the patient saw or sees the world felt as if that was the only alternative possible if, for example, the patient was to maintain any continuity of being or self-organization. Despite these caveats about the development of analytic trust, I would still say that for most clinicians interpretive efforts early in the treatment can either serve to disrupt a patient or put the patient into a position of having to comply with the analyst's treatment method and perspectives.

Analytic Trust and Transference Cycles

Various authors (Ellman 1991, Freedman 1994, O'Shaugnessy 1981) have conceived of an analytic treatment as containing at least several cycles. Each cycle embodies a dominant transference–countertransference theme that, when adequately understood and worked through, begins the advent of the next cycle. It is the transition between cycles where disruptions in the analytic process frequently occur. This is particularly the case with patients who use defenses such as splitting or projective identification and who early on in the treatment are incapable of self-observation with regard to transference phenomena. For this type of non-symbolizing patient (Freedman 1994, Steingart

1995), what the analyst perceives as transference is seen by the patient mainly in realistic terms.

Usually the main transition that a patient goes through occurs at the start of treatment or the first cycle in the treatment process. During the beginning phase of the treatment, analytic trust has to be established before there is a space for interpretation to serve a therapeutic function. This is particularly the case with transference interpretations. Premature interpretations often induce enactments and are at least one form of analyst-centered enactments. During the start of each new transference cycle, analytic trust to some extent has to be reestablished. Frequently the analyst is bewilded by this because the analyst has felt that the treatment has already achieved a working rhythm only to be disrupted by issues that seemingly had been dispensed with earlier on in the analysis. Aspects of analytic trust run through a treatment even to termination. During termination the analysand begins to fully trust the results of the treatment, and the analyst begins to more fully trust the analysand to take control of the analytic process.

Transference and Analytic Trust

After the opening phase of treatment the analysand shows signs that he or she believes (and has demonstrable reason to believe) that the analyst understands the subjective states that have arisen at the beginning of the treatment. The patient will then demonstrate that he or she can tolerate perspectives that are separate from their former subjective reactions.

During the initial phase of analytic trust the analyst has concentrated on issues surrounding the synthesis of experience (self-cohesion), issues that typically involve embarrassment and shame. The analyst is trying to feel the intensity of the person's feelings and to reflect back how they are at times disrupting the person's sense of self, how at times patients need to expel these feelings from their experience of themselves. In one way or another we are attempting to titrate the intensity of the person's feelings so that the experience of treatment is not overly aversive. Some patients may need in this vein to regulate the temperature of the room or the lighting, and our focus in this aspect of the treatment is to see how the boundaries of the treatment situation can accommodate the way the person experiences this new analytic world. Clearly I am dwelling on this in terms of how some narcissistic and borderline patients experience the analytic situation, but I would say that while some patients may go through this phase of the treatment more quickly, it is an inevitable part of all treatments.

When patients begin to include me in their object world, it is then that the possibility opens up to include aspects of the other within what may be the final part of the initial phase of analytic trust.

A hypochondriacal patient who has been exclusively focused on her body and the sensations attendant to certain experiences begins to recognize aspects of my waiting room or reading material, or a tie, and so forth. Along with that development, she is able to talk about the impact she has on others and not only about the toxins that her family and colleagues are pouring into her literally and symbolically. When this interplay begins (between self-experience and some consideration of the other), the analyst, it seems to me, naturally sits further back in his chair and elements of the unconscious fantasy begin to drift into the analyst's consciousness and are retained.

When the patient starts to include other perspectives, then I begin to think that transference elements now begin to be included into the person's self–object world. That is, the question of how pleasurable experiences have turned to unpleasant experiences becomes a leading focus of the transference. With narcissistic patients, there are usually two or three transference cycles before one is able to put transference experience into their experience of self and object relationships. The assumption is that transference is always present and is always coloring the intensity of affective experiences, even though it is not present in interpretable form. Transference manifestations during the first cycles are helping determine how quickly patients have to move the affect out of their psychological world. Before transference manifestations are interpretable, the analyst first has to show how self-experiences are disrupted by the intensity of affect and how the other is often experienced as an impingement. Transference is interpretable when the other is viewed as another[2] and is tolerated as a separate entity with at least some needs and predilections that are different than those of the analysand.

The question of analytic trust takes on a new dimension when interpretative efforts begin. The patient is now asked to see things from a different perspective, and the analyst has now presented his or her perspective in a way that typically involves a narcissistic investment. Although it is relatively easy to state the principle of analytic trust and give examples of how the analyst ought to proceed, in actuality there are always small breaks in trust during an analysis. This is particularly the case when, as Chused (Chapter 7 this volume) has stated, the analyst is invested in some result or effect from the interpretative efforts.

---

[2]This of course is at times a temporary recognition and one that will disappear and reappear in the transference throughout most of the treatment. I am maintaining that within some transference cycles the other is viewed as another and then within that cycle it is possible to consistently interpret transference manifestations. The other viewed as another is something that happens in a fuller way at the end of the treatment.

Ms. W. (the patient with hypochondriacal concerns) began to develop an idealizing transference relationship with me as analytic trust was being established. It became clear to her that I was the perfect analyst and undoubtedly was an excellent husband (could do no wrong). Her husband on the other hand was totally denigrated and she was considering leaving him for he was not much better than her first husband. She was married to her first husband while her father was still alive and during this first marriage she would frequently leave her husband and return home to her father. Her father had taken care of her since her mother died when she was 3. He had never remarried. He died when the patient was 28. She had left her first husband before her father died (suddenly) and had married her second (present) husband shortly after her father's death. They had been married for ten years when she began her treatment. The marriage had been a stormy one and, after three children, her husband had from her perspective become increasingly abusive. Several months before she entered treatment the patient developed the thought that she had a brain tumor. This thought occurred to her because she felt that she had the same symptoms her father had developed when he had a brain tumor. She developed these symptoms at a time when she and her husband were undergoing particularly severe marital difficulties. It was shortly after the development of her thoughts about her brain tumor that she decided to enter treatment.

An idealizing transference began at about the same time Ms. W. first recognized other events in the world besides her bodily concerns. Gradually others populated her thoughts and after her transference became consistent, I began to interpret her wish for a man to protect her from her many fears (that she had started to confide in me). She responded to this by telling me about her difficulties with her first husband and how she always felt better when she returned to her father's home. We began to see how I was now a replacement for her dead father. As we came to understand this material, her symptoms started to intensify. Although the patient did not ostensibly blame me for her symptoms, nevertheless with the uncovering of her transference analytic trust was disrupted. Her ability to self-reflect was impaired and her belief in the treatment helping her was gone. To be sure, during this phase of the treatment the analysis couldn't help her; nothing could for she was dying of an inoperable brain tumor. I was spared because she wanted me to transmit her last moments to her children. Why did she develop these intensified symptoms? She had begun treatment in a panic for despite the fact that she had been through a number of diagnostic tests over a period of two years, she still believed that she had a brain tumor. Although this belief never went away during the first year of treatment, she no longer was preoccupied by her concerns. After my transference interpretations she again went into states of panic and, as far as I could tell, her anxiety was greater at this point than it had been before she entered treatment.

Clearly at this point in the treatment I regarded the patient as having a disruption in analytic trust. Ms. W. believed that no one understood her symptoms and she was finding no help from the myriad of specialists she was consulting. The idea that no one understood her symptoms was a manifestation of the new transference. I had not fully understood that when I had interpreted her need for a powerful father figure she felt bereft of any figure to help in her state of need. My interpretation suddenly took away the only figure she could depend on in fantasy. I also realized after this series of interpretations that I no longer was in the same empathic stance that I had previously maintained. Had I been I would have been able to interpret her transference reactions in a more gradual manner, particularly, because her father had been such a central figure in her life. Her loss of trust therefore was in part due to the transition of transference states and in part due to the fact that I no longer was as filled with her subjective states as I had been. My investment had changed to an investment in understanding, and this alteration in perspective was experienced by the patient as part of my withdrawal from her. What occurred then was in effect a cessation of the analysis, for the symptom was becoming more problematic for the patient. She began to desperately search for help from the medical community for what she now knew was a fatal condition. As she went to many doctors in a variety of specialities I became increasingly irritated. I felt that my irritation was under control, but I also found that my interpretative efforts became more intense and I ingeniously developed new forms of the same type of interpretations. The patient was complaining about her symptoms not only to doctors but also to virtually anyone who would listen to her. This I began to realize was embarrassing to me and after some understanding of my embarrassment, I realized some of the meaning of the intensification of her hypochondriacal concerns. This came later in the treatment in what I would describe as another transference cycle: we came to understand that while she desired to believe that her father/analyst could provide all that she needed, there was a split-off aspect of her that yearned for her lost mother (aspects of herself) and was also unable to meet this aspect of her self for it contained in fantasy so much destructive potential. The partial untying of the bond to her dead father led to her beginning to search for other help and, at the same time, this condensed image began a search to reunite her with aspects of her self and the mother (object) she simultaneously longed for, hated, and believed she had destroyed. Moreover her enactments with her husband were constant proof to her that only her father could save her and no one else had the power or interest to care for her. This sequence went on not only with her husband(s) but also with many of her friends who were constantly disappointing her, whereupon she would remove them permanently from her life.

That there is still some narcissistic disequilibrium is evident because I am tempted to write a more complete history of this case. It is hard to stop the case description for I want to tell the reader that later in the treatment the enactments ceased (or at least diminished in intensity) and Ms. W. was able to give up her symptoms and begin to have a more fulfilling relationship with her husband and her friends. For now, however, the question is how one would classify the enactments that occurred. Her enactments seem clearer to me. As the transference was interpreted to her, she began to enact a behavioral pattern that took the place of everything else in the analysis. She could only talk about her anxiety or the medical tests that she was undergoing once again. All of her thoughts were related to her symptoms; there were no daydreams or dreams or other "incidental" thoughts that she brought up in the analysis.

My enactments seem similar to a description that Kohut (1968) provided in one of his early papers. In that paper the analyst was unwilling to tolerate a beginning twinship transference as I was unwilling to tolerate my patient's idealization. My intolerance occurred as I began to feel or think (unconsciously) that she was responding not really to me but to some fantasized figure that had little to do with me. I felt not present in the room, and this caused a degree of narcissistic disequilibrium. To maintain my equilibrium I behaved as an analyst "should"; I interpreted and I interpreted quickly and fully. I would maintain that my initial interpretations were also fueled by resentment at not being included more fully in her object world during the initial phase of treatment. When she then completely excluded me by going to other doctors, I began to regain my equilibrium (because I more clearly felt my resentment) and began to arrive at a different position on what was transpiring in the analysis.

In this rendition there is a postulated break in empathy after the beginning phase of the treatment. When Ms. W. began to include elements in the treatment that included the other as at least a form of another, I too rapidly interpreted her transference manifestations. I did this because I was unable to tolerate her idealization of me. This lack of tolerance occurred because the idealization had the form of obliterating me as a real object in her world. In this form of idealization the transference is relatively complete and the patient's self-observation is relatively impaired. For her I was an idealized object whose only desires were to see her happy and successful in her marriage and career. This form of transference is, in my experience as an analyst and supervisor, one where the analyst is frequently stimulated toward enactments. Moreover when this type of enactment occurs, the analyst's ability to hold and contain is diminished. This further leads to a series of enactments where the analyst may stick to his interpretation because "the material points to the correctness of the interpretation." This rationalization is a way of allowing the analyst to be a real object in the analysis and fends off the patient's desire (need) to utilize the analyst as a particular type of transference object. Parenthetically, in intense negative transference states where the analyst is attacked, there is even more of a tendency toward enactments.

Are enactments restricted to the occurrence of intense transference states? In the formulation that I am proposing, enactments are more likely during states of intense transference because all the "real" aspects of the analyst are likely to be obliterated during these states. Thus in a less intense transference patients are more likely to have the ability to observe themselves and others, and aspects of the analyst will be represented. This formulation should not be confused with the reality of my errors in creating a difficult analytic situation in the above example. Rather, I am maintaining that to the extent analysts do not experience themselves in the treatment situation, then to that extent most analysts will have an increased tendency toward states of narcissistic disequilibrium. Moreover, I am also postulating that the analyst facilitating the unfolding of transference requires a delicate balance not easily maintained. Freud, for example, could rarely if ever tolerate the consistent manifestation of a transference state. It is of course easy to be anachronistic in looking at Freud's struggle with transference. One may either idealize his concepts and actual treatment or criticize him in a manner that does not fully appreciate the struggle of simultaneously creating and attempting to utilize a new treatment method. Chused (Chapter 7 this volume) also points to the difficulties that an analyst faces in attempting to achieve the delicate balance that allows for consistent and gradual unfolding of interpretable transference reactions. This is a balance that allows space for the patient to create an illusory (and simultaneously real) relationship that we call a transference relationship. In thinking about the difficulties inherent in allowing the patient this type of transitional space, I am taken back (as many analysts have been, for this is a frequently quoted example) to a countertransference difficulty that Kohut (1968) briefly described (this example was alluded to before) in one of his first articles on the treatment of patients with narcissistic conflicts (not Kohut's term). He portrayed a patient in what he termed a beginning twinship transference. This patient began the treatment by enumerating the similarities between herself and the analyst. She told the analyst that it was clear to her that he was Catholic. The analyst demurred and informed the patient that he was not Catholic. Because it was the beginning of the treatment I will fantasize that the analyst felt that he was being "honest" or "authentic" in his reply to the patient. In this example, however, the patient did not ask whether the analyst was Catholic but simply stated that she was sure that the analyst and she were born into the same religion. Why would an analyst respond in this manner and not allow the patient to fill the analytic space with the analyst she wished to create?

To paraphrase Kohut's answer, the analyst was deprived of even the acknowledgment of having a separate existence. The analyst was in short reduced to a mirroring object with no separate personality or proclivities of his own. I would suggest that this type of narcissistic mortification occurs frequently, even when the analyst wants to be a good-enough analyst. In this example there is the implication that the patient had narcissistic difficulties because she was developing a twinship transference. Kohut in this paper stated that such patients place a special burden on the analyst. Granting that this is the case, it may be that we have underestimated the extent to which transference analysis is typically a narcissistic burden to the analyst. I am suggesting that allowing space in the analytic situation for the patient to create transference objects is a factor that frequently disrupts the analyst's narcissistic equilibrium. In response to this disruption, analysts either attempt to put an aspect of themselves in the treatment situation or attempt to distance themselves from the emotional impact of the transference. In a previous discussion I have suggested that each theoretical position has enactment potential inherent in the assumptions of the position. The classical position and the Kleinian position in one form or another stress the patient's receptivity to interpretations and thereby rid themselves of the need to continue empathetic attunement with the analysand. Being the silent, critical analyst and being the overinterpretative analyst are two ways of insulating oneself from becoming emeshed (engulfed) in the patient's transference world. The interpersonal analyst's confrontations are a way of becoming real in the patient's world and disrupting the unfolding of the transference. In the position that I have outlined, the stress on entering the patient's world can lead to an excessive holding environment and can leave the analyst in a position holding and containing while interfering with the unfolding of transference cycles, particularly negative transference states. This stereotyping of positions is not intended as a serious critique but rather as a brief illustration of the ubiquitous nature of the tendency to enactments regardless of theoretical position. The serious point is a belief that each position has built-in modes of enactments.

Analytic Ideals, Classical Tradition, and Narcissistic Equilibrium

If I am correct in the assertions that I have put forth, then given psychoanalytic history it is not surprising that the topic of enactments has taken so long to enter center stage in psychoanalytic discourse. In the United States the classical tradition made the topic of enactments difficult to talk about and a mythology grew around the issue of countertransference. The mythology consisted of the idea that if analysts had reactions to their patients, they were not fully analyzed. Thus I assume a number of analysts were filled with shame at some of their reactions and, not infrequently, attempted to put their shame into the patients they were seeing in analysis. It was not unusual for analysts to put their frustrations into the patient by declaring the analysand unanalyzable. This stance led to both shame about the analyst's countertransference and to a type of idealization of the distant analyst. This idealization has in recent years suffered the fate of idealized objects: ridicule, degradation and, by and large, abandonment. It is unfortunate that the quiet analyst has been associated with the distant analyst. Thus, at the very least, the assertion that enactments are frequent in the analytic situation seems a refreshing antidote to a type of denial that has been present, particularly in the psychoanalytic literature in the United States. Some may consider this last sentence too harsh. Yet it must be conceded that, at the very least, the classical position has put forth a type of ideal that few if any analysts have realized.

Both Freud's and Kohut's theories of narcissism would state that when an ideal is not realized there will always be some narcissistic disequilibrium. I would postulate that many analysts have been suffering under the burden of the classical ideal. When Sandler, Jacobs, McLaughlin, and Renik (Chapters 3, 5, 6, and 8 this volume) began to write about the analyst's role in a new way, they immediately drew the attention of analysts within and outside of the Freudian tradition. They raised the possibility of easing the burden that the classical ideal has placed on many analysts.

It is possible to conclude that there are at least two different narcissistic disruptions that occur within an analytic situation: (1) the difficulties inherent in the analytic situation that would ordinarily occur between analyst and analysand, particularly in establishing analytic trust and facilitating the unfolding of transference, and (2) the ideals that have been stated by classical analysts that have led to analysts' refusal to report certain routine countertransference problems. These ideals have produced shame in many analysts that has both affected analysts reporting enactments and affected the analytic process in many analyses.

If we look at the first point, it is possible to consider enactments as typical narcissistic reactions of analysts who are unable to tolerate a given transference situation. Given the still prevalent pejorative view of narcissism, this interpretation may even be worse than silence in helping to free analysts to talk about their countertransference tendencies. Moreover to consider all enactments as narcissistic responses to the patient's transference must sometimes be incorrect. Still in all, I consider it a tenable hypothesis and think that many of the examples used in this book could be understood as disruptions in the analyst's narcissistic equilibrium. Let us assume that this is correct and that enactments are the result of the analyst being unable to tolerate the narcissistic difficulties that are present when the patient uses the analyst in a manner that does not acknowledge the analyst's unique personal traits. If this occurs and analysts begin to recognize and understand their reactions, a great deal of information may be garnered about the nature of the transference and the reasons for the analyst's narcissistic disequilibrium. Thus if one accepts this as a normal occurrence, it is possible not to be incapacitated by this reaction.

Enactments and Analytic Trust

In previous chapters it seems that the term enactment is used in at least three different ways and that two of these usages overlap with older concepts. When Jacobs (Chapter 5 this volume) uses the term enactment, he is clearly discussing countertransference enactments, and if he had written this chapter twenty-five years ago he might have entitled it countertransference actions or, more likely, confessions of a countertransference-ridden analyst. It is my view that the term countertransference has several meanings that are not mutually compatible, and so I propose that in place of countertransference enactments we utilize the term analyst-induced enactments. This term then includes any factor that might influence the analyst toward enactments. Thus an enactment may be seen as a result of projective identification or as a result of the analyst's own psychology. There is an assumption in the use of the term enactment that some interaction between analyst and analysand is always taking place. An analyst-induced enactment only designates that the analyst is the primary actor in this activity. A state of narcissistic disequilibrium is one common factor in analyst-induced enactments.

A break in analytic trust is always associated with patient-induced enactments. The enactment may occur within or outside the analytic situation, overlapping with older notions of acting in and acting out. In this definition there is no conceptual distinction between activity inside or outside the analytic situation. The distinction is one of degree, which is usually determined by the locus of activity. More concretely, if a patient is secretly enacting outside the treatment situation, this usually indicates a more severe break in analytic trust than if something is enacted within the analytic situation.

The final designation is mutual enactment, for which there is no earlier overlapping concept. Mutual enactment corresponds to McLaughlin's definition of enactment (Chapter 6 this volume) and refers to "events occurring within the dyad that both parties experience as being the consequence of behavior in the other" (p. 80). In patient- or analyst-induced enactments, the other party may or may not be aware of the enactment. In mutual enactments, both parties by definition perceive the other's role in the activity. Usually mutual enactments result in or reflect impasses in the treatment situation. These enactments come at a time when analysand and analyst perceive that the treatment is not of maximal or perhaps of any benefit to the patient. Mutual enactments may take other forms than the ones presented in McLaughlin's chapter. It may be that both patient and analyst decide not to talk about certain issues. This decision may be perceived by both parties as being a result of the other's vulnerabilities or inability to deal with certain issues. For example, an anorexic patient perceives that her analyst is usually a good-enough analyst but is uncomfortable talking about issues that deal with food intake. The analyst similarly does not bring up issues around food intake because he thinks that the patient is not able at this point to deal directly with these issues. This is an example of an activity (a mutual inhibition) that may or may not be perceived as an impasse, but obviously indicates that the issues surrounding one of the patient's symptoms will not be discussed directly. This may involve conscious suppression on the part of both analyst and patient.

This last example raises the question of whether mutual enactments necessarily reflect a therapeutic impasse. It may be that neither patient nor analyst is ready to discuss the unconscious meaning of the patient's symptoms, and this mutual enactment or inhibition may be therapeutically beneficial. It does, however, mean that analytic trust is not fully established, because neither analyst nor patient is able to trust that the other will be able to utilize the efforts in a manner that will be therapeutically useful.

A final question that I will consider (but not answer) is the therapeutic efficacy of enactments. Renik's example (Chapter 8 this volume) shows us that enactments can be therapeutically efficacious. He implies that enactments typically carry the therapeutic action in an analysis. Grand (Chapter 9 this volume) disputes this view, but to finish this chapter I will only look at one other aspect of enactments and analytic trust. In a perfect analysis, analytic trust will be developed and there will be few if any major disruptions during the course of the analysis. In fact analytic trust over the course of the analysis should develop and become increasingly bidirectional as the analysis continues. I have never conducted an analysis that went as smoothly as this hypothesized perfect analysis. More typically there are disruptions in trust during an analysis, and during these periods there is a higher probability of enactments. It may be that we should think of an ideal analysis as a different type of analysis, rather than as one that is somehow superior to other forms of analysis. Some types of patients perhaps require enactments to be able to fully experience aspects of a fantasy during the course of an analysis. We might say that actions (or enactments) by the patient are a necessary condition for understanding the transference. Some patients may not be able to develop analytic trust unless they test the analyst by disrupting the treatment. This is particularly the case with patients who have undergone certain types of trauma.[3] Moreover some patients do not believe their transference reactions unless they become "real" in the treatment. The act of self-reflection for this type of patient destroys the "reality" of their experience. This type of transference reaction in my experience always leads to enactments and therefore at least periodic disruptions in analytic trust. These breaks may be the only way that the patient and analyst can continue the cycle of analytic trust throughout the treatment cycle. Therefore it seems to me that for some patients enactments are probably a necessary and common event. This may be a necessary condition for the full development of analytic trust. That is, for some patients it may be essential to enact certain conflicts in order to be able to fully trust the analytic situation.

Summary

In this chapter I have tried to advance some concepts and definitions, but I have not fully stated firm conclusions about the nature of enactments. I believe the topic is more complex than has been so far acknowledged in the literature, and a full discussion should be performed in the context of a theory of technique. Having said this, it follows that the discussion that I have furnished is of necessity inadequate; with this in mind, I offer some tentative summary statements.

If we agree that enactments are a common occurrence in many treatments, how do we understand why this is the case? If I restrict myself to the classical literature, it is possible to state three converging factors:

1. Analysts frequently attempted interventions (particularly interpretations) before analytic trust was established. This led to enactments, or worse led to declaring the patient unanalyzable.
2. The impact of transference has always been underestimated. *It is a more difficult task than previously realized for the analyst to maintain what I have termed narcissistic equilibrium.*
3. The sense of shame that the classical tradition has induced has made it difficult to even talk about the factors that lead to narcissistic disequilibrium.

If it seems that my comments are reserved for the classical tradition, this is far from the case. It is my view that many if not all psychoanalytic positions

---

[3]A patient whose father abandoned her and her mother (when the patient was 4½) had to leave the session early to avoid my ending the session, which for her had traumatic implications. It took her several years to understand the meaning of this action.

attempt to evade the full impact of transference in the analytic situation.[4] It may also seem as if I am writing in a manner that implies that all patients can be treated if the analyst is skillful enough in establishing analytic trust and in dealing with the difficulties of transference manifestations. Although the question of analyzability is an important one, it too represents issues that are vast and difficult to encapsulate. Here I can only say that to some extent the issue of analyzability has been utilized to evade difficult situations that many analysts have faced. These issues have now been opened up and it remains to be seen how the issues of analyzability will fare in the future. Despite this caveat, it seems clear that some patients would be difficult for most (perhaps all) analysts to treat no matter how the analyst positions himself or herself. Thus the difficult patient is not simply a manifestation of the analytic world's inadequacies; rather, there are some patients who evoke enactments that tend to destroy the treatment. These patients may be unanalyzable, but I think that we know too little about patient–analyst interaction to make this statement in any form except a probabilistic one. This type of statement indicates that at this time there are some patients who have a high probability of eliciting unresolvable mutual enactments.

The topic of enactments shows us first that the field of psychoanalysis is beginning to truly look at itself in a more open and honest fashion. This can only be considered an advance no matter what position one takes about the nature of enactments. However, even the phrase *the nature of enactments* repeats a tendency that is all too present in psychoanalytic discourse. We tend to write (and perhaps think) in terms of absolutes and dichotomies. The question of whether enactments promote the therapeutic action of psychoanalysis should undoubtedly be a more precise and differentiated one. The question perhaps should be posed in terms of the type of enactment and the type of anxiety the enactment engenders. Moreover, patients' tolerance of the anxiety and their ability for self-observation should be evaluated. Thus if a patient experiences intense and unendurable annihilation anxiety the enactment will have a great probability of having the effect of hurting the treatment as opposed to the situation where a patient experiences tolerable castration anxiety. Even this statement is not truly clinically relevant, for it is possible that once having experienced intense and for a time seemingly unendurable anxiety patients may develop a greater trust in the process when they see that both they and the analyst can go on being (to paraphrase Winnicott [1954]). Perhaps the best criteria we can use is whether the patient withdraws or is able to tolerate the

---

[4]The explication of this last statement awaits a fuller examination of different theoretical clinical positions.

regressive elements that are usually present in an enactment. Winnicott has stated that when patients withdraw from the analytic situation they are, in effect, attempting to cancel object relations and at best present aspects of what he called the false self. When the patient withdraws from the analytic situation, I have found that this calls for a renewal of analytic trust and for a period of cessation of interpretive efforts. Perhaps we can study the effect of different types of enactments and begin to recognize those that promote certain aspects of the analytic process as opposed to the type of enactments that tend to disrupt or destroy analytic trust and, at times, the analytic relationship. More precise concepts then may allow us to formulate a dynamic theory of technique that includes the bidirectional nature of enactments. Hopefully this volume is a step in that direction.

REFERENCES

Brenner, C. (1976). *Psychoanalytic Technique and Psychic Conflict.* New York: International Universities Press.
—— (1982). *The Mind in Conflict.* New York: International Universities Press.
Ellman, S. J. (1991). *Freud's Technique Papers; A Contemporary Perspective.* Northvale, NJ: Jason Aronson.
—— (1997a). *An analyst at work.* In *More Analysts at Work,* ed. J. Reppen, pp. 91–115. Northvale, NJ: Jason Aronson.
—— (1997b). Criteria for termination. *Psychoanalytic Psychology* 14(2):197–210.
Freedman, N. (1994). More on transformation enactments in psychoanalytic space. In *The Spectrum of Psychoanalysis: Essays in Honor of Martin S. Bergmann,* ed. A. K. Richards and A. D. Richards, pp. 93–110. Madison, CT: International Universities Press.
Kohut, H. (1968). The psychoanalytic treatment of narcissistic personality disorders: outline of a systematic approach. *Psychoanalytic Study of the Child* 23:86–113. New York: International Universities Press.
O'Shaugnessy, E. (1981). A clinical study of a defensive organization. *International Journal of Psycho-Analysis* 62:359–369.
Rapaport, D., and Gill, M. M. (1959). The points of view and assumptions of metapsychology. *International Journal of Psycho-Analysis* 40:153–162.
Steingart, I. (1995). *A Thing Apart: Love and Reality in the Therapeutic Relationship.* Northvale, NJ: Jason Aronson.
Winnicott, D. W. (1954). Withdrawal and regression. In *Collected Papers: Through Paediatrics to Psychoanalysis,* pp. 255–261. London: Tavistock, 1958.

Credits

Index

Abend, S. M., 111, 170
Abstinence, neutrality and, 136–137
Abt, L., 38
Acting out, 19–28, 37–61
  acting in versus, 48–49
  action, defense, and reality, 50–54
  actualization and, 42–44, 65
  body language and, 24–25
  concept of, 37–38
  definitions, 19–20, 41–42, 47–48
  Freud and, 40
  genesis of, 21–24
  hysteria and, 28
  interpretation and, 25–27
  pejorative context, 80
  reconsideration of, 38–42
  repetition, regression, and working
      through, 54–57
  transference and, 44–47
Action, 169–181
  acting out, defense and reality, 50–54
  character enactments, 171–176
  developmental regression hypothesis
      and, 176–179
  overview, 169–170
  thought and, 135–136
Actualization, acting out and, 42–44, 65
Alexander, F., 94n1, 116, 126

American Psychoanalytic Association,
    38
Analytic trust, 187–197, 199–201
  countertransference, 189–190
  transference, 191–197
  transference cycles, 190–191
Arlow, J. A., 52, 65, 108, 177
Aron, L., 142
Awareness, enactment and, 111–113

Baudry, F., 171
Benedek, T. F., 161
Beres, D., 38, 53, 56
Bibring, E., 55n11
Bion, W., 84
Dird, B., 15n10, 53, 104, 114, 115, 134, 146
Blos, P., 37, 57
Blum, H., 37, 52
Body language, acting out and, 24–25
Boesky, D., xii, 65, 107, 113, 125, 131,
    141n3, 146, 185
Brenner, C., 48, 51, 55, 140, 150, 187
Breuer, J., 2, 3, 4, 5, 8, 9, 171

Calef, V., 37, 50
Character enactments, action, 171–176
Chused, J. F., xii, 116, 125, 136, 144, 149,
    154, 158, 174, 184, 185, 192

Corrective emotional experience,
    enactment, 115–121
Countertransference, 29–36
    analytic trust, enactment, 189–190
    case study, 34–36
    character enactments and, 174–176
    defined, 29
    enactments and, 63–76, 129–138, 142.
        See also Enactment
    positive value of, 29–30
    role relationship and, 33–34
Cowitz, B., 51
Curtis, H., 48

Dare, C., 29, 30
Darwin, C., 112
Defense
    acting out, action and reality, 50–54
    Freudian methods, 5, 6–10
Developmental factors, acting out, 21–24
Developmental regression hypothesis,
    action and, 176–179
Diatkine, D., 44, 54
Dora case (Freud), 10–15

Eagle, M., xiii
Ego-syntonicity, acting out and, 53–54
Ekstein, R., 160
Ellman, P., xiii
Ellman, S. J., xiii, 1, 187, 190
Emde, R., 106
Enactment
    action and, 169–181. See also Action
    analyst's contribution to, 84–88
    analytic conscience and, 124–125
    analytic trust, 187–197, 199–201
        countertransference, 189–190
        transference, 191–197
        transference cycles, 190–191
    assumptions, 183
    awareness and, 111–113
    clinical examples, 81–83
    concept of, xi
    corrective emotional experience,
        115–121

    clinical example, 118–121
    described, 115–118
    countertransference and, 63–76
    countertransference enactment, 113–
        114, 129–138
    definitions, 184–187
    evocative power of, 93–109
    Freudian legacy, 15–16
    historical perspective, 77–78
    implications for, 88–90
    insight and, 157–167
    projective identification and, 83–84
    psychoanalysis and, 78, 121–124, 197–
        199
    psychotherapy and, 126–127
    shared behaviors, 80–81
    term of, xiii–xiv, 77–78, 139–140, 183
    transference–countertransference
        enactment, 114–115
    ubiquity of, 78–80
    utility of, 149–155
Etchegoyen, R. H., 165
Externalization, transference and,
    30–31

Fenichel, O., 19, 20, 21, 22, 25, 27, 39, 40,
    49
Fine, B. D., 49, 170
Fleming, J., 161
Fliess, W., 13
Freedman, N., 186, 190
French, R., 116, 126
Freud, A., 20n1, 25, 37, 38, 42, 170
Freud, S., xi, xii, 1–17, 24, 29, 38, 39, 40,
    41, 42, 43, 44, 45, 46, 47, 51, 52, 54,
    55, 56, 77, 79, 89, 112, 114, 115,
    135, 136, 139, 141, 150, 171, 180,
    196, 198
Freudian methods, 1–17
    Dora case, 10–15
    enactment and, 15–16
    suggestion and, 3–10
    therapy and, 2–3
    transference and, 1
Friedman, L., 116, 145

Gay, P., 13
Gediman, H. K., 160
Gill, M., 42n3, 51n9, 73, 89, 127, 190
Goodman, N. R., xiii, 174
Grand, S., 138
Gray, P., 49, 89
Greenacre, P., xii, 26, 38, 49, 50, 56
Greenson, R., 52
Grinberg, L., 43, 52
Grossman, W., 44

Hartmann, H., 41
Heimann, P., 29, 30
Hoffman, I., 89
Holder, A., 29, 30
Hypnosis, Freudian methods, 2–3
Hysteria
    acting out and, 28
    Freudian methods, 2, 3–10

Infante, J., 37
Insight, enactment and, 157–167
Interpretation
    acting out and, 25–27
    of countertransference, enactment
        versus, 132–133

Jacobs, T. J., xii, xiii, xiv, 78, 93, 108, 111,
        113, 185, 199
James, W., 112
Johan, M., 132

Kanzer, M., 38, 45n6
Katan, A., 23, 100
Kernberg, O., 145
Kohut, H., xiii, xiv, 116, 196, 197, 198
Kris, A., 125

Langs, R., 65
Laplanche, J., 42, 48, 139
Lipton, S., 40, 116
Loewald, H., 37, 40, 51, 52, 54, 55, 116
Loewenstein, R. M., 42, 100

MacDougal, J., 66
Mahler, M. S., 170, 177, 178
Marill, I. H., 145, 146
McLaughlin, J. T., xii, xiii, xiv, 16,
        48, 78, 79, 84, 88, 102, 103,
        136, 145, 149, 157, 183,
        199
Miller, I., 52
Mitscherlich-Nielsen, M., 43, 52
Modell, A. H., xiii
Moore, B. E., 38, 49, 52, 170
Mosher, P. W., 77

Neubauer, P. B., 140
Neutrality, abstinence and,
        136–137
Newman, K., 117

Ogden, T., 83
O'Shaugnessy, E., 190

Poland, W., 88, 93, 117, 125
Pontalis, J. B., 42, 48, 139
Projection, transference and, 30–31
Projective identification, enactment and,
        83–84
Psychoanalysis, enactment, 78, 197–199.
    See also Freudian methods

Rangell, L., 37, 38, 41, 45, 140
Rapaport, D., 190
Raphling, D. L., 158, 174
Reality, acting out, action and defense,
        50–54
Reed, G., 154, 155
Regression
    acting out, repetition and working
        through, 54–57
    developmental regression
        hypothesis, action and,
        176–179
Reich, A., 64
Reich, W., 170
Renik, O., xii, xiii, 116, 129–138, 141n3,
        145, 174, 184, 200

Repetition, acting out, regression and working through, 54–57
Resistance, Freudian methods, 5–6
Rexford, E., 38
Robertiello, R., 55n12
Role relationship, countertransference and, 33–34
Role-responsiveness, countertransference and, 29–36. *See also* Countertransference
Rosen, J., 49
Rosenfeld, H., 41

Sampson, H., 116
Sandler, J., xii, 29, 30, 37, 40, 42, 43, 46, 66, 79, 88, 94, 97, 145, 157
Schwaber, E., 89
Searles, H., 165
Segel, N., 50n7
Settlage, C., 116
Shapiro, R., 83
Simon, B., 44
Smith, H. F., 158
Stein, G., 22
Stein, M., 49, 56, 66
Steingart, I., 141n2, 190
Sterba, R., 51n8, 53n10
Stern, D., 79, 106
Stolorow, R. D., 142
Sugarman, A., 142n4
Suggestion, Freudian methods, 3–10

Tarachow, S., 53
Transference
  acting out and, 39, 44–47
  analytic trust, enactment, 191–197
  character enactments and, 174–176
  Freud and, 1, 13–14, 39
  projection and, 30–31
Transference–countertransference enactment, 114–115
Transference cycles, analytic trust, enactment, 190–191
Tyson, R., 131

Van Dam, H., 53n10
Van Gaard, T., 55
Van Waning, A., 140, 141

Wallerstein, R. S., 127, 160
Weinshel, E., 150
Weiss, E., 40
Weiss, J., 116
Weissman, S., 38
Werman, D. S., 6
Wilson, A., 142n4
Winnicott, D. W., 31, 202
Wolf, E., 66
Wolkenfeld, F., 160
Working through, acting out, repetition and regression, 54–57

Zeligs, M., 49